ANSWERS FOR THE
Honest Skeptic

ANSWERING SKEPTIC OBJECTIONS
TO BIBLICAL CHRISTIANITY

TED EVEN

ISBN 978-1-0980-3738-3 (paperback)
ISBN 978-1-0980-3739-0 (digital)

Christian Faith Publishing, Inc.
832 Park Avenue
Meadville, PA 16335
www.christianfaithpublishing.com

Printed in the United States of America

This book is first dedicated to my Lord and
Savior Jesus Christ—to him who
has created all, be all glory forever and ever!

As it concerns those whom he created, this book is
dedicated to Nancy:

My sweetheart, my best friend, and my wife.

Without her love, patience, and encouragement,
this large endeavor would have been much more difficult.

PREFACE

Please note that many of the "objections" within this work are so involved that they could well be a whole book all on their own. So while this author has certainly purposed to make each objection thorough enough to do justice to the subject, at the same time, I have also endeavored to make the answer to each one as short as possible. Perhaps all objections which have been covered do not necessarily either apply to you or spark your interest. That's perfectly okay. We'll just say they were written for some other reader than yourself—shall we?

Ultimately, I have tried to answer most all of the common objections which *the honest skeptic* may wrestle with. But please feel free to read and contemplate the answers to just those objections which may spark your personal interest.

However, if you wish to just start at the beginning and read all of them, that would be my first recommendation simply because there is *new information* within each objection which is vital in one's search for the overall truth. Admittedly, there is also some overlap of information with some of the objections, just because "repetition" can be a good teacher concerning those things which are of more importance. However, no matter whether the whole book is read or just parts, it is my sincere desire that you would not only meet the "real Jesus" but also understand that he is all about perfect love toward you and all men. And as your creator, he only wants the best for you, which not only includes a right and loving relationship with him but also his awesome eternal life which is truly beyond our comprehension.

In part three of our series, we'll also be discussing many different conflicting religions in our world which all not only claim to have the truth but also the only way of eternal salvation. And by way of simple and reasonable testing, we'll be exposing whether or not they be true or false as a belief system. However, it must be stated up front that it is certainly *not the adherents* of any false religion (or belief system) which this author is against but only those *false teachings* within that religion or belief system which deceive men away from the one and only true God and his eternal salvation. And in part three of our series, which discusses false religions, I will be of course reminding the reader of this good motive, just so my sincere and loving intentions may not be misunderstood.

As the Bible clearly teaches that God himself does not wish that any should perish, neither should any who follow him (2 Peter 3:9). In verses like Jude v. 3, God's word also clearly teaches all Christians to *"earnestly contend for the faith which was delivered to the saints"* as the eternal life of men is literally at stake. For those of you who may already know Christ and have always just wondered about many of the topics covered in this work, it is sincerely my hope that your faith in Christ will be truly strengthened and you will be able to honestly defend it to a greater capacity in these last days we are living in before the return of Christ.

All scriptures are in bold, and the Bible versions being quoted from are the King James Version, Amplified Version, Revised Standard Version, New International Version, New King James Version, and the New Living Translation.

INTRODUCTION

During the middle ages, knights were the most courageous warriors in this world. Knights were gallant, strong, and kept their honor by defending the honor of their king. Dressed in their suits of armor, they were unafraid to face the mightiest of opponents in defense of their kingdom. Since any lasting kingdom must be established in truth if it is to endure, it was indeed even a spiritual battle between truth and deception which also raged in the hearts of those knights which did do mortal combat for their king.

You may well be thinking, *Yes, that was then, but now the world has changed and the days of such chivalry are long gone and over.* But are they? Is the battle between good and evil really over? Is the battle between truth and deception over? I think not. Are even real kings and kingdoms upon this earth just faded memories of the past? I think not.

For in truth, my friend, it has long been predicted within the Holy scriptures of that ancient book we call the Bible that there is a real, physical, but eternal kingdom of God which will soon be established upon the whole earth! And even now, Christ, the King of kings, continues to send out his knights into that same battle between truth and deception that men may know him and dwell in his eternal kingdom to come.

Many have held belief that it is heaven itself which will be the main eternal dwelling for all men of sound faith and character. But what are such misguided notions founded upon? For the holy scriptures themselves have always taught that the earth we dwell on will endure forever and that the *"meek shall inherit"* it (Psalms 78:69; Revelation 11:15; Matt. 5:5).

Surprised? In fact, the Bible teaches us that this soon coming kingdom on earth will not only be eternally inhabited by all those who have believed in Christ but will be the awesome and beautiful likes of which this world has never seen! Indeed, as it is written:

Eye has not seen, nor ear heard, neither has it entered into the heart of man the things which God has prepared for them that love him. (1 Cor. 2:9)

If you do not yet believe in the Bible, perhaps you just haven't encountered the basic honest evidence which soundly validates it. For example, did you know this remarkable book has already foretold in their exact order the last three world-dominating kingdoms on earth within only a few of its great prophecies? Hundreds and hundreds of years before their fulfillment, these major world empire predictions were given to the Jewish prophet, Daniel, during the Babylonian kingdom (about 606 BC). They explicitly foretold that the next world-dominating kingdoms following Babylon would be none other than the Medo-Persian kingdom, then the Greek kingdom, and then the Roman kingdom—in that exact order (Dan. 2:38–45, 7:3–9, 8:1–21). And just as history cannot lie, those prophecies through Daniel which spanned roughly 2,000 years after his time proved 100 percent accurate without flaw!

But let us not stop there, for these were not the only world-dominating kingdoms which were foretold to come within those awesome prophecies. Following the Roman empire, which we already know to be history by at least 500 years, the prophet Daniel also foretold that an eventual short kingdom will be ruled by that man known as the "Antichrist" with the ten nations which will give him their aid (Dan. 8:23–25; Rev. 17:10–13).

While this most wicked kingdom is by far the shortest of all (only three and one half years long), unlike all kingdoms before it, it is foretold to literally dominate all "peoples, tongues, and nations" on earth with its one world government and nearly cause the extinction of the human race (Rev. 13:7; Is. 24:6; Matt. 24:22)! But before the world will be destroyed by the Antichrist, many prophecies within the Bible also foretell that Christ himself, the King of kings, will once again step back into human history and throw down the Antichrist from his wicked throne to finally establish his everlasting realm on earth which has no end (Dan. 2:34–35, 2:44–45; Rev. 19:11–21).

Nearly 3,000 years of human history has transpired since those amazing prophecies were given to the prophet Daniel, and three of the five predicted world-dominating kingdoms have proven 100 percent accurate in their exact succession. And now the world races toward a one-world government which the Bible tells us is a prerequisite to the rule of the Antichrist.

Coincidence? I think not. My friend, no other so called "holy book" in the world has even dared to lay out 3,000 years of human history in advance to prove its divine authorship through such large prophecies. And what of these next two world-dominating kingdoms to come? Was it just the prophet Daniel who specifically foretold of them? Nay, my friend, for it was at least twenty some other prophets and apostles of the Holy Bible who also foretold of these very same two coming kingdoms!

And considering these major prophecies are accompanied by many smaller detailed prophecies attached to them, which have also proved accurate so far, it is quite amazing to say the least. The mathematical probabilities of these small and large predictions all coming true together in their exact foretold sequence by mere random reckless chance could hardly account for all their accurate fulfillments so far! After all, thousands of human freewill decisions were also involved in these major prophecies all coming true, and only someone who is "all-knowing" could have known which world dominating empires would commence in the exact order they did. However, if in fact our eternal God and creator who is "all-knowing" desired to clearly reveal himself to his own creation by foretelling the detailed future way in advance, then such astounding prophecies (along with hundreds of others within the Holy Bible) begin to make some real sense.

Depending upon one's source and how that source chooses to divide up Bible prophecy, the exact number of predictive prophecies contained within the Bible can vary. Nevertheless, did you know that the Bible itself contains *roughly* 2,500 predictions of the future and all but about 500 of them have already been fulfilled with undeniable historical accuracy? Would it not then be rather heedless and hasty to just throw such power of prediction aside? For why would the Bible's potential to accurately predict our future be any less than its potential to have already predicted the past with accuracy?

Indeed, my friend, if one was to bring such powerful evidence of these many fulfilled prophecies into any earthly civil court for examination, would not the burden of proof that this great book is false be upon the unbeliever? And so, with at least the fair trial it deserves in any civil court, shall we not bring this uncommon book under our honest examination together?

Of course, if you have already predetermined that any honest evidence presented would matter not and sway you not, then shall we not fairly conclude that your present stance is just one of mere emotion? However, if honest evidence does indeed hold sway in your good heart then, my friend, you would quickly prove your good worth in any lasting kingdom. Nevertheless, at this present time, it might just be you who is the honest skeptic, saying within yourself, "I cannot yet believe in your Christ, his coming kingdom, nor the Holy Bible which tells of them, for as of yet, I've not encountered the sound evidence required for them." Well, my friend, it has long been said that a skeptic retains his honor as long as he remains an *honest skeptic*; for the honest heart will always find the truth no matter how long the journey to get there.

Let us then fairly face the facts. Honest evidence for the truth will only guarantee one's belief in the truth if they themselves are honest with that evidence. But all the honest evidence in the world presented to those dishonest would accomplish about as much as putting good coin in a bag with holes. However, since honesty is a personal choice of the human free will, then all men can be basically honest enough to arrive at the truth if they should so choose. And if you be that honest skeptic, undoubtedly, your sincere objections to the Bible could well vary. Therefore, it is precisely for those valid objections which this extensive work was penned to address.

> A skeptic retains his honor as long as he remains an honest skeptic—for the honest heart will always find the truth no matter how long the journey to get there.

What therefore is your weapon of choice, my friend? Shall we not ride out together with a sincere heart to do battle against the very lies and deceptions which do hinder the truth of reality? Let us then once and for all place the claims of this ancient book on fair trial and address with honesty those objections of the unbelieving skeptic which have been so prevalent among men. What say you?

Foretold by the one who is "Ancient of Days" almost twenty centuries ago, the basic account within the Holy scriptures which predict God's coming kingdom on earth has echoed down through the long deplorable corridors of humanity still awaiting its awesome fulfillment in an exact time undisclosed to man. However, as time continues to elude those who would restrain it, the irreversible signs of our present day, which continue to just confirm Bible prophecy, have plainly mounted up to confuse scoffers and skeptics alike, reminding even an unsuspecting generation such as ours of those awesome words which rumble down out of eternity:

Surely I come quickly. (Revelation 22:20)

TABLE OF CONTENTS

Part I—We Have a Creator

Objection 1:   I Don't Trust Any Bible-believing Christian Sources in My Search for Truth Because They Are All Biased 17

Objection 2:   There Is No Personal God 21

Objection 3:   I'm an Atheist 27

Objection 4:   I Don't Believe in Intelligent Design 43

Objection 5:   I Believe in Evolution 60

Objection 6:   What About All the Evidence for Prehistoric Cavemen Who Lived in the Stone Age? 95

Objection 7:   If the Global Flood of Noah's Day Was Real, Why Can't We Find the Ark Today? 112

Objection 8:   If God Is Loving and Just, Why Wasn't Noah's Ark Even Large Enough for Anyone Else of the Pre-Flood World Other Than Just Noah's Family? 126

Objection 9:   How Can the Bible Even Be in Compliance with Science When It Is So Full of Fantastic Miracles? 134

Objection 10:   I Believe All Life Came from Aliens 158

Objection 11:   I Already Believe in God 178

Objection 12:   I Don't believe in Just one God (Monotheism); I believe in Many Gods (Polytheism) 182

Objection 13:   If God Is Real, Why Doesn't He Just Show Himself Plainly to the World? 195

Objection 14: I Was A Bible-believing Christian for
               Many Years…But Now I'm an Atheist............203
Objection 15: I'm an Agnostic 215
Objection 16: I Already Know the God of the Bible Is
               Real; I'm Just Ripping Mad at Him for
               All the Pain in My Life! 239
Objection 17: I Believe the Reason for the Moral
               Collapse of Mankind Is Because Many
               Won't Get More Involved in Politics...............245
Objection 18: If the God of the Bible Created
               Everything and Is Perfect and Loving,
               Then Where Did Evil Originally Come
               From? 262
Objection 19: I'm a Good Person, and I've Done the
               Best I Can 285
Objection 20: Aren't We All Children of God?......................310
Objection 21: I Don't Believe in Sin 314
Objection 22: All Spiritual Truth Is Just Relative to
               One's Own Perspective 321

PART I—WE HAVE A CREATOR

Objection 1

I Don't Trust Any Bible-believing Christian Sources in My Search for Truth Because They Are All Biased

Some may feel that when it comes to the search for the truth, they really cannot trust any Bible-believing "Christian" sources, because they believe them to be all "biased" from the start. It is certainly easy to understand why "trust" in any source which claims to know the truth cannot be built upon the personal biases of men. I wholeheartedly agree. However, interestingly enough, in many cases, the very same people who are reluctant to look at "biblical" sources in their search for truth are surprisingly quite open to exploring many other sources from other "belief systems" without any complaint that those sources are *predisposed* toward the belief systems which they advocate.

The simple truth is that most all people who hold to a given belief system (or religion) must also have their personal biases and/ or starting premises! And even those who may not yet hold to any given belief system (or religion) have their biases too, no matter what source they are searching! I have yet to find any exceptions.

Humanly speaking, it would be rather impossible for anyone to not "see the world through their own eye glasses" to some degree. Technically, Buddhists could be "biased" toward Buddhism in some way... Humanists could be biased toward humanism in some way... Mormons could be biased toward Mormonism in some way... and Bible-believing Christians could be "biased toward biblical Christianity in some way, etc. But the critical question is: Do the personal biases or starting premises of men actually have the power to deceive us away from the real truth if the real truth is self-evident through sufficient honest evidence?

For example, in any civil court of law, what do the judges go by for their arrival at the truth? The personal biases or starting premises of men? Or the honest evidence regardless of the biases of men? If civil court judges go by the honest evidence regardless of the biases of men, then why use the starting premises of men as an excuse not to search a certain source for the truth when it is ultimately the honest evidence which determines all truth for those honest?

> Do the personal biases or starting premises of men actually have the power to deceive us away from the real truth—if the real truth is self-evident through sufficient honest evidence?

So then I guess the only real question for us all is: Are we willing to conscientiously and carefully comb through the honest evidence with an open heart and see just where it would actually lead? In other words, the spiritual truth based on honest evidence is fully recognizable by the honest soul apart from any false or true premises he or she would even start with. And since each belief system deserves a "fair trial" in the courtroom of our conscience, if we really want to know the truth, why be derailed in the beginning of one's search for the truth with the fact that most all men must technically have some personal biases or starting premises?

As we've already mentioned, even those who might reject a certain source because they are "concerned about biases" also have plenty of biases of their own as well. Therefore, the bottom line in our search for spiritual truth is that if a man is honest with himself and the evidence which he encounters, even a wrong starting premise or bias will inevitably be corrected in his own conscience, and he or she will discover the real truth no matter what it is.

So then I guess the only real question for us all is: Are we willing to conscientiously and carefully comb through the honest evidence with an open heart and see just where it would actually lead?

Personal Motives in Our Search for Spiritual Truth

Of course, in one's search for the truth of reality, our continuing objective cannot be to attach ourselves to just those spiritual beliefs which may have personal appeal. It should be to just "find the truth," no matter which "camp" it lives in. After all, those who just want to "be right" and disregard honest evidence to the contrary can only have an emotional view and are still reasonably disconnected from reality. Obtaining "the truth" on any subject should not be about anyone trying to be important or satisfy their personal wishes. On a much more sober note, it should only be about human wellness and human survival. Throughout all recorded human history, lies and deception have consistently proven to bring mankind harm, suffering, and death. And it would seem that dishonesty fueled by unfounded fear within one's quest for spiritual truth is certainly no exception.

However, the healthy motive in our search for spiritual truth should always be to simply find the truth of reality supported by honest evidence, no matter what that truth is. Why? Simply because we know only the truth of reality itself can give us the real life, love, and fulfillment we truly need.

Conclusion

Learning to discern truth from error when establishing your spiritual beliefs can definitely be exciting when you find yourself getting somewhere in the process. But undoubtedly, you will also encounter the biases of men along the way and maybe even some of your own biases as well. However, since reality itself has always required the honest evidence which must support it; our greatest concern should not be so much with the personal biases of men as it should be with just finding that solid evidence, which supports reality and making sure that we are truly *honest* with ourselves when we encounter it.

OBJECTION 2

There Is No Personal God

I can understand exactly where you are coming from! What God? Where is He? I've never personally seen him! After all, why on earth should you believe in a personal God you cannot personally see? Now if you could physically see him, touch him, and talk face-to-face with him, that would be different. But to accept that there is a personal God who created us just because someone says so is ridiculous! Yes, many Bible-believing Christians know just how you feel because they too used to hold your same convictions; that is, until God revealed himself to them in a way they could not honestly deny.

However, in many cases, God may not have revealed himself to them until they *sincerely* sought him. Atheists who have asked God to reveal himself to them may have been in a real critical situation and needed help or answers desperately. And yet, others may have just been sincerely curious. But whatever the case, going by the millions of testimonies of Bible-believing Christians who did not know Christ, it would seem that God himself not only can be found by those sincerely seeking him but actually desires to be found!

It is, of course, common knowledge that the theory of Darwinian evolution asserts that "there is no personal God" and all we see in our earth and universe is just the *shaky* scientific results of random reckless molecules and atoms which have collided with each other over billions of years. And before there were even atoms and molecules, somehow...*nothing* started it all!

So ultimately, according to the Darwinian evolutionary view, when you boil the theory down far enough, "everything must have come from nothing." And the fact that man has never scientifically observed this fantastic phenomenon (something coming from nothing) throughout all of recorded human history should somehow not be a problem for those desiring to hold to true science!

According to the Darwinian evolutionary view, when you boil the theory down far enough—everything must have come from nothing.

Other "belief systems" (such as the "New Age Movement") have also clearly denied the Bible's claim of a "personal" trinity God who created all of humanity in His own image. Some belief systems may teach that all mankind and the world around us came from mere impersonal "chance" or maybe just an impersonal "force" of some kind (as taught in the movie *Star Wars*). Yet, other belief systems may even hold that the entire universe is just an illusion of the human mind and does not really even exist as our mind perceives it to exist. The Hindus and Buddhists seem to be some of the main proponents of this pantheistic view to their own degrees.

Others, who are at least "deists" of some kind (those who believe in a God), may reject the evolutionary belief that there is no God at all because they can clearly see that the earth and all in it is an intelligent "effect" which certainly must have some kind of an intelligent "cause" behind it. Nevertheless, many such deists also reject the idea of a "personal" God. Some of these deists may just believe in a monotheistic God who is some kind of a cosmic eternal power or mind out there beyond the universe we see, but he (or it) is not at all personal and cannot be known.

Albert Einstein seemed to gravitate toward this view. Other non-Bible-believing deists may actually believe in some kind of a non-cosmic monotheistic God who has *some kind* of a distant personality but is still so transcendent from his own creation that he cannot be defined by human concept at all. In other words, he's way beyond having any personal relationships with his own creation. He simply wound up the universe like we would a clock and then let it go until it unwinds and he has to wind it up again…or make a new clock.

But then we must ask, why would an impersonal God even create us at all if he never wanted any kind of a relationship with us? It really doesn't make much sense, simply because it lacks any meaningful purpose.

However, upon reasonable reflection of this incredible world around us teeming with people who need loving relationships and are very "personal" in nature (hence the word "person"), it would certainly seem this basic reality alone is not exactly a "feather in the cap" of those completely denying an intelligent "personal" creator "behind it all." Why? Even addressing man's existence from a purely rational or scientific standpoint alone, just the basic scientific law of "cause and effect" would indeed seem to forbid any nonpersonal or non-intelligent "force" behind it all.

Science has long discovered and recognized that no "effect" can be *greater than* its "cause." In other words, the cause of something is always greater than the effect of that cause. If you kick a ball, the force of your kick must always be greater than the force of the ball (immediately after the ball starts rolling). I don't believe true science has found an exception yet. And when we rationally apply this same basic law of "cause and effect" to man's existence, it would then be only reasonable to believe that whoever brought the human race into existence is also superior to us in our own *personal* nature as our "cause."

For example, if all mankind (characterized with intelligence and creativity) has always been "*personal*" in nature, needing close relationships which require love and communication, it would only be reasonable to believe our "cause" (*who*ever it was) would also have to be fully characterized by all of these very same things as well. With just this basic scientific understanding then, our "cause" must certainly be a "person" who is like us desiring relationships, etc., rather than mere "chance" or some "impersonal force" which, of course, is not a person at all. Almost always, the spiritual beliefs of mankind fall into one of the following different categories:

1. Atheism—The belief that there is no God (an example being Darwinian evolution).
2. Agnosticism—The belief that man cannot know for sure if there is a God (which can also encompass the uncertainty of any truth whatsoever).
3. Monotheism—The belief in a single divine eternal creator being who is supreme (examples being biblical Christianity, the Muslim religion, the Catholic religion, Judaism, etc.).
4. Polytheism—The belief in many different gods (examples being Greek mythology, Viking folk religions, native American Indian religions, Egyptian beliefs, etc.).
5. Pantheism—The belief that everything is God and God is everything (examples being Hinduism, Buddhism, The New Age Movement, Scientology, etc.).

When we apply the basic law of "cause and effect" to man's existence, it would then be only reasonable to believe that whoever brought the human race into existence is also superior to us in our own *personal* nature as our "cause."

But obviously, we can easily see that just the basic *personal* reality of all mankind inevitably makes little to no sense with the very "impersonal" belief systems of atheism, agnosticism, and pantheism, and probably even "polytheism," which typically teaches that we cannot have a close personal relationship with the "gods" that they suppose to exist. And that's probably why the largest religion in the world is still "monotheism" today.

While the basic *"personal"* reality of all mankind inevitably causes the impersonal belief systems such as Darwinian evolution, Hinduism, Buddhism, the New Age movement, etc. to fall fast out of favor, amazingly enough, it is indeed in perfect harmony with the monotheistic view of biblical Christianity. The Bible has always taught that man was created in the very image of God who is a person (Genesis 1:26) and that the invisible attributes of our personal creator can be clearly seen by the things He made, especially us (Romans 1:20).

Additionally, the central theme throughout the Bible is that God desires to restore a right and loving relationship with all mankind (John 3:16; Matthew 22:37). And not only has the Bible always taught these basic things which fully cooperate with the well-proven law of cause and effect, but it has always taught that God, our cause, is much *greater* than us as a perfect eternal being. But when you apply this reasonable "cause and effect" principle to man's existence in the case of "impersonal" evolution, the New Age Movement, or any other belief system which rejects a personal God, then it would indeed seem they go completely against it and the obvious great sea of very *personal* human life we observe around us. Why, even the entire animal kingdom is "personal" in nature and has the fingerprints of the very same personal creator all over it! And this is undoubtedly why, as we'll discuss in our next objection, atheists, as well as agnostics, have always been a much *smaller* percentage of the world's overall population.

Conclusion

And so because mankind has always been very "personal" in nature, the honest truth is that neither the nonpersonal "theory of evolution," the "New Age Movement," Hinduism, Buddhism, atheism, agnosticism, or even nonpersonal deism can make any sense with this basic reality and simply do not begin to explain the real very *personal* world as we all know it. If you're one who's just not sure yet if the personal God of the Bible actually exists, just do what millions of people have already done. With an open and sincere heart, simply ask God to reveal himself to you in a real way that you can understand, and see for yourself what happens in your life afterwards. You may be amazed at how God really answers you if you give him just a small chance with a small amount of faith.

If you are a strict atheist who has been quite adamant about the nonexistence of the personal God of the Bible, then just sincerely pray the following simple prayer and see for yourself what happens in your life afterwards:

"God of the Bible, if you exist, which I adamantly deny, I believe it is your responsibility to reveal yourself to me. Therefore, I now *sincerely* ask you to reveal yourself to me in a way I can understand and prove me wrong."

OBJECTION 3

I'm an Atheist

"Atheism" itself is simply the belief that no creator deity (or deities) exist and is probably quite old as a "belief system" within traceable human history. But no matter how *old* this obscure belief system is, typically, only a *smaller percentage* of the human race has historically actually held to atheism. This seems to be the case whether one researches the Hebrew, Egyptian, Oriental, Babylonian, Persian, Greek, or Roman cultures, for most all of them held to a belief in a deity (or deities). And today's world is little different, even when considering those who believe in Darwinian evolution. According to the Pew Research Center online, world religion statistics were roughly as follows as of September of 2016:

84 percent of the world is religious;

16 percent of the world is unaffiliated with any religion;

And of the religious (84 percent): Monotheists make up 55 percent, Reincarnationists make up 22 percent, and Folk religionists make up 6 percent;

And of the Monotheists (55 percent): Christians make up 32 percent, and Muslims make up 23 percent;

And of the Reincarnationists (22 percent): Hinduism makes up 15 percent, and Buddhists make up 7 percent;

And of the unaffiliated (16 percent): Agnostics (those unsure of a God) make up 11 percent, and Atheists (those who flatly deny the existence of God) and free thinkers make up about 3 percent.

Atheism may even be on the increase today, but nevertheless, if it follows its general pattern throughout traceable human history, it will still remain an obvious minority in the world's overall population, even though it may rise and fall statistically within that smaller percentage. Some statistics may try to project that atheism/agnosticism or even the nonreligious will completely dominate the world by such and such a year. However, such projections must rely upon all moral (and other) trends fully accommodating an atheism "takeover" (a never observed phenomenon in the recorded history of man).

But this is not something anyone can say with absolute certainty, unless they are "omniscient" (all-knowing) as it concerns our future filled with probably trillions of human freewill decisions! The human race has always been full of surprises as it reacts to many things like world economics and even world wars which have their real influence upon man's spiritual beliefs.

For example, even WWI and WWII had its real influence on the world's spiritual beliefs. And I can assure you that if the book of Revelation really does unfold in our very near future, it too will greatly skew such projections as an atheist "takeover!"

Additionally, many (even atheists) may not be aware of this basic reality, but typically, the highest percent of atheists are mainly comprised of *younger people*! And as the age of man increases, the percentage of atheists within those higher age brackets *dramatically decreases*. For example, according to Pew Research Center, in their "Religious Landscape Study," the basic age distribution among atheists are basically as follows:

Ages 18–29 represent 40 percent of atheists;
Ages 30–49 represent 37 percent of atheists;
Ages 50–64 represent 14 percent of atheists;
And ages 65 and older only represent 9 percent of all atheists.[1]

That in itself is quite interesting indeed. One must certainly ask why such an obvious decline in atheism as the age of man increases?

---

[1]   Pew Research Center. "Religious Landscape Study"

The entire human race in most every culture has always held that with more age comes more wisdom. Nobody *honest* can deny that basic fact. And in light of that universal truth, we certainly should be able to say the same for self-proclaimed atheists! Thus, we must fairly conclude that real "wisdom which comes with age" would even lead the atheist away from their own obscure belief system.

Also, it should be noted that just like "Satanists," both atheists and agnostics are also quite *dis-unified* and disagree with each other even in their more *basic* convictions of reality. However, such *basic* disagreements are not generally characteristic of other belief systems. But no matter what small percentage of the world *professes* to be atheist, and no matter how dis-unified they are among themselves in their basic beliefs, one must still ask the basic question: "Is there really even such a thing as a true atheist?"

The Heart and Mouth of Man Have Always Been Connected

The Bible has always taught us that "*[o]ut of the abundance of the heart, the mouth speaks*" (Matthew 12:34). This simply means that whatever is truly in the heart (or spirit) of a man, that is what is truly reflected when they speak. According to the Bible, this is because God created us in his own image so that our heart (or spirit) gives command to our mind and our mind in turn gives command to our body—in that order (James 1:14–15). Science may not have yet verified that man even has a spirit (beyond weighing people before and after death), but it has certainly confirmed that our mind commands our body. So once again, even though this basic "order of man's function" taught within the Bible may go *beyond* our present scientific discoveries, it certainly does not go *against* the scientific discoveries which we have confirmed.

So, if "*[o]ut of the abundance of the heart, the mouth* (truly) *speaks*," then what people say with their mouths, even out of emotion, can certainly be a reflection of their true heart beliefs. This is not only taught within the Bible, but society in general seems to also recognize this basic truth. In a court of law, the verbal confession of witnesses would have no power unless it represented their true heart beliefs. Similarly, the "verbal/heart" connection is why a parent may scold one of his children for saying something which is simply not good.

So relating this same "verbal/heart" connection to the atheist, what has probably come out of the mouth of every atheist that has been in a serious life threatening situation? Probably the same thing that has come out of the mouth of every other person who has been in a serious life-threatening situation—"Oh my God!" But if an atheist truly believes in his heart there really is no God, why would they, along with everyone else, consistently say "Oh my God!" in serious life-threatening situations?

Similarly, what has probably every atheist done at one time or another when they've suddenly lost control or gotten hurt? Probably the same thing that every other person has done who has suddenly lost control or gotten hurt—they have taken God's name in vain! And more than likely, many times when they've wrongfully taken God's name in vain, they've also been specific enough to say the name of God's Son in vain—"Jesus Christ."

So what is my point? When asking an atheist if they believe in God, they *may not willingly admit to you* that they believe there is a God because they are just as capable of "living in denial" as anyone else who is living in denial. But when they go through the above the situations, they just can't hide the fact that they too are no different than anyone else who really believes in their heart and conscience that there is a God! And many times, they demonstrate that they even believe that Jesus Christ is God, simply because they specifically take his name in vain. Hmm…interesting.

> But if an atheist truly believes in his heart there really is no God, why would they, along with everyone else, consistently say "Oh my God!" in serious life threatening situations?

How about the "agnostic?" Again, the "agnostic" is someone slightly different than an atheist in that *they say* they just *aren't sure* there is a God. According to the agnostic, there might be a God or there might not be a God; *as they say*, they just can't *be sure*. But what has probably come out of the mouth of every agnostic that has been in a serious life-threatening situation? The same thing that has probably come out of the mouth of every other person who has been in a serious life-threatening situation—"Oh my God!" (or maybe they even take the name of "Jesus Christ" in vain?).

But again, if an agnostic really *can't be sure* in his heart that there is a God, why would this be? Why doesn't the agnostic say "I don't know for sure" when he pounds his finger? Why doesn't the "New Ager" take "Buddha's" name in vain when they pound their finger if, in fact, they believe just as much in Buddha as they do Jesus Christ? Why does the unbelieving world (those who reject Christ) specifically pick on "Jesus Christ" when they "pound their finger" if, in fact, they really don't believe in their hearts that he is the one and only true creator?

Why doesn't the atheist, evolutionist, or the New Ager take the name of "Mother Earth" in vain if they really believe in just "Mother Earth" and not "Father God?" My friend, I've never heard anyone say "Mother Earth" when they pound their finger. Have you? But even if you have, more often than not, you've probably also heard them specifically take Jesus Christ's name in vain as well. And why would that be? When they consistently and specifically take Jesus's name in vain, is it then just some "figure of speech?" But why then don't they consistently and specifically take any other name in vain for their "figure of speech?" These are certainly some very fair and reasonable questions which clearly point to the fact that our one true God and creator is undeniably tied into the very conscience of every atheist and agnostic who has verbally admitted the reality of God when experiencing a crisis, etc.

> Why does the unbelieving world specifically pick on "Jesus Christ" when they "pound their finger" if they really don't believe in their hearts that he is the one and only true creator?

Our Human DNA Is Actually a "Book" Storing All Our Personal Information

With all the order displayed within it (such as page numbers, etc.), and the intelligence, meaningful purpose, art, and design, do you believe that this book that you are reading right now could have ever written itself without the aid of an intelligent creator? Even given billions of years in some random evolutionary process, do you believe this book could have ever written itself and come together in its bound book form laid out just as it is without the aid of an intelligent creator? Let's all *be honest*; whether you gave it billions of years or trillions of years, our well-proven law of entropy, which states everything by itself just tends toward ruin and gets more disorderly with the passing of time, would honestly make any such belief rather ridiculous, would it not?

But did you know that scientists have now discovered that your human DNA is actually a much larger, more sophisticated, and intelligent "book" than even the one you are reading, which stores all of your personal information within it? Your DNA "book" actually determines the color of your hair, the color of your eyes, the length of your eye brows, the shape of your ears, your height, your metabolism, how long your toes are, the shape of your face, and literally everything there is to know about your entire person.

And yet, many have been deceived into believing that the human being (which of course includes our human DNA, cell structure, etc.) actually just came together completely on its own through some random, reckless, haphazard process of evolution without any aid of an intelligent creator whatsoever! And not only the entire human race, but also the whole animal kingdom, all the plant life, all the marine life, and everything else in our entire universe, which is full of the very same complex order, design, and purpose. And considering most forms of life on this planet also have many complex systems built within them which all must work together with great precision in order to sustain delicate life, it most certainly would go against our well-established scientific law of entropy to believe it all just came about through the random, reckless, haphazard chance of some evolutionary process which did not involve an intelligent creator.

Therefore, if you can truly believe all of nature (including the human race) with its great order, design, and meaningful purpose just evolved all on its own without the aid of an intelligent creator, then you can also believe this book you are reading right now evolved completely on its own without the aid of an intelligent creator as well! But if you simply refuse to believe this book evolved completely on its own for many sane obvious reasons, then very reasonably, you must equally refuse to believe all of nature (including the human race) with its much greater order, design, and purpose just evolved all on its own without the aid of an intelligent creator. And amazingly enough, long before modern scientists discovered our human DNA is actually a "book" containing all our personal information, roughly 1,000 years before Christ, King David, inspired of the Holy Spirit, actually wrote in Psalm 139:16 that just the way God made us is contained in such a "*book*" as our DNA! Once again, the Bible is *way ahead* of modern science—and very reasonably it should be if, in fact, it is the inspired word of our very own "all-knowing" creator.

The Second Law of Thermodynamics (or "Entropy")

According to both evolutionary and creation scientists today, our sun is burning off its own mass at about a rate of four million tons per second! And obviously, since the sun has not ever been observed to regenerate new mass, all observable science so far teaches us that once mass is burned off the sun, it is not regained. Thus, it does not take a rocket scientist to conclude that given enough time, one day, the sun will simply run out of mass to burn. And scientists have also observed that what is true of our sun is true of the stars as well, and one day, our entire universe will eventually experience what they've come to call a "heat death." In fact, all of what we see in nature around us is constantly deteriorating and going from a state of order to disorder just like our sun and stars. This constant deterioration is one of the most well-proven laws of science known as the "Second Law of Thermodynamics."

However, if we could hit a reverse button and go back in time, our sun and stars would just gain more and more mass until our universe would eventually reach a state of "wholeness" or perfection. And this would, of course, line right up with the Bible's teaching that our universe had a beginning at some point when God did, in fact, create everything perfect before man's sin entered his perfect creation. And even scientifically, such a "beginning" would inevitably point to some "beginner" who was the actual cause of that beginning, especially if that beginning was indeed in some state of perfection compared to what we observe today. But if we were to hit that same reverse button, really, how does the random, reckless, haphazard process of evolution *honestly* fit with the inevitable state of wholeness or perfection of our universe back in time? The simple honest truth is that it doesn't!

> If we could hit a reverse button and go back in time, our sun and stars would just gain more and more mass until our universe would eventually reach a state of "wholeness" or perfection.

Scientists have also observed that the universe is expanding. And similarly, if we reverse the expanding universe which we observe, then we must conclude that all planetary bodies were indeed closer together than they are now. And given enough time reversing the expansion process, many scientists today have generally concluded that our universe must have had an actual beginning before it started to expand. Even Albert Einstein eventually admitted that because the universe apparently had a beginning that it also must have had a "beginner" or a creator of some kind, even though he rejected the God of the Bible because he just couldn't reconcile a loving God with the suffering he saw in the world.

However, in our objections 18 and 23, we discuss from a spiritual view point just why our loving creator had to allow all the suffering we see in the world for a season within his overall prophetic plans for man. And this very necessary dual reality, which encompasses the "life-giving normal" and the "death-giving abnormal" is probably a biblical reality which Einstein himself may have had a difficult time reconciling if he did not understand the basics of God's word very well. Nevertheless, most scientists today now finally accept that the universe did at least have a beginning of some kind, which has been a starting point for some evolutionists to have faith in a God, simply because "a beginning" points to some kind of a "cause" for that beginning, namely "a beginner." For lack of a better term, shall we just call him God? As the scientific "Kalam Cosmological Argument" essentially concludes: "If indeed our universe must have had a beginning, then our universe also must have had a cause or 'beginner.'"

Since most of the modern scientific community agrees on the fact that everything inevitably had to have a beginning, then the inevitable conclusion that there was a "cause" or "beginner" of everything is rather inescapable. And not only a beginner, but an intelligent "personal beginner" as we already discussed in our "Objection 2." In this real sense, and by way of analogy, our whole universe could just be compared to some old deteriorated farmhouse out in the country. If you just came upon an old deteriorated farm house out in the country somewhere, several basic things should be obvious about it:

1. Going backwards in time, at one point, it was new in a state of wholeness when it had its "*beginning*" and did not show basic deterioration.
2. Because it obviously had a beginning, it also must have had some *intelligent creator* "*cause*" who was necessarily behind its beginning.
3. Because it had an intelligent creator who was the cause of it, it must have been created for a specific purpose which is self-evident through the design it was given (which, of course, is a "shelter for mankind" in this example).

While the Bible's explanation for our universe lines up perfectly with these three realities in our universe, it also does the very same with all things man-made (which have always demanded the need for a creator behind them). However, how does the Theory of Evolution line up with the fact that everything man-made has an intelligent creator behind it if, in fact, it maintains that the far more complex intelligence which we find in all of nature just evolved on its own? The simple truth is that it doesn't!

The Theory of Evolution not only goes completely against the reality and science we all know to be true with anything man-made which consistently has a creator behind it but also violates both the First and Second Laws of Thermodynamics! And the fact that many things within nature are either much larger or smaller than anything manmade should be rather irrelevant to the honest soul as even the things man-made vary in size on a smaller scale. It is true that within nature, we find the "life-giving normal" and the "death-giving abnormal." However, if we understand all of the natural world around us with the Bible, then everything we observe in nature that is either good or bad fits perfectly with just what the Bible has always taught. In the beginning, God created everything perfect before man's sin entered his perfect creation and caused its deterioration. And the Second Law of Thermodynamics then is essentially just the honest scientific evidence for the effects of man's sin upon God's perfect creation.

> While the Bible's explanation for our universe lines up perfectly with all things man-made (which demand the need for a creator behind them), the theory of evolution of course does not.

Evolutionists may indeed assert that there was some "big bang" (instead of God), which started our universe to expand, and may even believe that all universes started with some kind of a big bang, kind of like fireworks all going off on Fourth of July. And they may even believe that the whole process took billions or even trillions of years. However, no matter how many universes evolutionists imagine or just how they imagined they all had their beginning or how many years it all took to unfold, they still cannot escape the inevitable need for an intelligent personal "cause" at the very beginning of it all. By insisting that our universe began with a "big bang" instead of God, they are just delaying the inevitable reality that even if there was a big bang which started our universe, it too had to have had a "beginning" and an intelligent cause or "beginner" behind that.

Even if all the universes exploded like a bunch of fireworks, each in their own time over billions of years, you still have to ask the basic reasonable question: Who created and set off all the fireworks in the first place? And while the Bible reasonably answers all those questions, the Darwinian theory of evolution simply cannot answer them with anything other than "everything ultimately came from nothing."

However, such an answer not only defies all scientific realities we've observed but also even the conscience and common sense of a ten-year-old! And that's exactly why some of our greatest scientists like Sir Isaac Newton and Albert Einstein totally rejected the idea that the universe somehow began on its own or from "nothing." To them, it was even more ridiculous than insisting that anything man-made just popped into existence on its own or from "nothing," simply because the universe and all of "nature" actually displays much more intelligence than anything man-made! Many atheists may try to say that there is really nothing which forces the need for a creator. But obviously, many things, including what we just said, does very reasonably force the need for some kind of an intelligent creator behind it all.

The Concept of Man's "Thankfulness"

Many an atheist (or agnostic) have expressed the fact that they are indeed thankful for many good things in their lives. If you are a self-proclaimed atheist (or agnostic), perhaps you have even specifically mentioned many things you were thankful for during the Thanksgiving holiday over the years. For example, you may have expressed thankfulness for your family which surrounded you at the Thanksgiving dinner table. Or perhaps at times in your life you have expressed thankfulness for just being alive. Or perhaps for having good health or having a spouse when so many do not. Or perhaps many times you have just been "thankful" for the nice day. However, no matter which of these and other good things you've been thankful for in your life which ultimately man himself could not have given you, even you're expressed appreciation of these things really makes no sense with true atheism!

You see, really, any "thankfulness" on the part of man is always a two party concept which by nature and definition *necessitates both a giver and a receiver.* Thankfulness can never truly be directed to just "thin air" or "no one." The "receiver" is always thanking a personal "giver" or the personal source of their gift received. Thus our common expression, "Thank you." However, our common expression, "Thank you," does not even fit with the theory of Darwinian evolution which would be a completely nonpersonal source for those good things we can think of which simply could not have come from mankind. For example, when's the last time you heard anyone say, "Thank you, evolution, for the nice day?" or "I'm thankful to evolution for this sunset?" It simply would make no sense.

Even if an atheist claimed to "thank evolution" for a nice day, it would make little sense simply, because evolution (if it were true) would have had no choice in producing that nice day. Thankfulness really only makes sense with a giver who had a freewill choice in the process of giving. Either way, "thankfulness" for anything which could not have come from man on the part of the atheist makes very little sense indeed. This is why even an atheist thankful for a nice day must be thanking a personal giver source for that nice day within their heart. Thus, general thankfulness as well as the "you" in "thank you" always makes the giver source we are thanking a person, whether it be the person of God or your fellow man. And so just the common ability of most all atheists and agnostics to be "thankful" for those things which could not have come from man is just more evidence that God really does exist in their heart, mind, and conscience—even though, once again, they may be quite unwilling to openly *admit it* to their fellow man.

> Just the ability of atheists to be "thankful" for those things which could not have come from man is just more evi-

dence that God really does exist in their heart, mind, and conscience...

The Edge of Eternity Also Exposes the Reality of God in the Hearts of Men

It is true that many a soldier waiting before battle has received Christ as their Savior. And many of them have testified that they thought themselves to have been true atheists beforehand. Why would this be? Simply because deep down in their heart and conscience, they always knew Christ was their creator, Lord, and Savior; they were just *unwilling to surrender to that reality* until their very life was on the edge of eternity.

My point is obvious and clear. The Holy Bible is right once again as it has always taught that every man in his or her heart and conscience knows, without a doubt, there is a God simply because God himself put the reality of himself in us all when he created us (Ecclesiastes 3:11). But some are just unwilling to verbally admit it, which of course is another issue altogether! Let's take a look at Romans 1:20:

> **For the invisible things of him from the creation of the world are clearly seen, being understood by the things that are made, even his eternal power and Godhead, so that they are without excuse: because that, *when they knew God, they glorified him not as God,* neither were thankful; but became vain in their imaginations, and their foolish heart was darkened.**

The Right Question Finally Asked

Thus, the right question we should be asking isn't "Is there a God?" but "Why would anyone be unwilling to admit there is a God when they already know in their heart there is indeed a creator?"

Finally, we are now asking the right question. Going by the simple testimonies of many professing atheists who have come to believe in God, there are probably a variety of irrational/emotional reasons we could cite. We'll just consider a few of them:

1. Anger toward God—Atheists/agnostics who have come to believe in God of the Bible have certainly admitted afterwards that they were either consciously or unconsciously angry with God because of painful experiences they've been through in their lives. I think we've all been *misguidedly* mad at God sometime or another if we are honest. However, in the case of some atheists/agnostics, it was indeed their extreme anger toward God that forbade them to even acknowledge his existence.

    Understanding that this reason for not believing in God is only "emotional" and not at all based on any "honest evidence flatly disapproving God's existence," this gives us some insight into human behavior. It is also very interesting to note that most all serious atheists/agnostics who insist that there is no God are not even seriously looking for God! They are quite rare indeed.

    Let's be honest; it's not like their lifelong dominant dream is to find God! The truth is that anyone will greatly decrease their ability to find the truth if they really don't even want to know the truth in the first place! But strangely enough, if you notice, for some reason, they are always talking about the God they don't believe in! Nevertheless, if atheists/agnostics are not really even seriously looking for God, this too points to just an emotional reason for their denial of God. After all, why would they seriously look for God or "spiritual truth" if their hearts are too hardened or blocked with anger, bitterness, or rage toward God? However, strangely enough, many such atheists will try to convince you their position is the most rational and scientific!

2. Money and power—Many atheists/agnostics who have come to Christ have also admitted that they were not even seeking "the truth" (or God) because the power and money they had in their lives blinded them from seeing their true need for God."

Simply put, because they have their security in money, some atheists may refuse to even acknowledge their need for God. However, power and money will only satisfy us so much, and then we finally learn that those things do not really give us "life" either. History has shown us this in the lives of men repeatedly. For example, people who marry others just for power or money usually find this out. And even the rich and famous realize the extreme limitations of their power and money when they come to draw their last breath as they can take none of it with them.

3. Pride—Of course, all men wrestle with a certain amount of pride every day; nobody is perfect. But dominant pride is undoubtedly one thing that has hindered all men in their desire to know God and have a right relationship with him through Christ, atheists and agnostics being no exception. A basic biblical definition of humility is "dependence upon God" (James 4:8–10). And a basic biblical definition of "pride" is "independence from God" (Jeremiah 13:9–10). I guess it is rather simple to know that an atheist is rather "independent from God" if he refuses to even *admit* his existence! Therefore, if one goes by the Bible's definition of pride, it would just follow that pride itself must inevitably be a foundation under their atheism to some degree. And some atheists may even wrestle with a combination of all of the above and more.

> If atheists/agnostics are not really even seriously looking for God, this too points to just an emotional reason for their denial of God.

Conclusion

However, if we notice, none of the above reasons to reject the existence of God have anything at all to do with any discovered honest evidence, which *"flatly disproves the existence of God."* They only consist of either mere material things or emotions which have pulled the heart of man away from his own creator. So why do atheists and others specifically take the name of Jesus Christ in vain? Simply because they already know in their heart and conscience that Jesus Christ is the one and only true creator of all things (Colossians 1:17) and that truly *"there is no other name under heaven given among men by which we must be saved"* (Acts 4:12).

So if you happen to be a professing atheist reading this and know in your heart you need a major change in your life, consider that along with many other things, even the reality of "love" in this world doesn't make much sense with the Theory of Darwinian Evolution. But it does make complete sense with the Bible, which has always taught that God is the very source of all true love (1 John 4:8).

Even if you have been an atheist who has been adamantly against the existence of God, that still doesn't change the reality of God's awesome love for you! None of us are any better than anyone else. And every one of us can escape the destruction of our own sin nature if we want to.

After thirty-five years of being a Christian, I can personally testify that it was God's love which ultimately changed my life for the better. But if I had never given Christ a chance to even reveal himself to me, then I know I would have never gotten the healing I needed. If you are one who is tired of running from God and you want to personally experience his awesome unconditional healing love for you, I invite you to just take that first small step of faith by sincerely praying the prayer of salvation located at the end of this book. No matter what your past is like, God loves you and sincerely wants you to be a part of his awesome eternal kingdom!

Jesus said, "I am the resurrection and the life. He who believes in me, will live even though he dies; and whoever lives and believes in me will never die..." (John 11:25–26)

OBJECTION 4

I Don't Believe in Intelligent Design

Typically, atheists, evolutionists, or agnostics may reject the certain idea that any "intelligent design" can be easily seen in the world around us. And in a *partial* sense, such a view of the world around us is *somewhat* understandable. Because while to them there might *seem* to be "intelligent order" within nature, they may be more focused on the "disorder" within nature. For example, instead of seeing the awesome intelligence within the human body full of complex systems, which all must work together with great precision in order to sustain delicate life, some may be more focused on the disorder of deformities and diseases which often assail human health. However, just to begin with, we observe that there is probably much more "order" (which we call the "normal") within nature than there is "disorder" (which we call "abnormal"). So does the smaller reality of "disorder" within nature really cancel out the obvious "order" and intelligence which we plainly see within all nature? Or are they two completely separate realities within nature which exist for two completely separate reasons and are just forced to coexist for a time just as the Bible teaches?

While some atheists or those adhering to religions such as the "New Age Movement" may easily acknowledge all the obvious "order" in our universe and earth, they may still reject the idea that all that order came from an "intelligent" source or being who actually had to create it all. Instead, they may just believe that all the obvious order and complex systems in our universe, which all must work together with much precision in order to sustain delicate life on earth are just a result of the random, reckless, haphazard chance of some evolutionary process.

Even if they believe that all the matter and energy which brought about all the complex order we see in our universe just "always existed," they still may believe that given enough time (billions of years), all the complex order we see in our world and universe today all came about from complete "disorder" all by itself. But of course, the rather large problem with such a *blind belief* is that *never* within the natural sciences has mankind *ever observed* order coming out of disorder *without the aid of an intelligent being behind it!* Yes, without an intelligent being causing it to happen, order coming from disorder is a *special* reality which science has never been privileged to observe! But this special unobserved phenomena is precisely what the entire Theory of Evolution is based on!

For example, which is much more realistic to believe: A brand-new car being manufactured by a tornado ripping through a junk yard for millions of years? Or a brand-new car being manufactured in a factory full of people who purposely put much labor and thought into it? One scenario fairly represents the Darwinian Theory of Evolution, and the other fairly represents biblical Christianity.

Scientists have definitely observed disorder coming from order (for example, human beings full of order can wreck things, like their own lives) but *never* have they observed order (especially complex order) being brought about by complete disorder *without an intelligent being behind it to make it possible.* In fact, as we've already mentioned, one of the most proven laws of science is the law of entropy which essentially states that everything tends toward ruin or disorder (from a state of order) if just left to itself without an intelligent being involved.

Again, to illustrate just how impossible or "incredible" it would be for all the order and complex systems in our universe (which all must work together with much precision in order to sustain delicate life on earth) to come from the random, reckless, haphazard chance of some evolutionary process, it would be far more "incredible" than a tornado ripping through an automobile junkyard and leaving behind in its destructive wake a fully functional 747 airplane all fueled up and ready to fly!

My friend, if we are all to be *honest with ourselves*, it wouldn't matter if the tornado ripped through that same junk yard for trillions of years, it would still do just the opposite of anything constructive! Scientifically, when it comes to order coming from disorder, *more time* has always proven to just be an enemy, not a friend! And to think that believers in evolution are willing to stake their very eternity on this very impossible unscientific process which we have never been privileged to observe is quite amazing indeed.

Scientists have *never* observed complex order being brought about by complete disorder *without out an intelligent being behind it to make it possible.*

The truth is that hands down, most people (including children) can easily see even "superior intelligence" to our own in the world around them no matter which facet of nature is being observed. Why then would some insist on denying any intelligent design within nature? Perhaps some just may not want to *admit* "intelligent design" simply because it would lead to the inevitable conclusion that there is an "intelligent designer" behind all creation around them? But what would be their problem with an "intelligent designer" behind all creation if that were in fact true? Perhaps some may just find it difficult to reconcile the idea of an intelligent creator God who has given "order" to creation and at the same time allowed all the "disorder" and suffering they also see within creation. In other words, how could a loving creator possibly allow so much suffering in the world?

Therefore, some might just find it emotionally easier to reject the idea of an "intelligent designer" altogether if they can't reconcile the suffering they see in the world with a loving God (a subject we cover much more on in "Objection 23)." But of course, that would be a completely different emotional reason for rejecting an intelligent creator and not at all a scientific one. We must certainly remember that because they too are human, even evolutionary scientists are quite capable of drawing their scientific conclusions from an emotional standpoint! Or perhaps, other evolutionary thinkers may just refuse to acknowledge an intelligent creator because they want to run their own lives and be their own "god" without him. But really, if we are honest, none of these reasons for rejecting an intelligent creator are at all scientific, for they are more of a personal emotional nature, which really has little to do with real science.

Anything Which Obviously Has an Intelligent Purpose Always Means Some Intelligent Creator Must Have Been Behind It

When looking at anything man-made, it is obvious that there was an "intelligent designer" behind it. When we see order, design, art, or creative/meaningful purpose in anything man-made, we intuitively know there was some person with intelligence who gave it its "order," "design," or even artistic creativity *every single time without one single exception!* This is not only true now with everything man-made but has been true as long as recorded history bears witness.

When something is true every single time without any exceptions, this should cause us to take note and add it to our definition of "reality." For example, when we see the fins all in a row on an airplane engine, we know they were constructed just that way with an intelligent purpose by an intelligent being. All men know intuitively just within their conscience that it could not have come about through some mere haphazard random reckless chance of events, simply because all haphazard events of nature tend only toward disorder or ruin, not intelligent order and careful design, especially with a meaningful life-giving purpose.

As we've already mentioned, this basic reality has been referred to by scientists as the "Law of Entropy" or the "Second Law of Thermodynamics" (left to itself, *everything* tends toward ruin or disorder), and it is one of the most well-proven laws of science. But amazingly enough, believers in evolution still actually believe their haphazard theory is more "scientific" than is the Bible which reasonably teaches us that an intelligent creator must be behind all that shows intelligence and meaningful purpose.

Why is it that when we look at Mt. Rushmore, we don't say, "Wow, erosion over millions of years sure is an amazing thing! Look how it formed the heads of our four presidents with such accuracy of their likeness!" No one says that, because it would be absolutely foolish to do so. Well, really, when you boil the Theory of Darwinian Evolution down, it is even more foolish, simply because it is even much more unrealistic, teaching that all of nature (which is much more complex than Mt. Rushmore) came about without the aid of an intelligent being! Just why doesn't anyone believe that the Mt. Rushmore art came about from some evolutionary process? Just because there were historical witnesses which can confirm the human artist behind Mt. Rushmore? Of course not.

Because the simple truth is, whenever we see creation, design, art, and order (even if we can't confirm anyone having witnessed the creator or the creation of it), we *always know* intuitively in our conscience that there was some intelligent being behind it to make it happen! And if the human body, animals, or even plants are far more complex and full of design than the four presidents carved into Mt. Rushmore; then *honestly,* why would anyone even begin to believe that they simply evolved on their own through millions of years of haphazard random reckless chance which has always just tended toward ruin and disorder?

Once again, if *everything* man-made *always* has an intelligent person/creator behind it, then how can it be that everything in nature around us (plant life, sea life, animal life, and human life) does not have an intelligent creator behind them when, in fact, they are clearly superior in design, intelligence, and purpose than anything man has ever made?

For example, we know the human brain, eyes, nose, etc. were created with superior intelligence to our own, simply because man cannot yet fully understand them. In fact, man is way behind when it comes to fully understanding most all of nature around us as well, whether it be under the microscope, outer space, or anything in between! Therefore, if an atheist or evolutionist (who admittedly possesses some intelligence) cannot begin to grasp the millions of marvels in the world around them, which are full of order, creative design, art, and obvious meaningful purpose, then how could that atheist or evolutionist begin to insist they are without an intelligent designer behind them? This would be like a man on foot saying that a cheetah has no speed at all when he couldn't begin to keep up with the cheetah on foot! If you are starting to see that the whole "no intelligent design" stance has always been characterized with obvious inconsistency (some might call it hypocrisy), I guess I would have to agree with you.

For yet another example, if the atheist (who admittedly has some intelligence) cannot understand or tell you how to make a *seed*, then how has he the right to say seeds were not made with intelligence? Instead of "seeds," one could plug anything in nature around us, which cannot be created by man into the above question, and the answer would essentially be the same. The atheist simply does not honestly have the right without being rather *hypocritical* in doing so. Only the day when that atheist can understand and create all that he sees in nature around him will he have the right to say they were not made by an intelligent creator who has superior intelligence to his own intelligence.

Just so, only the day when a man on foot can outrun a cheetah would he have the "true credentials" or "clout" to say "the cheetah has no speed at all." My friend, simply put, the *honest truth* is that atheism or evolution, which denies an intelligent creator behind all of nature, which is even more full of order, design, and intelligence than anything man-made, makes absolutely no sense at all!

Some may say they have a hard time believing there is an intelligent creator behind all creation simply because *they've never personally seen God create anything themselves.* But it gets right back to our example with Mt. Rushmore. The main reason we know the Mt. Rushmore art did not come about through some evolutionary process isn't because man has personally witnessed the men who carved it. Most men (including you and me) did not personally witness the artists of Mt. Rushmore create their images. But *we all reasonably believe* they were created by *someone intelligent* who carved those specific images for a meaningful purpose.

If a realtor walks you through a bunch of houses, the thought that those houses somehow evolved into being over time on their own, just because you've never personally met the carpenters who built them, would be rather ridiculous, would it not? In fact, most people never actually meet the carpenters who built their home…yet I've never ever heard anyone believe that their house evolved completely on its own over time because of it. And if you added billions of years to such a notion, it would just look all the more ridiculous. In fact, when you think about it, most people never meet the designer/creator of most man-made things they encounter during their entire lives. And yet, no one seriously believes they just evolved into existence over time (especially over billions of years) and that the intelligent designer/creator of those things doesn't exist.

But one might contend that the real reason is just because we have all at least seen many men create most things man-made, and *this is why* no one doubts an "intelligent creator" behind anything man-made which they encounter throughout their life. Thus, just seeing mankind create things which are manmade is what really causes our belief in an intelligent creator behind all man-made things. While this *partial explanation* may help us believe, it's certainly not the main reason we believe that an intelligent being made all things man-made.

Let's explain. Like we already said, the main reason we believe there was an intelligent creator behind Mt. Rushmore isn't because there were historical witnesses which can confirm this truth (although that might help). It is simply because we can easily see the design, art, and meaningful purpose in it, and those things quickly register within our conscience that an intelligent creator was behind them!

For example, if all things man-made were *completely haphazard* without any order, design, art, or creative/meaningful purpose whatsoever, no one would be able to confirm that any particular man-made thing which they encountered (without its creator present) had an "intelligent designer/creator" behind it. In fact, if they never personally witnessed the creator of a certain thing which is only full of haphazard disorder, no one could confirm it had an intelligent creator, even if all they ever previously witnessed were men creating completely haphazard things without any order, design, art, or creative purpose! Therefore, the real *main reason* man can recognize an "intelligent designer/creator" behind anything man-made (without its creator present) isn't just because we have all seen men creating things man-made. It's because that thing has definite intelligent order, design, art, or creative/meaningful purpose *which always registers as proof for a creator in our conscience.*

Even haphazard man-made "modern art" has enough obvious evidence pointing to its intelligent creator, just because it does have some meaningful order and purpose in the way it is displayed, etc. But if you were to take away *all order, design, art, or creative/meaningful purpose* in things man-made, there would simply be *no way of confirming* that they had an intelligent creator behind them without seeing the intelligent creator of them. Only if you actually saw (or had reliable witnesses who saw) someone creating something completely haphazard could you confirm there was even a creator behind it!

> The real *main reason* man can recognize an "intelligent designer/creator" behind anything man-made (without its creator present) isn't just because we have all seen men creating things man-made.

All of Nature Has Order, Design, Art, and Creative/Meaningful Purpose

Even though there may be some disorder, all of nature also has order, design, art, and creative/meaningful purpose. For an obvious example, almost everyone knows that an intelligent being must have placed all the stars in the sky simply because of the many obvious "connect-the-dot" pictures which our stars form. For just some examples of the pictures which our stars form, here are their names we have given them because of the obvious pictures they form:

1. Virgo—The Virgin
2. Centaurus—The Centaur
3. Bootes—The Coming One
4. Libra—The Scales
5. Scorpio—The Scorpion
6. Serpens—The Serpent
7. Hercules—The Mighty One
8. Sagittarius—The Archer
9. Capricornus—The Sea Goat
10. Aquarius—The Water Bearer
11. Draco—The Dragon Cast Down
12. Pegasus—The Winged Horse
13. Lupus—The Wolf
14. Lyra—The Harp
15. Crux—The Cross
16. Aquila—The Eagle
17. Sagitta—The Arrow
18. Piscis Australis—The Southern Fish
19. Corona—The Crown
20. Taurus—The Bull
21. Cancer—The Crab
22. Leo—The Lion
23. Argo—The Ship
24. The list goes on…

Let's be honest, the notion that all of these many star pictures of real animals and people formed on their own through the mere random reckless haphazard chance of evolution would be absolutely absurd and an insult to human intelligence. That would be essentially no different than believing that the faces carved into Mt. Rushmore evolved on their own just through erosion! But we all know that someone both powerful and intelligent had to put these many stars in their exact positions to form these specific amazing pictures which are visible from earth!

And the even more interesting thing is that if these many star pictures were observed from any other planet than our own, they would most likely be completely unrecognizable! So that means that whoever put them in the heavens must have done it for just the inhabitants of the earth which, by the way, is a reality that even favors the fact that there is no life on other nearby planets.

And while all these realities do no favors for the theory of Darwinian evolution, they only confirm the Holy Bible and the Christian faith. But not only can Bible-believing Christians see the obvious intelligence in the pictures which stars form, but so do the Greeks, New Age astrologers, evolutionary scientists who study astronomy, and many others. Not only can we see they communicate obvious and specific "connect-the-dot" pictures, but Bible-believing Christians can easily see that they specifically depict many of the truths taught within the Holy Bible. Coincidence? Again, I think not. The truth is. my friend, that man did not actually invent "dot-to-dot" pictures; but it is fair to say that the same being who put the stars in the sky did! For lack of a better term, shall we just call him God? In fact, if God wanted to undeniably reveal himself to honest mankind, what a better way to do it? As it says in Psalm 19:1:

The heavens declare the glory of God; the skies proclaim the work of his hands.

The list of obvious examples of intelligent design built right into nature could go on and on for some time. But really, when you think about it, the stars (and their pictures) alone should pretty much do it for the honest soul. In the last fifty years or so, scientists keep discovering new things in nature, which simply demand intelligent design. For example, scientists have discovered that the Bombardier beetle has two tail pipes in its rear to blast any would-be predators with literal fire! But it has to mix two chemicals together just prior to being threatened for such an intelligent feat to occur. But how can the haphazard chance of evolution account for such a timely complex intelligent scenario? Let's face it; that insect has to be part scientist to mix those two exact chemicals together at just the right time in order to defend itself! It really doesn't make much sense for anything completely haphazard to bring about something else which requires complex life-saving precision. And yet, that's about all we find in all of nature that it is full of many such different systems which all require complex precision in order to function properly to protect life on earth.

> It really doesn't make much sense for anything completely random and haphazard to bring about something else which requires organized complex life-saving precision.

For another example, the Leaf Hopper insect literally has a set of teeth gears built into its back legs in order to shoot forward at a high speed and evade predators, etc. And the amazing thing is that the gears are of such a design as to be a superior design to any gears which man had manufactured prior to our discovery of the gears built into this insect. Is this the first time intelligent man has learned something from nature? If truth be told, most of man's inventions come from copying nature to a large degree. If someone can believe that such gears built right into an insect just haphazardly evolved on their own with no one intelligent behind their making (for a meaningful purpose), then they must at the same time believe all of our man-made gears (of inferior design) have evolved on their own as well! But I think if we are all *honest* with ourselves, neither one could have simply evolved on their own without the aid of an intelligent being behind them.

Because there is order, design, art, and creative/meaningful purpose in all of nature around us, even little children can understand and or believe that there is a personal creator/God behind it all, even though they have never seen God, read the Bible, or even been taught that there is a God. And because we can see that the order, art, and design, we observe *"normal"* nature has the meaningful purpose of preserving life or saving life; we can also reasonably conclude that the intelligent being which created it is also consistently loving! After all, where are all the complete bad designs in nature which purposely and consistently take life?

Yes, there is the abnormal corruption of obvious good designs which give death (which is fully explained by our sin corrupting God's perfect creation), but there are no obvious and consistent bad designs in nature which purposely and consistently take life (which would point to our creator being unloving). Nevertheless, while "seeing our intelligent creator would certainly help us believe," this certainly does not mean one *has to* "see" our intelligent creator in order to really believe he is real if, in fact, all things which he has created are full of order, loving design, art, meaningful purpose, and even superior to man's intelligence.

Many Reliable Historical Witnesses

In addition, just because we (or anyone we may know) may have not personally seen our creator God on earth creating anything, that certainly doesn't at all mean that no man ever has! In fact, many reputable historical figures claim that not only they have personally seen God but that thousands of others from all walks of life have indeed seen God as well, whether it be real historical people like Abraham or Moses in Old Testament times or the thousands of real people who personally met Jesus Christ during New Testament times and personally witnessed the creating attributes of almighty God in miraculous power flowing through him. Therefore, what should we reasonably do with all the testimonies of the apostles and the many other early Church Christians if there is no real evidence which would obviously discredit them as character witnesses?

I believe what any civil court of law would do. Even a court of law would say their historical testimony must be considered valid if there is no sound historical evidence against them. They must be considered innocent (or credible and telling the truth) until proven guilty! And so again, just because we have not personally seen God on earth creating anything, this means very little in light of two basic facts:

1. There are many united historical credible witnesses which claim to have not only seen God but also claim to have personally witnessed the creating attributes of almighty God in miraculous power (Genesis 18:1–3; Exodus 33:18–23; Luke 1:1–4; John 1:1–14, 14:7–11; Acts 1:1–11; 1 Corinthians 15:4–8; 1 Timothy 3:16; 2 Peter 1:15–18; 1 John 1:1–3). And when they also all agree with each other on the exact character of God and just what his specific purpose and plans for all mankind are, then such unification also testifies to them telling the truth as well.

2. In a very real sense, we have all seen God just through his "fingerprints" all over his own creation, which consist of order, design, art, and meaningful purpose! Similarly, our civil courts have always recognized that human fingerprints (which have a design) are *always* sure proof of a specific person, simply because they have a *specific design*. Why then wouldn't the order, design, and art "fingerprints" all throughout nature be considered sure evidence for the person of God who created nature? The truth is that all the awesome things in creation we can see should easily give us the faith to believe in him whom we cannot yet see.

The Obvious Intelligence Built into Raw Foods

When we've eaten the same foods our whole lives, it may be easy to overlook the obvious fact that they were purposely and specifically made to be consumed by humans! For example, every one of the raw foods in nature are easily handled and consumed by humans. They can all not only be easily harvested by man, but many of them are also easily consumed by man in their natural state. For example, many raw foods like bananas, celery, grapes, plums, green beans, berries, mushrooms, Brussels sprouts, carrots, etc. fit right into the human mouth for consumption. And many more of those raw foods we find in nature are not much bigger and can just be eaten like an apple, because they easily fit into the human hand as well. Peaches, pears, tomatoes, onions, avocados, oranges, grapefruit, cucumbers, potatoes, and the list goes on. And even the larger raw foods such as watermelon, squash, cauliflower, broccoli, cabbage, etc. can be easily harvested and consumed by humans. And honestly, such a reality certainly goes far beyond mere haphazard random reckless chance bringing all that consistent evidence for a creator who specifically designed the raw foods for human consumption.

> All the awesome things in creation we can see should easily give us the faith to believe in him whom we cannot yet see.

Let's again be honest; there are no watermelons the size of donkeys (which cannot be easily harvested by man)! And honestly, why wouldn't we see many such larger inconsistencies in the realm of raw foods which are not compatible with human consumption if *haphazard* evolution were really true?

If evolution were true, we would be forced to believe all this is just a mere coincidence over the last 6,000 years, simply because evolution is based upon only a haphazard, random, reckless chance of events. But if indeed our creator (who is very personal in nature) specifically created all raw foods for the human body (and animals), then this "size" reality of our raw foods would make much more sense! If haphazard, random, reckless evolution were at all true, very reasonably, we would certainly *not* expect all the raw foods to be just the right *consistent* size for human harvesting and human consumption. Instead we might expect some very inconsistent and unmanageable raw food sizes. And we would also expect that probably over half of them would not even be fit for human consumption!

Just how can any random, reckless, haphazard process produce only the consistent life-giving results as we plainly see in all the raw foods designed perfectly for human consumption? We must remember that any haphazard process will only bring about inconsistent haphazard results! In fact, not just raw foods, but many other realities of planet earth all basically indicate that it was specifically "Taylor made" for the survival of human race. The consistent temperature ranges of the sun, the winds consistently staying mild enough for human survival, the soil being largely conducive for vegetation growth, and *a whole host* of other basic realities which *must all work together* for human survival inevitably point to a creator who lovingly intended human survival.

If evolution were really true, then other raw food realities (which are far beyond the haphazard, random, reckless chance of evolution) would have to be explained as well. For example, if you cut a carrot in half (the short way), you'll notice that it looks similar to the human eye. And amazingly enough, carrots, when eaten, are good for your eyes. Just a coincidence? Maybe if carrots were the only raw foods having a specific design which aids specific human body part health! If you cut a tomato in half, you'll notice it has four chambers inside just like the human heart. And amazingly enough, tomatoes are good for the human heart when eaten. Similarly, if you look at the silhouette of a hanging bunch of grapes, it is shaped like the human heart. And amazingly enough, grapes are good for the human heart. Avocados are shaped like a human female womb and take nine months to grow. And amazingly enough, they are good for the female womb. Also, eggplants and pears are shaped like the female womb, and they too are good for the female womb.

Similarly, figs which are full of seeds and hang in twos are good for increasing the mobility and count of male sperm to prevent male sterility. Walnuts look similar to the human brain, and amazingly enough, studies have shown that they are specifically good for the human brain when consumed. Kidney beans are, of course, shaped just like the human kidney, and once again, they are good for maintaining kidney function. Celery, Bok Choy, Rhubarb, and other similar raw foods look similar to human bones. And amazingly enough, they all specifically target human bone strength.

Sweet potatoes look like the human pancreas and actually balance the glycemic index of diabetics. Olives assist the health and function of human female ovaries. Oranges, grapefruits, and other citrus fruits look just like the mammary glands of the human female and actually assist the health of the breasts and the movement of the lymph in and out of the breasts. Onions look just like the body's cells. And amazingly enough, today's research shows that onions help clear waste material from all of the body's cells. The working companion, garlic, also helps eliminate waste materials and dangerous free radicals from the body. And, of course, the list goes on—hopefully you get the point. If haphazard, random, reckless evolution were true, we would be forced to believe that all these specific special relationships were just a mere coincidence! However, simple *honesty* in the heart and conscience of man should convince us otherwise.

Conclusion

Yes, it is difficult to understand just why some atheists or evolutionists insist on rejecting "intelligent design" when they (who admit to having some intelligence) cannot even understand the purposeful design within much of creation. And because of this confusing self-contradiction within their "no intelligent design" beliefs, one must reasonably conclude that their beliefs are essentially based more from mere "*emotion*" rather than fortified with the abundant honest scientific evidence we might expect of a belief system which claims to explain the very origins of all life around us.

But is it even possible that a person could choose such an entire false belief system such as Darwinian evolution just for emotional reasons? Well, our emotions are not only very powerful things, but they are quite deceptive simply because they don't seem to respect age, sex, education, rational thought, or even reality itself. In other words, no matter what the age, sex, education, or rational understanding a person might have, mankind has always had a *great history* of making even his most important choices in life through mere emotion rather than the honest evidence which supports true reality. For example, as you probably already know, people often pick out their houses, cars, and spouses for emotional reasons, only to find out later that they were deceived by their emotions because they ignored the honest evidence which was connected to the reality that their choice would end in pain.

And if we can be deceived by our emotions with houses, cars, and spouses, why not with our "spiritual belief system" as well? Yes, people are very emotional beings, and this even includes evolutionary scientists as well! And the fact that people are very emotional about even their spiritual beliefs may indeed explain just why there are so many different spiritual belief systems in the world (which includes evolution), which all "claim to be right," even though we know they're not because they directly contradict each other within their basic doctrines and views of reality.

Let's face it; because all the existing spiritual belief systems in the world contradict each other in just their basic doctrines, we are rather forced to conclude through simple reason that they are either all wrong, or all but one of them must be wrong and based upon mere emotion rather than the honest evidence which reality has always required. Ultimately, when it comes right down to it, the Theory of Darwinian Evolution teaches us that all obvious "intelligence" found within nature (including ourselves) came from "nothing," while biblical Christianity teaches us that all obvious "intelligence" within nature came from our highly intelligent creator who is the source of all "intelligence."

Which one honestly sounds the more scientific and reasonable to you? If you can see the obvious truth that there most certainly must be a very intelligent creator behind all the complex life which we cannot yet even fully comprehend and want to finally give the God of the Bible a chance to reveal himself to you in a way you can't deny, I invite you to just take that first small step of faith by sincerely praying the prayer of salvation located at the end of this book. No matter what your past is like, God loves you and sincerely wants you to be a part of his awesome eternal kingdom!

Jesus said, "I am the resurrection and the life. He who believes in me, will live even though he dies; and whoever lives and believes in me will never die..." (John 11:25–26)

OBJECTION 5

I Believe in Evolution

The Theory of Darwinian Evolution may not be considered a "religion," per se, simply because it rules out a personal God. However, it is just as much a "spiritual belief system" as any God-believing religion, simply because it too has its own answers to the basic spiritual questions, which all religions in the world attempt to answer in their own way, such as:

1. Where did we come from?
2. What is our purpose in life? Or why are we here?
3. Where are we going when we die?
4. What (or who) is the true source of all life?

Darwinian evolution may just give us very different answers to the above questions than does biblical Christianity, but it nevertheless answers them. Its answers to the above questions are basically the following:

1. Where did we come from? Dirt, sunlight, heat, water, chemicals, the big bang explosion, which all came from "nothing." But evolution believers simply cannot explain where these things even came from or how life actually came from "nothing," which is non-life. Therefore, just like biblical Christianity, it too is a *completely "faith-based"* belief system—*not science based.* The only difference is that it probably takes much more faith to believe all life on earth

60

came from nothing (or nonlife) than it does to believe all life on earth came from the living person of God who is the source of all life.

2. What is our purpose in life? Or why are we here? To self-ishly just survive, even if that includes eliminating what you deem an inferior race of people or anything which is considered a threat to over all human survival. Since you are nothing more important than mere protoplasm washed up on some beach, your purpose in life is just to somehow evolve over millions of years, even though no one has ever observed such a long and very boring process. And because your purpose is just to survive physically, the only love you could give or receive throughout such a long boring process is purely "selfish love," which is really no love at all if you think about it.

3. Where are we going when we die? You will just be recycled back into nature starting with worm food. You have no spirit which finds its home with a creator. You're just dust or dirt, and as soon as you die, you just become part of the very impersonal cosmos. Bloodshed, suffering, death, and pain are absolutely essential to the process of evolution and will continue for the entire human race as long as it ever exists with no escape from it ever.

4. What (or who) is the true source of all life? There can't be a self-sustaining loving perfect God which all life came from, just because it goes beyond our very limited intelligence. But evolutionists cannot explain where all life did come from either, other than from nothing, which certainly seems to be a violation of what little intelligence we've proved to have.

When asking any believer in evolution why they believe in evolution, they usually assert that it is "science" backed and, therefore, the "logical choice." And then when asked if they mean the kind of science that can be tested and observed like with the scientific method, they usually say something like, "Most definitely." Then when you ask them if they can give you *just one clear example* of one "kind" of creature evolving into another "kind" (which "Macro" or "Darwinian" evolution necessitates) *which can be "observed,"* they can only give you examples of one "species" of a "kind" evolving into another "species" of that same "kind" and simply cannot provide any clear examples of Darwinian evolution taking place under the observation of man in all of recorded human history.

Let's expound a little bit on that. When a finch bird with a little beak evolves into a finch bird with a larger beak, this is only an example of "micro" evolution—not "Macro" or Darwinian evolution. The bird is still a bird. This is only one "species" of a "kind" evolving into another "species" of that same "kind." Most every scientist on planet earth wholeheartedly believes in this kind of evolution because it is "observable science" both in the fossil record and within recorded human history. However, in the science world, a dog and a bird are considered two completely different "kinds" of animals. And no one in recorded human history has ever observed a dog evolving into a bird or vice-versa. Nor has anyone observed any other "kind" of animal evolving into any other kind of animal. And if, in fact, it were true or even possible, then why on earth do we not observe all the different "kinds" of animals even *wanting* to crossbreed with each other?

But as it has always been observed, you can even put two different "kinds" of animals (which are even rather similar) in a cage together for months, and they will not crossbreed with each other. They may try to kill each other, but they would never even attempt to seriously crossbreed! In addition, if macro evolution were true, why has the fossil record and or recorded human history completely denied us this precious evidence for the obvious crossbreeding of two completely different kinds of animals?

> If, in fact, Darwinian evolution were true, then why on earth do we not observe all the different "kinds" of animals even *wanting* to cross breed with each other?

Even though this is what the "Theory of Evolution" has taught in all school textbooks, it is not at all "observable" science, especially since *one single clear obvious example* of it has not been found or observed in all of human history! The simple truth is that if the Theory of Darwinian evolution were true, we'd easily find thousands and probably even millions of fossils which would obviously show all the many different "kinds" of animals evolving into other "kinds" of animals in different intermediate stages. But since these many necessary intermediate fossils have never been found by the professional scientific community within the last 150 years, what should we honestly conclude?

The truth is that we should have found *thousands* of these intermediate fossils by now if Darwinian evolution were basically true. But we haven't. And that, of course, is a big problem for the honest soul, because that itself is the very heart of the theory of evolution, not just some little side issue. If the biggest part of any theory is simply missing, how can anyone expect *honest* people to believe in it? That's like expecting people to climb into an expensive fancy car without an engine and believe it will transport them! If the very "engine" of a theory has always been missing after 150 years of modern scientific scrutiny and research, should it not be humbly abandoned as "provable science" to save the human race from further embarrassment? And that's exactly why the "Theory of Evolution" is still referred to as a "theory" to this day, simply because the very heart of its claim has not yet been "observable science" just as the "scientific method" reasonably requires.

> If Darwinian evolution were true, we'd easily find thousands of fossils which would show all the many different "kinds" of animals evolving into other "kinds" of animals in different intermediate stages.

Let's face it; it is not at all anything close to proven science if *one clear example* of "Macro" evolution still cannot be provided after all this time. Even Darwin himself was deeply troubled by the fact that no certain fossils proving "Macro" evolution could be found by the end of his own lifetime. He very reasonably thought that if evolution from one "kind" to another was indeed the basic explanation of life that there should have been not just one but *many clear examples of it found in the fossil record* by the end of even his own life. If Charles Darwin knew that even after 150 years we haven't found the many intermediate fossils required to confirm evolution, he likely would have abandoned his own theory long ago.

Additionally, if he had even known about the very intelligent complexity of the cellular world which scientists have discovered in the last fifty years, it is very doubtful indeed that he would have even continued with his own theory on that basis as well. As everyone now knows, the "cell" (no matter what of) is anything but "simple" and has many complex systems within it which all must work together in order to sustain life!

The First Deception—The Theory of Evolution Is Based Upon Real Science

Many evolution believers have been deceived into believing that the Theory of Evolution is based upon real science. However, we've just exposed that the Theory of Evolution is still waiting for its *basic scientific backing* after well over 100 years of modern scientific investigation. And also considering it cannot explain just where everything evolved from, one must realize that it too is ultimately reliant upon 100 percent faith for the *origins of life,* just like any other "God-based" religion in the world which cannot rationally explain where God himself came from. So where's the basic science which "backs" it in light of that? Where did the original explosion, heat, water, dirt, or microorganisms come from?

The Theory of Evolution really has no *sensible scientific* answer to these questions. In fact, to simply say (or personally believe) "everything came from nothing" is no more sensible or scientific than if we were to say that the book you were reading right now "came from nowhere!" Let's face it; if "everything came from nothing," then not one thing truly even exists! Sounds scientific? Or 100 percent faith-based for its origin of life?

Again, one must be *honest* with themselves about these things if they ever hope to find the truth. The honest truth of the matter is that the Theory of Evolution is just as much a "faith-based belief system" as is biblical Christianity, simply because it too is ultimately based on 100 percent pure faith (not science) *for its explanation of origins* in the chain of supposed "evolutionary" life. In fact, as we've already mentioned, it takes far more faith to believe "everything came from nothing" rather than believe everything in creation which displays intelligence, order, and purpose came from an intelligent eternal being who we just cannot fully comprehend. Because even though God may reasonably go well beyond our understanding of science, at least he does not go against the science we do observe and understand like the Theory of Evolution does! However, in any case, the point is that for our explanation of life and reality, all we have to choose from are "faith-based belief systems." The only question is, which "faith" is truly in harmony with real science and other honest evidences, like historical, archaeological, etc.?

> The theory of evolution is just as much a "faith-based belief system" as is biblical Christianity simply because it too is based on 100 percent pure faith (not science) for its explanation of *origins*...

The Second Deception—Biblical Christianity Is Not Confirmed by Real Science

As for biblical Christianity being "unscientific" as many evolutionists assert, nothing could be further from the truth. In fact, for the last several centuries, many, if not most of our greatest scientists were indeed Bible-believing Christians who made many of the world changing discoveries we rely upon today! And in many cases, it was, in fact, the truths of the Bible itself which aided them in their discoveries!

Presently, in the US today, about half of scientists are creation scientists who believe in a "creator God" behind it all (rejecting Darwinian evolution), and many of them believe in the Bible. For example, the late Henry Morris, who was a creation scientist, was a pioneer in the modern sciences in that he showed how the Bible is in complete harmony with our scientific discoveries so far. In other words, it has never been at odds with real science, but rather real discovered science just supports it. For example, he mathematically calculated that all the different "kinds" of animals would have easily fit into Noah's Ark (given its biblical dimensions) with plenty of room for their food, etc. Today, the Answers in Genesis Ministry located in the northern tip of Kentucky has even built a full-sized Noah's ark according to biblical dimensions just to show the world how realistic the biblical account of it was. If you haven't yet seen it, please just take a day and see it for yourself—it is truly amazing!

Henry Morris also noted that the worldwide fossil record was in complete harmony with what the Bible taught as it clearly showed that millions of both plants and animals worldwide were quickly buried and could not have died decaying rapidly as we know animals do today, which really leave us almost no fossils at all. Also, when commenting on global processes and their indication of the earth's age after his whole life's career in studying earth science and the other sciences, Henry Morris stated:

> "It is widely taught today that the earth is 4.6 billion years old and that the universe is anywhere from 8 billion years old to eternally old. The Bible, on the other hand, indicates the universe to be only thousands of years old, and all known human history (as recorded in the historical annals of Egypt, Sumeria, and other ancient nations) also is limited to the same basic time frame."

The great ages needed to make Darwinian evolution appear feasible are based mainly on a handful of very slow radioactive decay processes (uranium to lead, potassium to argon, etc.). These must each be based on at least three unverifiable assumptions:

1. Known initial boundary conditions (assumption of no initial radiogenic lead in the uranium/lead mineral).
2. Isolated system (no ingress of components of the system during the time it is functioning).
3. Constant rate of process (no effect of environmental radiations or any other force on the decay rate).

"None of these assumptions are capable of either proof or disproof since conditions are unknown prior to recorded history. And all are known to be wrong in almost all natural processes today. On the other hand, there are scores of worldwide natural processes which even with the above "uniformitarian" assumptions, will indicate ages far too brief for Darwinian evolution to be feasible...Therefore the weight of scientific evidence (entirely apart from the definitive and conclusive biblical revelation) is that both the earth and universe are young (p. 1505).[2]"

Henry Morris adds:

"The existence of a transcendent creator and the necessity of a primeval special creation of the uni-

---

[2] Morris, Henry. *Defender's Study Bible*. Grand Rapids, Michigan: World Publishing, Inc., 1995

verse is confirmed by the most basic principles of nature discovered by scientists:

1. The law of causality, that no effect can be greater than its cause, is basic in all scientific investigation and human experience. A universe comprising an array of intelligible and complex effects, including living systems and conscious personalities, is itself proof of an intelligent, complex, living, conscious person as its cause.

2. The laws of thermodynamics are the most universal and best proved generalizations of science, applicable to every process and system of any kind, the first law stating that no matter/energy is now being created or destroyed, and the second law stating that all existing matter/energy is proceeding irreversibly toward ultimate equilibrium and cessation of all processes. Since this eventual death of the universe has not yet occurred and since it will occur in time, if these processes continue, the Second Law proves that time (and therefore, the space/matter/time universe) had a beginning. The universe must have been created, but the first law precludes the possibility of self creation. The only resolution of the dilemma posed by the First and Second laws is that "in the beginning God created the heaven and the earth." The so-called big bang theory of the origin of the cosmos, postulating a primeval explosion of the space/mass/time continuum at the start, beginning with a state of nothingness and then rapidly expanding into the present complex universe,

contradicts both these basic laws as well as scripture (p.3).[3]"

Some evolutionary thinkers today will try to insist that within their belief system there was no beginning of the cosmos but rather that it "always existed." However, as Henry Morris well put it, "Since this eventual death of the universe has not yet occurred and since it will occur in time if these processes continue, the Second Law proves that time (and therefore, the space/matter/time universe) had a beginning."

Evolutionary thinkers will sometimes respond by saying, "Yeah, but Bible-believing Christians say that 'God' always existed, so what's the difference?"

The obvious difference is that we can scientifically observe the Second Law of Thermodynamics actively at work in all the earth (and observable cosmos), but no one has ever scientifically observed that the Second Law of Thermodynamics was actively at work in the person of our creator. Thus, there is no equal comparison, and the possibility, of course, still exists that our creator always did exist as much as that reality goes beyond the comprehension of his creation (which it should, if our self-existing creator created us). Therefore, while basic observable science has easily disproved evolution or the idea that everything always existed, it certainly has not disproven the aseity (self-existence) of an eternal creator. So if the cosmos could not have come from "nothing" and could not have "always existed" without contradicting these very basic laws of science, then it is certainly "checkmate" for the Theory of Evolution as a personal intelligent creator of all is the only honest option left. And that is exactly what all our great contributing scientists listed below reasonably concluded as well:

---

[3] Morris, Henry. *Defender's Study Bible*. Grand Rapids, Michigan: World Publishing, Inc., 1995

Other Well-Known Bible-believing Scientists of the Past and Their Discoveries

Joseph Lister—Antiseptic surgery

Louis Pasteur—Bacteriology, bio-genesis law, fermentation control, Pasteurization, Vaccination and immunization

Isaac Newton—Calculus, dynamics, law of gravity, reflecting telescope

Johann Kepler—Celestial mechanics, physical astronomy, ephemeris tables

Robert Boyle—Chemistry, gas dynamics

Georges Cuvier—Comparative anatomy, vertebrate paleontology

Charles Babbage—Computer science, actuarial tables, calculating machine

Lord Rayleigh—Dimensional analysis, modern analysis

James Clerk Maxwell—Electrodynamics, statistical thermodynamics

Michael Faraday—Electromagnetics, field theory, electric generator

Ambrose Fleming—Electronics, thermionic valve

Lord Kelvin—Energetics, thermodynamics, temperature scale, trans-Atlantic cable

Henri Fabre—Entomology of living insects

George stokes—Fluid mechanics

William Herschel—Galactic astronomy, double stars

Gregor Mendel—Genetics

Louis Agassiz—Glacial geology, ichthyology

James Simpson—Gynecology, chloroform

Leonardo Da Vinci—Hydraulics

Matthew Maury—Hydrography, oceanography

Blaise Pascal—Hydrostatics, Barometer

William Ramsey—Isotopic chemistry, inert gases

John Ray—Natural history

Bernard Riemann—Non-Euclidean geometry

David Brewster—Optical mineralogy, kaleidoscope

John Woodward—Paleontology

Rudolph Virchow—Pathology

James Joule—Reversible thermodynamics

Nicholas Steno—Stratigraphy

Carolus Linnaeus—Systematic biology, classification system
Humphrey Davy—Thermo-kinetics, mine safety lamp
Joseph Henry—Electric motor, galvanometer, self-induction
John Herschel—Global star catalog
Francis Bacon—Scientific method
Samuel Morse—Telegraph

Interestingly enough, and probably unknown to many atheists today, many of the above discoveries were directly aided by specific scriptures of the Bible itself. For example, Matthew Maury actually discovered the "currents of the ocean" for easiest marine travel in Psalm 8:8, which teaches us that there are indeed *paths of the sea.* The following are other great scientific discoveries which have always been in the Bible (written by an inspired prophet of God sometimes thousands of years before they were even discovered by modern science):

Evaporation—Psalm 135:7; Jeremiah 10:13
Condensation—Job 26:8, 37:11, 16
Condensation nuclei—Proverbs 8:26
Precipitation—Job 36:26–28
Run-off—Job 28:10
Oceanic reservoir—Psalm 33:7
Snow—Job 38:22
Hydrologic balance—Job 28:24–26
Springs in the sea—Job 38:16
Principle of Isostasy—Isaiah 40:12
Shape of the earth—Isaiah 40:22; Job 26:10; Ps. 103:12
Rotation of the earth—Job 38:12, 14
Gravitation—Job 26:7, 38:6
Rock erosion—Job 14:18,19
Glacial period—Job 38:29,30
Uniformitarian's—2 Pet. 3:4
Dinosaurs—Job chapters 40 and 41
Size of universe—Job 11:7–9, 22:12; Isaiah 55:9; Jeremiah 31:37
Number of stars—Genesis 12:17; Jeremiah 33:22

Uniqueness of each star—1 Corinthians 15:41
Precision of orbits—Jeremiah 31:35,36
Circulation of atmosphere—Ecclesiastes 1:6
Protective effect of atmosphere—Isaiah 40:22
Oceanic origin of rain—Ecclesiastes 1:7
Relation of electricity to rain—Job 28:26; Jeremiah 10:13
Fluid dynamics—Job 28:25
Blood circulation—Leviticus 17:11
Psychotherapy—Proverbs 16:24, 17:22
Biogenesis and stability—Genesis 1:11, 21,25
Uniqueness of man—Genesis 1:26
Chemical nature of flesh—Genesis 1:11,24, 2:7, 3:19
Cave men—Job 12:23–25, 30:3–8
Mass energy equivalence—Colossians 1:17; Hebrews 1:3
Source of energy for earth—Psalm 19:6
Atomic disintegration—2 Peter 3:10
Electrical transmission of information—Job 38:35
Rapid transportation—Daniel 12:4
While the earth revolves around the sun, it also has its own orbit revolving around the earth—Psalm 19:4–6

While the above list is, of course, only partial, it verifies that although biblical Christianity may well go beyond human reasoning (as does any belief system), it certainly does not go against what scientific realities have been discovered. And not only has the Word of God always been in complete harmony with our well-established natural sciences, but also *far ahead* of our scientific discoveries in many cases!

For example, Job 38:24 says, "*By what way is the light parted, which scattereth the East wind upon the earth?*" Did you know that modern meteorologists only more recently (within the last fifty years) discovered that the sunlight actually causes wind patterns? And yet this 4,000-year-old verse of God's Word plainly disclosed this information a long time ago. Again, in Job 38:16 it says, "*Hast thou entered into the springs of the sea?*" But it wasn't until 1977 that scientists even confirmed there were "springs" in the ocean floors. And I can assure you that the list of modern scientific discoveries trailing far behind the Bible goes on.

The Bible, Our History, and the Discoveries of Archaeology All Agree with Each Other that Man Has Always Lived Right with Dinosaurs

While evolutionists typically maintain that dinosaurs died out sixty million years before mankind even "evolved" into existence, the Bible has always taught that man has always lived right with dinosaurs (Job chapters 40–41). In fact, one can just Google "Cryptozoology" and see that Cryptozoologists who spend much of their time investigating the subject believe there are, in fact, still dinosaurs alive with mankind on planet earth today! Whether we are talking about the many relatively recent sightings of the "Loch Ness Monster" (of which commonly describe a "Plesiosaurus" dinosaur) or just the hundreds of encounters which historic sailors have claimed to have had with marine-type dinosaurs from the 1500s through the 1800s, it would certainly seem that so many people of good reputation simply could not have all been lying straight-faced to the world in their many testimonies!

For many today, "dragons" are thought of as being just a myth. However, there are many evidences which would lead us to believe they were just another type of dinosaur which died out only a few hundred years ago. In fact, in some of our dictionaries as recent as 1946, part of the definition of *dragons* is "now rare." All in all, there is much evidence that many different types of dinosaurs were still alive and well on planet earth only hundreds of years ago.

For example, it is common knowledge among archaeologists that the North American Indians carved many pictures of obvious *living* dinosaurs on the walls of the Grand Canyon. Why, if they did not actually see living dinosaurs? They didn't carve pictures of just the skeletons of dinosaurs; they carved pictures of only living dinosaurs just as though they were completely familiar eyewitnesses of them.

My friend, such archaeological evidence does not exactly favor the Theory of Evolution. Similarly, from Ica, Peru, we have over 500 burial stones (called the "Nazca Burial Stones" dating from 300 BC to 800 AD), many of which have the carved pictures of men living right with live dinosaurs, some of which show men even riding dinosaurs! And since some of these "Ica" stone carvings even accurately show round circle patterns for the skin of their dinosaurs, which archaeologists now know is only unique to thick dinosaur skin, we can be quite certain these Indians were actual eyewitnesses of real dinosaurs living among them. How else would these Indians have known what the skin of dinosaurs looked like? Carving into these burial stones was just their way of preserving history for following generations. So did it work? Or were their careful record efforts all in vain? It would certainly seem they were in vain, at least for the evolutionist.

And why did the Vikings carve in long-necked dragons/dinosaurs on the front of their sailing vessels if they never actually encountered such creatures at sea? If they wanted to portray their own military might at sea, would it have made any sense whatsoever to just put some "make believe" creature (which no one was familiar with) on the front of their vessels to intimidate their foes? I don't think so! But it would make perfect sense for them to position one of the most fierce creatures *already known to man* on the fronts of their ships to represent their military strength.

Similarly, you can go to Babylon—Iraq today—and still see unmistakable long-necked dragon/dinosaur creatures carved into the ancient stone walls of Babylon which Saddam Hussein was trying to rebuild and preserve. Again, none of this kind of honest evidence is a "feather in the cap" of evolutionists which insist that such creatures died out *millions* of years ago!

Also, it is also common knowledge among reputable historians that Alexander the Great gave us written record that when he conquered parts of what is now India in 326 BC, his soldiers were actually scared by a "great dragon" which lived in some cave they encountered. Evidently, the Indians of the area worshiped it and implored Alexander not to slay it with his army. And Alexander honored their wish. Nevertheless, they recorded the length of the massive hissing creature sticking half out of the cave to measure about seventy cubits (over 100 feet) in length.

Similarly, Onesicritus, one of Alexander the Great's lieutenants, stated that the Indian "King Abisarus" kept other "serpents" that were between 120–210 feet long! At that length, clearly, these were also a type of dinosaur as well! Herodotus, Aristotle, and other Greeks also wrote of man witnessing many live dinosaurs. Additionally, Marco Polo even wrote of many obvious live dinosaur encounters along his travels. The historical records of the Chinese also clearly testify that they lived right with live dinosaurs, especially dragons.

Morvidus was the king of the Britons from 341 to 336 BC. And as recorded by Geoffrey of Monmouth, Morvidus was eaten by a large sea dragon which came out of the Irish Sea. Evidently, the inhabitants of the western shores were being devoured by the creature, and in an attempt to stop it, Morvidus met the beast in single combat and used every weapon he could against it to no avail.

According to Geoffrey, the monster lunged at him and "gulped down the body of Morvidus as a big fish swallows a little one." Then, of course, you have the written accounts of the "Wawel dragon" given to us from the twelfth century AD, and the dragon St. George slayed around 300 AD.

Pliny the Elder, a Roman author, naturalist, and philosopher, also describes in good detail just how the tenacious dragons of his day preyed on the large elephants of India in his written records. Then again, a man by the name of Saxo Grammaticus, in his work, *Gesta Danorum*, relates the account of the Danish King Frotho and his fight with a giant dragon/dinosaur reptile. Evidently, a local man had firsthand knowledge of the beast and wanted to help the king get rid of the dangerous monster. He thus described the serpent to the king:

> "Wreathed in coils, doubled in many a fold, and with a tail drawn out in whorls, shaking his manifold spirals and shedding venom…his slaver (saliva) burns up what it bespatters…remember to keep the dauntless temper of the mind; nor let the point of the jagged teeth trouble thee, nor the starkness of the beast, nor the venom…there is a

place under his lowest belly whither thou mayest
plunge the blade…"

Obviously, what was described by this real person in history to a Danish king was a real live dragon-type dinosaur which lived in the region. And just as obvious, it was of good enough size to threaten a king and was no mere modern animal known to us today as its saliva literally "burned up what it bespattered." And there are many other such accounts of dragon type dinosaurs from *Ulysses Aldrovandrus, The Epic of Gilgamesh, Beowulf, Silius Italica, The Henham Dragon, Glamorgan*, etc. And none of these well-known accounts are even listed in our bibliography, just because any one of them can be so easily "Googled."

So just what do evolutionists do with so many *credible historical records* if they insist dinosaurs all died out *sixty-five million* years ago? Obviously they can't have it both ways with such a massive time gap between both views. Could it be that evolutionists who seriously maintain that dinosaurs all died out millions of years ago deny all the obvious evidence which we've discussed because their stance is one of mere emotion which just gives them freedom from God? After all, they didn't live sixty-five million years ago, and they certainly don't even have any historical records from then to back up their fantastic position. And if there are many historical records like the ones we've touched upon which strongly validate the Bible's clear teaching that man has always lived with dinosaurs, when it comes to this subject, whose belief system is based on *only blind faith*? And whose is based on honest historical evidence?

Relatively Recent Sightings of Dinosaurs Still Living Today

In his book titled *Shipwrecks and Sea Monsters*, author Randall Reinstedt even shows a real picture of an obvious marine dinosaur which washed up on the beach on the coast of Monterrey California in 1925 (pg. 167).[4] It unmistakably had a neck about twenty feet long which simply does not match any such large marine creatures

---

[4] Reinstedt, Randall. *Shipwrecks and Sea Monsters.*

we are familiar with today. However, such a skeletal structure would, in fact, easily match the marine-type dinosaur which we have called the Plesiosaurus.

Additionally, some time ago, the front cover of *Time Magazine* featured a picture of an obvious dinosaur-type marine creature (looking a lot like a Plesiosaurus) which was found by a Japanese fishing vessel in 1977 off the coast of New Zealand. Evidently the *only half-decayed* corpse of the long-necked creature was pulled up from 900 feet down and was approximately thirty-two feet long and weighed about 4,000 pounds! Plesiosaurus-like creatures have also been reported by Aboriginals in far North Queensland, Australia (pg. 345).[5]

Similarly, the natives today which surround a large swamp in the middle of Congo, Africa, testify of their common sightings of marine-type dinosaurs living in that swamp. And, of course, there are the many sightings of "Loch Ness" marine-type dinosaurs in Loch Ness Lake located in the Scottish Highlands. Many may think that these "Loch Ness" sightings are only relatively recent (1933 and on), but historical sightings of "Loch Ness" marine-type dinosaurs actually date back 1,500 years!

Archaeologists have even unearthed old riverbeds in Texas which actually have both the contemporary footprints of man and dinosaurs trapped together as a result of Noah's global flood![6] Really, how much more proof does one need that man has always lived right with dinosaurs just as the Bible teaches, if they are just honest with such evidence?

And, of course, the obvious answer as to why not many dinosaurs are left today (and most all clearly extinct) is because historical mankind has killed them off for a variety of reasons. Some of those main reasons include just the protection of civilizations, the gain of food and medicine from their deaths as well as being killed off just for sport. It is little different than the fact that there is only a handful of grizzly bears left today compared to the thirty some million grizzly bears which roamed the West just 100-plus years ago!

---

5   *CEN Technical Journal*, Vol. 12, no. 3. 1998
6   Hovind, Dr. Kent. *Dinosaurs and the Bible*. CSE Ministry. 2006

Human nature within hunters of all past cultures probably all "loved a challenge," just like hunters still do today. Sometimes ignorant skeptics have asked the question, "Well, if man has always lived with dinosaurs, then why aren't 'dinosaurs' by name even mentioned in the Bible?" Well, the main reason is, of course, because our particular modern term *dinosaur* was only more recently invented in 1841 by Richard Owen! However, the Bible just calls the very same creatures by a different name—namely *dragons*. To expect the historic records within the Holy Bible which are 2,000–4,000 years old to use all our modern terms today is really quite unrealistic indeed. Nevertheless, the King James Version actually mentions *dragons* (referring to what we now call dinosaurs) about thirty-four times. While the Bible's general term, *dragon*, may certainly include (depending upon context) what we call a "dragon" today; in a broader sense, it refers to *all dinosaurs* in general as both the context and description of "*dragons*" within the Bible bear witness to this fact. And, of course, this just makes sense if what we know to be a "dragon" today is, in fact, just another type of dinosaur. When referring to marine-type dinosaurs, the Bible just refers to them as "*dragons of the sea*" (Psalm 74:13–14; Isaiah 27:1–2).

All this honest evidence strongly confirms from a wide variety of sources that ancient man lived right with dinosaurs—and that the very long ages assigned to Darwinian evolution are not even close to true.

The *biblical* proof that man lived right with dinosaurs is quite obvious. In Job 40:15, when God is talking right to Job, he plainly states that he created land animals right with mankind:

Behold now Behemoth (meaning "huge beast"), which I made with thee...

In Job 40:17, the Behemoth is clearly described as a massive beast having a tail like a *"cedar tree,"* which certainly rules out any living creatures known to man today and undoubtedly refers to what we know as a giant Sauropod dinosaur! And why would God ask Job to *"behold now Behemoth"* if Job didn't know what that particular dinosaur looked like? Let's face it; a large dinosaur with a tail the size of a cedar tree would certainly be pretty hard not to behold, and I'm sure Job saw more than one in his lifetime.

Yes, it is quite obvious that God here is talking to Job about the great Behemoth dinosaur just as though Job himself were very familiar with him. Also, according to Genesis 1:24–31, God made all land animals and mankind both on the sixth day, and that is exactly why God says to Job *"[w]hich I made with thee."* Most Bible scholars date the book of Job to be around the time of Abraham (2,000 BC). In Job chapter 41, God also talks to Job about the great *"Leviathan"* sea dragon, just as though Job himself were very familiar with him as well. Isaiah was God's prophet for the nation of Israel in about 700 BC. In Isaiah 27:1, even though he is symbolically comparing Satan with *Leviathan*, Isaiah also confirms that *Leviathan* was *"the dragon that is in the sea."* In verse 19–21, God says to Job about the Leviathan:

> **Out of his mouth go burning lamps, and sparks of fire leap out. Out of his nostrils goeth smoke, as out of a seething pot or cauldron. His breath kindleth coals, and a flame goeth out of his mouth.**

Leviathan's whole description in Job chapter 41 is clearly that of a large fire-breathing dragon which dwells in the sea. And the plain archaeological/historical evidence which we've discussed so far is only a fraction of what has been discovered which not only confirms the truth of the Bible but also easily discredits the *long ages* assigned by evolutionists (between man and dinosaurs) who just want you to take their word for it.

Well, many people have not only been fooled into just "taking their word" for the long ages they assign between man and dinosaurs but also the age of the earth as well. Just the fact that the long ages they assign to the earth keeps drastically growing by billions of years should certainly be a red flag to anyone sensible.

For example, in 1770, the evolutionist, George Buffon, officially declared that the earth was 70,000 years old (pg. 151).[7] Then in 1905, evolutionists officially stated that the earth was two billion years old (pg.50).[8] Then in 1969, evolutionists changed their mind again and stated that the official age of the earth was 3.5 billion years old.[9] And today, it is common knowledge that evolutionists basically believe the official age of the earth is now 4.5 billion years old.

Hmm...something is not quite right with all this. Do you see it too? According to their very "professional" and "accurate estimations," the earth actually got older at a rate of twenty-one million years per year, just in the last 220 years! I don't know about you, but that sure doesn't build much trust with me, especially for a belief system which seriously claims to represent reality for everyone and has a serious impact on the eternal destinies of men should their theory be wrong!

Where's Any Basic Evidence for Ape-Human Evolution?

If we humans actually evolved from half-ape and half-man creatures as the Theory of Evolution actually requires, then why don't we see many half-ape and half-man creatures alive and running around on our planet, if we see many fully formed apes and fully formed humans alive and running around on our planet? And if we, in fact, evolved from the ape, and archaeologists can find both many fully formed human skeletons and fully formed ape skeletons, why can't they reasonably find *just as many* transitional ape-men skeletons?

---

[7] *Integrated Principles of Zoology.* 1996
[8] *Newsweek Magazine.* July 20.
[9] *Minneapolis Tribune.* Monday, Aug. 25, 1969

Let's just be once again *honest with ourselves*; if Darwinian evolution were really true, we would fully expect to find hundreds and hundreds of "missing links" transitional skeletons between man and apes. And reasonably, why not if we find hundreds and hundreds of both ape and human skeletons? But in 150 years, scientists have not even found *one clear obvious example* of a transitional skeleton between apes and man, which has not turned out to be either fully human, fully ape, or an actual hoax! All we really have is ape skeletons, human skeletons, deceptive hoaxes, and evolutionary imaginations.

And if Darwinian evolution were true, why don't we reasonably find hundreds and hundreds of transitional fossils for the evolution between all other kinds of animals as well? Did outer space aliens come down and steal all the transitional fossils and skeletons and just leave us the fossils and skeletons for all the fully formed kinds? Of course, the notion is absurd—about as absurd as the Theory of Evolution! My friend, if you are presently a believer in evolution, I encourage you to really think for yourself and not blindly just take their word for anything!

And as we've already mentioned, if Darwinian evolution were true, why don't all the different kinds of creatures still naturally even try to crossbreed with *other kinds* of creatures? They all of a sudden just decided not to evolve anymore because mankind is now watching for the last 6,000 years? Why, not even insects try to reproduce with other kinds of insects! When's the last time you saw a bunch of bees try to reproduce with a bunch of flies? The chances of seeing such a ridiculous thing is the very same chance that Darwinian evolution is true!

Again, why don't even many similar "kinds" of land animals like raccoons and skunks naturally desire to crossbreed with each other if Darwinian evolution were really true? You can put them in a cage together for months, and they might kill each other, but they won't crossbreed! In fact, let's continue to state the obvious. I know this is absurd, but if Darwinian evolution were really true, we would also honestly expect humans to just *naturally* want to crossbreed with apes if that is our nearest ancestor in the supposed evolutionary chain of life, and there is no such thing as "God-given morals." But seriously, how many believers in evolution do you see even desiring to do such a thing?

The truth is that it is a rare thing indeed for any human to even want an ape for a pet! My friend, when you *honestly* think about it, even the very basic reasonable evidence for Darwinian evolution has always been completely missing! Additionally, if you can stand in front of the mirror and seriously believe that your awesome body (which obviously surpasses anything man-made) just somehow evolved completely on its own, then you must also believe it is equally possible for this book, which is far less complicated than the human body, to have just evolved on its own without outside intelligent aid. Once and for all, we must see that such an unrealistic belief would *necessitate some basic dishonesty* once all the simple facts are on the table.

What About Our "Tailbone?"

Some will ask, "If man was created by God and made in His image, then why do we have a 'vestigial tail?'" Actually, the term *tailbone* is a more modern misleading term coined by evolutionists, which is actually *not even a medical term* at all. The proper term for the small triangular bone at the end of the human spine is the "coccyx." And the word *vestigial* is not accurate either, because it means "left functionless from the process of evolution." And medical science has long known that the "coccyx" bone is far from functionless as it would have been difficult for the human race to reproduce without it! There are at least twelve different muscles attached to the small vertebrae located at the end of the sacrum bone, and they are far from functionless, just as they are far from the result of an evolutionary process.

Perhaps the coccyx is functionless for those who believe it is, but obviously, the rest of the human race uses theirs. Even all the apes which have one use theirs as well. Let's face it; when God created man, he had to end the human spine somehow. So he just decided to end it with a purpose like everything else he created. To believe that our coccyx bone used to be some kind of a long evolutionary monkey tail is to believe that our nose used to be some kind of a long evolutionary horn sticking out of our head to attack wild beasts! Speaking of "wild," as hopefully you can see, nothing runs more wild than the imagination and blind assumptions of some evolutionary thinkers!

> To believe that our coccyx bone used to be some kind of a long evolutionary monkey tail is to believe that our nose used to be some kind of a long evolutionary horn sticking out of our head to attack wild beasts!

Isn't Our Appendix Proof for Evolution?

Some have also fallen for the notion that our appendix is also left over from evolutionary processes, just because *some* medical researchers have been unable to figure out its *full* purpose. While evolutionary thinkers may quickly label the appendix to be "vestigial" or useless, the whole medical field today certainly does not at all share this opinion. For example, *most doctors* now recognize that one of its *main* purposes is being a "safe house" for beneficial bacteria living in the human gut. We must be careful not to believe that some things in the human body have no purpose, just because man can technically live without them. You can live without a lot of body parts, but that doesn't mean you will live as well as you would have with them working properly!

For example, technically, one can still live without the gallbladder, but that doesn't mean the gallbladder is "vestigial" and has no purpose when working properly. Its purpose is to hold liver bile before it enters the large intestine. Similarly, the appendix is no different than our gallbladder (or tonsils). It may occasionally have to be removed because it may malfunction due to man's poor diet (and or just sin in the world), but that's our fault, not our creator's who originally made both the human body and the food for it perfect before sin entered his perfect creation.

> You can live without a lot of body parts, but that doesn't mean you will live as well as you would have with them working properly!

Man Is a Spiritual Being

Animals, birds, and fish have always been primarily concerned with just survival (food, shelter, a mate, and surviving from predators). However, though humans are also concerned with survival as well, we humans have always had a "spiritual" dimension which transcends the sole physical survival focus of the animal kingdom. Thus, books like this one are written! Thus, all the churches in the world. Clearly, humans are "spiritual" as is plainly evident by all the religions in the world. Humans have not only always desired to have a spiritual relationship with each other, but the evidence is rather abundant for man's search for a relationship with his own creator as well. And if "godless" evolution was really true, why on earth would this dominant reality be throughout the entire recorded history of man?

However, once again, the Bible is in complete harmony with this reality as it has always taught that God is spiritual and that man was created by God in his image, just so we can have a spiritual relationship with him. Literally millions upon millions have testified that they do have such a relationship with God, and even today, biblical Christianity is the largest unified religion in the world. However, the Bible does not at all teach that animals were created to have the same spiritual relationship with God as humans can have. The fact that *most* humans on the planet have historically desired *some kind* of a spiritual relationship with God their creator certainly does not "check out" with Darwinian evolution, which typically rejects any idea of a personal creator! Again, we must stop and think for ourselves of the obvious!

> The fact that *most* humans on the planet have historically desired *some kind* of a spiritual relationship with God their creator certainly does not "check out" with Darwinian evolution...

Does Darwinian Evolution and the Bible Mix?

Some rather deceived "Christians" have desperately tried to make the Bible fit with the recent theory of Darwinian evolution. In order to get around the six literal twenty-four-hour days of creation as recorded in Genesis, some professing Christians may assert that God actually used Darwinian evolution during Genesis's creation week. Theories like the "Gap Theory" and the "Day-Age Theory" all try to teach this very modern notion. But does Darwinian evolution and the Bible really mix? Let's once again look at the simple honest evidence and see for ourselves if it is even sanely possible:

1. First of all, as we'll cover in Objection 18, from a biblical perspective, it is simply impossible that God used any type of a Darwinian evolutionary process during creation week. Why? Simply because all suffering and death (which the process of evolution absolutely requires) are only a result of man's "sin" or "evil" which could not have come from God who is morally perfect and eternal. The Bible has always taught that sin, suffering, death, and bloodshed only came into God's perfect creation after Adam and Eve first chose to disobey God.

    Thus, from a biblical standpoint, any evolutionary process leading up to Adam and Eve which had to require suffering, bloodshed, and death would have been quite impossible. For according to the Bible, God himself is perfect and could never have been the author of the evil which would have brought about the pain and death required by evolution.

2. Secondly, verses like 1 Corinthians 15:39 make it abundantly clear that the flesh of mankind is actually different than that of animals, fish, and birds. In fact, it not only teaches us that the flesh of mankind is different from all other creatures but even teaches us that the flesh of animals is different than the flesh of fish, which is still yet different from the flesh of birds. And because verse 38 teaches that the "bodies" of men, animals, fish, and birds all have different "seeds" (or origins), their flesh which is all "different" could not have come from the flesh of each other but only from the unique "seed" of their own body. This too would make Darwinian evolution quite impossible indeed.

3. Thirdly, in Genesis during creation week, the Bible clearly teaches us that all creatures, whether they be animals, fish, birds, or Adam and Eve were *fully* created with absolutely no mention of any transitional creatures between Adam, the animals, fish, and birds!

4. Fourthly, even verses like Genesis 2:20 also indicate that God could not have used Darwinian evolution during a nonliteral creation week as it clearly states that none of the animals were even suited to be Adam's "helpmeet" (which literally means "helper like him"). And that's exactly why God created Eve who was suited to be a "helper like Adam." If God had actually used Darwinian evolution, and Adam actually came from the apes within the animal kingdom, then the apes would have been suitable to be Adam's helpmate, because Adam would have come from them, and they would have been "like him!"

    But as we already discussed in this objection, there is a huge gap in the abilities between even apes and mankind; not to mention the animal kingdom is completely lacking the whole spiritual dimension which man uniquely possesses so he can have spiritual relationship with not only his fellow man but also his creator.

5. Fifthly, there are more than a few verses which all make it abundantly clear that Adam and Eve were, in fact, the very first liv-

ing men which started the human race with no mention of any transitional ape men living before them, which Darwinian evolution mixed with the Bible would require. For example:

    a)   1 Corinthians 15:45—The first man Adam was made a living soul...

    b)   Genesis 3:20—And Adam called his wife's name Eve because she was the mother of all (human) living.

    c)   Jude vs. 14—And Enoch also, the seventh from Adam...

    d)   Mark 10:6—[f]rom the beginning of creation God made them male and female.

Because Genesis 3:20 clearly states that "*Eve*" was the "*mother of all* (human) *living,*" this then would obviously eliminate any "*living*" ape men which preceded her or Adam in the case of Darwinian evolution. Additionally, in Mark 10:6, Christ makes it abundantly clear that at the very "*beginning of creation,*" God created mankind, male and female and fully human. From this statement of Christ's, it should be obvious that the first "*male*" and "*female*" at the "*beginning of creation*" were fully human, going by the surrounding context in which Christ only refers to fully human husbands and wives who are mentally and spiritually capable of a marriage covenant!

Thus, because Christ said "*beginning of creation,*" there just could not have been any long process of evolution involving ape men prior to that. The Apostle Paul also taught that same reality in 1 Corinthians 15:45 when he very plainly stated that "*Adam*" was, in fact, the very "*first man,*" once again mentioning absolutely no transitional ape men which lead up to Adam.

Actually, the more one studies the Bible on this subject, the more one quickly discovers that in order to make evolution mix with the Bible's creation account, one has to pretty much undercut the authority of the entire word of God, which for the *true believer in Christ* should be absolutely *unacceptable*. And there are yet many other good biblical reasons as to just why God could not have used Darwinian evolution during a nonliteral creation week which time and written page simply do not permit us to discuss.

However, the above simple honest evidence which we have already revealed should easily make the mixing of Darwinian evolution and the Bible rather impossible for the honest soul. Another good, much more expanded resource on this particular subject which not only refutes the "Gap Theory" and the "Day-Age Theory," but Darwinian evolution in general is *The Genesis Record* written by Henry Morris.

All Complex Systems of Nature Require "Narrow Path" Precision in Order to Give Life

Just the human body alone has scores of different complex systems, which all must work together within their unique relationships in order to sustain delicate human life. Our nervous system, our digestive system, our immune system, our muscular system, our reproductive system, our circulatory system, and others must all function well and in special relationship harmony with each other in order to sustain human life. And this, my friend, is the direct opposite of the haphazard random reckless chance which Darwinian evolution teaches. If even one of those systems were to shut down, life itself would be seriously impaired or in most cases not even be possible.

And this is equally true with all animals, marine life, plants, and essentially all other life-forms on earth. Additionally, on a grander scale, scientists have easily discovered that all these different highly complex life-forms on earth actually need each other for mutual survival of all upon planet earth as well. For example, if we didn't even have bees to pollinate, we'd be in real trouble. If we did not have certain types of bacteria, we'd be in real trouble. If we did not have ants to do their job, we'd be in real trouble, etc.

And those are just a few creatures among thousands which we could cite that all must play their role in order for delicate life on earth to be sustained. So really, what we have are scores of highly complex systems within thousands of different creatures worldwide that must all consistently work together within an overall greater complex system of relationships with each other in order to sustain all delicate life on earth! And then you have the planetary bodies that all must be also in their precise alignments, cooperating with all living creatures on earth in order to sustain life. And because all these relationships which sustain life on earth have been consistent for thousands of years, it should be obvious to the honest soul that such precise life sustaining consistency is the direct opposite of any random reckless, haphazard process!

In other words, someone both loving and intelligent must be purposely maintaining all such consistent life-giving relationships, which must remain precise if they are to give life! Yet, evolutionists still insist that all these highly complex realities which all have *consistently worked together* with precision in order to sustain life on earth for the last 6,000 years (evolutionists believe for millions of years) just somehow did it through some haphazard, random, reckless processes which is just the opposite of the consistency and precision which all life on earth requires! However, the mathematical probability of all complex life forms arising on earth through some massive but completely aimless evolutionary process would be comparable to the probability of a monkey typing a perfect copy of the King James Bible without a single error (without a King James Bible to go by, of course).

In their way of thinking, evolutionists essentially believe that if enough monkeys typed long enough (for billions of years), eventually, one of them would type a perfect copy of the King James Bible! But the mathematical probability of such a phenomenon is, of course, ridiculous; not to mention that such an aimless process would essentially be the very same as gambling and is certainly as far from real observable science as one can get!

For example, the probability of just accidentally generating the very first verse in the Bible which has only forty-four letters ("In the beginning God created the heaven and the earth.") is one chance in (26) A 44 trials. Mathematically, this is equivalent to one chance in 181, 479, 392, 000, 000, 000, 000, 000, 000, 000, 000, 000, 000, 000, 000, 000, 000, 000, 000, 000, 000, 000, 000. And considering the King James Bible has a total of 3,566,480 English alphabet letters within it (many more than just forty-four), the probability of a monkey typing it perfectly through some random reckless process of chance is really out of the question for those honest with themselves!

And that doesn't even take into account that all such complex life on earth would have to also be more than just successfully generated for a moment, for all living systems would also have to be *consistently sustained* in their successful "living" state as well, just like they basically have been. And the fact that evolutionary or even "New Age" believers are willing to risk their entire eternal destiny on such very unrealistic "odds" is really rather a dangerous *unverifiable gamble* when one thinks about it.

Let's put it this way—the odds of winning every game in a gambling casino during just one visit would be much better than the Theory of Darwinian Evolution being even feasible. And yet, anyone would be very lucky to win only two games during a visit in the average casino!

Similar Design Does Not Automatically Mean an Evolutionary Process

Some evolutionary thinkers may just assume any similarities between different kinds is just *proof* that they evolved from each other. However, any general physical similarities (two eyes, two ears, one head, etc.) which humans do have with the animal kingdom isn't necessarily "proof" that we evolved from it so much as it simply reflects that it was just the same creator who created us and the animal kingdom with just "some similar good designs" for similar good life-giving benefits.

It is no different than when a car manufacturer creates many different models of cars. Just because all cars have general similarities (four tires, one engine, two headlights, etc.), it doesn't at all prove they must have somehow "evolved" from each other on their own. It just means that they had the same creator who used similar good designs in his creation for similar good reasons. Additionally, while modern scientists may not fully understand all the masterful "good designs" they encounter in all of creation, they really have never found any obvious "bad designs" other than the obvious abnormalities of the "good designs," which again can be reasonably explained by the horrible effects of man's sin upon God's perfect creation.

As it is, by far, *most* intelligent designs which we find in creation are "good" and would be classified as "normal," simply because they are "life-giving." However, if the haphazard, random, reckless chance of Darwinian evolution were really true, wouldn't we *honestly* find just as many (if not more) obvious "bad designs" within all of creation which are just transitions between them and those that are good designs? For example, human or animal babies born with major birth defects are quite rare compared to all those born normally. But why would this be if haphazard, random, reckless evolution was really true? The bottom line is that these many abnormal "missing links" simply cannot be sufficiently explained if the Theory of Darwinian Evolution was really true.

> If the haphazard, random, reckless chance of evolution was really true, wouldn't we *honestly* find just as many (if not more) obvious "bad designs" within all of creation which are just transitions between those that are good designs?

The Two Parallel Realities Which Coexist

In all of observable nature, there has always been what we call the "normal" (because it is both good and life-giving) and the "abnormal" (because it's accompanied by pain and death). The Theory of Darwinian Evolution may have an explanation for the rarer "abnormal," which is characterized by pain and death, because it *presupposes* that all life came about through haphazard, random, reckless chance, and teaches "survival of the fittest." However, such a haphazard, random, reckless "survival of the fittest" belief system really has no good explanation for *most* of what we observe in nature, which is the *consistent* good and life-giving normal.

For example, with its "survival of the fittest" mentality, the Theory of Evolution may be able to explain the hatred of Nazi Germany against the Jews, but it cannot explain unselfish human love, which we consider "the norm," because it is both good and life-giving. It may be able to explain the painful reality of a peer-pressured young mother aborting her baby, but it simply fails to explain why so many mothers would show great love to not only their own children but also to foreign children by adopting them. It may be able to explain, cruelty, pain, suffering, and disorder but cannot sufficiently explain the "norm"—that which is loving, good, orderly, and life-giving in nature. It may be able to explain tornadoes and all such natural disasters which are ultimately aftereffects from the global flood of Noah's time but cannot sufficiently explain just how all of the planetary bodies are kept in perfect alignment so as to sustain all delicate life on earth for all of human history.

Haphazard, random, reckless "survival of the fittest" evolution really has no good explanation for most of what we observe in nature, which is the consistent good and life-giving normal.

However, biblical Christianity has always had a very reasonable explanation for *both* the normal and the abnormal as the good and life-giving "normal" is just how all creation was before man's sin entered God's perfect creation, and the "abnormal" is the horrible effects of man's sin upon God's perfect creation. All the "goodness" and life-giving "love" in creation comes from our own creator who himself is the source of all that which is loving, good, consistent, orderly, and life-giving. And all the cruelty, pain, suffering, and disorder, comes from the horrible effects of man's sin which entered God's perfect creation totally against his will for a season of time.

Since both of these parallel realities have always been opposed to each other, it is not only reasonable to believe that they have two very different sources but that the cruelty, pain, suffering, and disorder which we presently observe is only *temporary*, because it can just bring death and could never have come from our creator who must certainly be morally perfect in order to be eternal. Therefore, only when we see our opposing world (with both the normal and the abnormal) through what the Bible has always taught does everything make any real sense.

Which came first? The chicken or the egg? Considering all eggs must be fertilized in order to even hatch a living animal, the answer should be rather obvious which one would have had to come first! Thus, just based on this simple question, there never really should have been any creation/evolution debate within the human race during the last couple centuries. Our creator really should be self-evident within the conscience of those honest with themselves.

Conclusion

If you happen to be a believer in Darwinian evolution who is reading this and know in your heart you need a major change in your life, consider that along with many other things, even the reality of "love" in this world doesn't make much sense with the Theory of Darwinian Evolution. But it does make complete sense with the Bible which has always taught that God is the very source of all true love, and mankind is created in his image (1 John 4:8; Genesis 1:26).

Even if you have been an atheist who has been adamantly against the existence of God, that still doesn't change the reality of his awesome love for you! Because he is your creator, no one loves you more than he does. So why cut off your greatest source of love? He knows all our faults and yet loves us unconditionally despite them. You probably can't say that for even many people in your life! If you would like to give your creator a fair chance to reveal himself to you, I invite you to just take that first small step of faith by sincerely praying the prayer of salvation located at the end of this book. No matter what your past is like, God loves you and sincerely wants you to be a part of his awesome eternal kingdom!

Jesus said, "I am the resurrection and the life. He who believes in me, will live even though he dies; and whoever lives and believes in me will never die..." (John 11:25–26)

Note: Another very good source which quickly exposes the Theory of Evolution as unscientific and false through overwhelming evidence is an easy to read paperback book titled *The Evolution Handbook* by Vance Ferrell, which is only about $10.00 online or free through Kindle.

OBJECTION 6

What About All the Evidence for Prehistoric Cavemen Who Lived in the Stone Age?

We've all heard evolutionary theories of "prehistoric cavemen" who lived back in the "stone age." And some young people in our school systems may have heard such evolutionary theories so much that they may have just assumed that everyone else believed them to be true as well. However, as we've already pointed out in Objections 2 and 3, most people on the planet still believe in a monotheistic creator God, and the simple truth is that only since Darwinian evolution was popularized in the last 150 years or so have we even heard of evolutionary terms like *"prehistoric cavemen."* In fact, before 150 years ago or so, terms like "prehistoric cavemen" simply cannot be found in historical writings. And because terms like *prehistoric* were actually invented by recent evolutionary thinkers, it essentially means *"belonging to the era before recorded human history."* But obviously, since no man has ever recorded that mankind even existed before our "recorded human history," such a fantastic era only survives in the wild imagination of evolutionary thinkers without one shred of any sure proof for it!

Obviously, this term, *prehistoric,* itself is quite *slanted* in favor of Darwinian evolution, simply because it *presupposes* that there was a primitive evolutionary human history before "recorded human history." At the same time, it also presupposes that "early man" was not even intelligent enough to speak or write like we can today and merely grunted "ugha-bugha" for millions of years. But obviously, those who came up with this term, "prehistoric cavemen," were not even around before "recorded human history;" and thus, we must just *blindly* take their word for it as their "theory" of this whole "ugha-bugha" era lacks any historical eye witness written accounts. This essentially means that scientifically, the whole theory of Darwinian evolution either stands or falls on fossil evidence alone, which certainly doesn't help their blind faith cause either!

Since no man has ever recorded that mankind even existed before our "recorded human history," the fantastic "prehistoric era" only survives in the wild imagination of evolutionary thinkers!

Often books promoting the Theory of Evolution will have pictures of furry half-ape, half-man creatures crouched in a cave near a fire using their crude stone tools. Or they will show progressive pictures of apelike creatures gradually evolving into modern man. However, as far as this Darwinian Paleoanthropology goes, we should keep in mind that these very personal interpretations from evolutionists are not yet at all the result of any solid scientific evidence which proves them and actually reflects a peculiar world view held by an overall minority in the world! In fact, Darwinian evolutionary thinkers must heavily rely on many such man-made drawings and or computer-generated pictures, simply because there is no obvious fossil evidence in museums which progressively displays man's evolution from apes.

In fact, there are an estimated 100 million fossils displayed in public and private collections covering over 300 million species, and after 150 years, we still do not have one obvious set of transitional fossils among any of them! Kind of like Jehovah's Witnesses have many times falsely proclaimed the date of Christ's return, more than once, evolutionary professionals have proclaimed to the world that they have discovered the remnants of half-ape and half-man skeletons. The Nebraska man, The Southwest Colorado man, the

Piltdown man, the Neanderthal man, the Peking man, the Java ape man, and Lucy, to name a few. But over time, they all proved to be either hoaxes fueled by men who wanted the world to believe in evolution or they turned out to be either fully ape or fully human specimens. But of course, evolutionists never broadcast these realities which simply expose the truth of God's Word. Please consider what actually came of these supposed missing links:

The Nebraska Man

For example, the "Nebraska Man," which was supposedly discovered in 1922 (in Nebraska), was imagined as a "missing link" all from a single tooth which later turned out to be the tooth of an extinct pig! Unfortunately, evolution professionals had even used the Nebraska Man as evidence in the scopes trial in 1925! Years after the scopes trial, the full skeleton of the animal was found. However, even today, the "Nebraska Man" continues to be misrepresented as scientific evidence for evolution in school text books. But where's the "real science" in such deception and dishonesty? Not to mention, it is a very "cheap shot" to specifically deceive ignorant school children (of all people) with the strategy that it would influence the next generation to believe in evolution.

The Southwest Colorado Man

Very similar to the Nebraska Man, the "Southwest Colorado Man" was also based upon a single tooth. It is now known that the tooth actually belonged to a horse (pg. 120).[10]

The Java Ape Man

The "Java Ape Man" was supposedly discovered in 1891 by Dr. Eugene Dubois, a fervent evolutionist. However, this discovery consisted of only three molar teeth, only a fragment of a left thigh bone, and a small piece of the top of a skull. And even these were found (in a year's time) scattered from one another over a distance of about seventy feet.

---

[10] Criswell, W. A. *Did Man Just Happen?* Grand Rapids, Michigan: Zondervan Publishing Co. 1973

To further complicate matters, these minor remains were found in an old riverbed mixed with the bones of extinct animals. Of the twenty-four European scientists who met to evaluate the find, ten said they came from an ape, seven said they came from a man, and only seven said they belonged to a "missing link." Other professionals, like the renowned professor Virchow of Berlin, said, "There is no evidence at all that these bones were even parts of the same creature" (pg. 120).[11]

Even Dr. Dubois himself changed his own theory, and his later conclusion was that the bones were the remains of some sort of small ape. However, even today, the "Java Ape Man" continues to be misrepresented as scientific fact in school textbooks. For those who are honestly looking for the real truth, the Java Ape Man being in school textbooks long after it was abandoned as a missing link is just another gross misrepresentation of scientific fact on the part of the evolutionist community.

The Neanderthal Man

The Neanderthal Man was discovered around 1900 in the Neanderthal valley near Dusseldorf, Germany. For years and years after the discovery, evolutionary professionals portrayed him to be a hunched over intermediate link between both man and ape. However, with the discovery of many more Neanderthal skeletons, it is now known that the Neanderthal Man was both fully erect and human. The "evolutionary professionals" who originally examined the bones of the Neanderthal Man and thought him to be a hunched over intermediate link between man and ape were rather deceived, because it just so happened that further scientific investigation revealed that the particular individual known as the Neanderthal Man must have had a severe condition of both osteoarthritis and rickets! Nevertheless, the Neanderthal Man has been portrayed as scientific fact in our school textbooks after the truth was discovered as well.

---

[11] Criswell, W. A. *Did Man Just Happen?* Grand Rapids, Michigan: Zondervan Publishing Co. 1973

The Piltdown Man

The Piltdown Man was supposedly discovered in 1912 by an amateur paleontologist, Charles Dawson. His discovery consisted of some bones, teeth, and primitive implements which he claimed he had found in a gravel pit in Piltdown, Sussex, England. He took his discovery to Dr. Arthur Smith Woodward, well-known paleontologist at the British Museum, and the remains were estimated to be about 500,000 years old. Over 500 doctoral dissertations were done on the Piltdown Man, and the media hailed the Piltdown Man as one of the greatest scientific discoveries.

However, in October of 1956, the entire discovery was finally exposed as a hoax. Using a new method to date bones (fluoride absorption), the Piltdown bones were found to be fraudulent. This just encouraged further investigation, which exposed that the jawbone actually belonged to an ape which had died within fifty years of the discovery. The teeth were purposely filed down, and the bones were discolored with bichromate of potash to disguise them (pg.120).[12]

Evidently, according to M. Bowden, the person responsible for putting the fake fossils in the pit at Piltdown was a man by the name of Teilhard de Chardin SJ, who was the author of more than one philosophical book which attempted to harmonize evolution with the Bible (pg. 35).[13] The fact that you've probably heard of the "Piltdown Man" and the others we've discussed confirms that they've been offered as real science to the community for decades. You probably have seen these frauds yourself more than once in school textbooks, etc. But as soon as they were discovered to be frauds, shouldn't the evolutionists have come clean and announced it and removed them from our school textbooks? Again, we can see that any false belief system must, to a large degree, survive on dishonesty.

---

[12] Criswell, W. A. *Did Man Just Happen?* Grand Rapids, Michigan: Zondervan Publishing Co. 1973

[13] Bowden, M. *Ape-Men—Fact or Fallacy?* Bromley, Kent, Canada: Sovereign Pub. 1977

Lucy

More modern-day speculations of human evolution have largely revolved around a 40 percent complete skeleton known as "Lucy." This particular skeleton was discovered from 1972 to 1977 in Ethiopia by a man named D. C. Johanson. In a 1976 *National Geographic* article, Johanson claimed that "The angle of the thigh bone and the flattened surface at its knee joint end…proved she walked on two legs" (pg. 790–811).[14]

However, since then, the knee joint end of the femur, Johanson's "proof," has proven to be pure conjecture. Anatomist Charles Oxnard employed a computer technique for analysis of skeletal relationships and has concluded that "Lucy" could not have walked upright, at least in a human way. While Chimpanzees spend a decent amount of time walking upright, they still do not walk upright as humans do and thus, based on the evidence, "Lucy" was probably a certain variety of an ape, like the Chimpanzee.

A Very Reasonable Explanation for Ancient "Cavemen"

However, while the Theory of Darwinian Evolution is still waiting for its basic scientific backing after 150 years of professional investigation, the Bible has always had a very good explanation for the fully human skeletons and crude stone tools which archaeologists have discovered in caves. You see, the Bible has always taught that the very first man, Adam, and the very first woman, Eve, were created fully human in the image of God. They were completely human with full intelligence and could speak and write with full human intelligence as well.

Of course, all historical human records would favor the Bible's clear teaching on this as even the earliest written records do not at all indicate even that "ancient" man was less intelligent or that he could not speak and write with full human intelligence. If this was, in fact, true, wouldn't our earliest historical written records at least indicate that fact of man's "evolved intelligence?" And this would also explain

---

[14] Johanson, Donald, "Ethiopia Yields First Family of Early Man." *National Geographic Magazine*, December 1976, Vol. 150, No. 6

just why after 150 years, we have not yet found one single set of transitional fossils when very reasonably, we should have found *thousands* by now if all animals and man did indeed evolve into their present state from lesser forms of life.

So not only is the Bible in complete harmony with all historical and fossil evidences discovered so far, but it also does, in fact, give us a very good explanation for all the evidence discovered of ancient man having to live in caves, using crude stone tools, etc. It's called the *"global flood,"* and it literally changed everything on earth at the time! You see, the entire human race had to essentially start all over again after the global flood of Noah's day. The full account of it is recorded in Genesis chapters 6–9. It basically describes Noah's flood as a time of God's judgment, because man's great evil had increased so much to finally warrant it.

The Bible plainly says that, "*God saw that the wickedness of man was great in the earth, and that every imagination of the thoughts of his heart was only evil continually*" (Genesis 6:5). More than interesting, one can even find plain written historical record of such a global flood (where only one family survived) in as many as 500 different cultures around the world (pg.2)![15] But where is such evidence which backs evolution's supposed "prehistoric era?" There is none! Again, they just expect you to take their word for it through *blind* faith.

While the minor details of each global flood account may slightly vary in these many different historical records from many different cultures of the world, they all agree on the basics, which would also seem to indicate that the basic biblical account of a global flood was a real historical event.

According to the Bible, the deep waters of the global flood judgment covered all the highest hills by fifteen cubits (Genesis 7:19–20) and destroyed everything but Noah's family and the animals on the ark (Genesis 7:21–23). And a year later, when they stepped out onto dry land, they might as well have arrived on another planet by way of a space rocket, because nothing was the same! We must understand that right after Noah's flood, the entire civilization of man world-

---

[15] Hodge, Bodie & Welch, Laura. *The Flood of Noah.* Green Forest, Az. Master Books. 2014

wide was wiped out, except eight very sober-minded souls! They were truly all alone with only the few tools and food they had to start over. And you can be sure, there certainly were no hardware stores or shopping malls!

> One can find plain written historical record of the global flood (where only one family survived) in as many as 500 different cultures around the world! But where is such evidence which backs evolution's supposed prehistoric era?

And undoubtedly, these eight people of Noah's family and or their close descendants lived in caves at times, simply because all trees were largely wiped out by the massive global flood. And according to creation scientists, they probably *moved around a lot* due to the earth's unstable conditions and the "Ice Age" which followed the flood. And all this reasonably explains why caves and temporary shelters worked out the best for mankind "starting over" right after the flood. This was probably because they were on the move, staying in caves was just easier for some than building shelters out of trees, which had to be scarce.

However, even all the evidence that men lived in caves which we do have does not at all say that Noah's descendants did not eventually live in plenty of man-made homes built out of trees as well, which just deteriorated with time. In contrast, the theory of evolution just makes the assumption that cave-dwelling mankind was not even intelligent enough to read, write, or even build normal man-made homes. But again, their blind assumption requires our *blind faith*.

After all, if Noah (at age 600) and his family were smart enough to construct the largest successful wooden vessel in recorded human history and survive the greatest known cataclysmic event known to historical man, then it should be quite easy to believe that they and their descendants were also quite intelligent enough to build and live in normal houses as soon as trees could grow again. And if the whole account of Noah's flood isn't true, then why do we find historic accounts of that same very unique global event within as many as 500 different cultures around our world today?

One must understand that just because the global flood and ice age both undoubtedly made the new civilization of man *look* pretty "primitive" for hundreds of years doesn't at all mean they were. Let's face it; this was a very unique and *completely devastating* global catastrophe which made it quite difficult for the human race to start over!

For as we've just mentioned, obviously, Noah and his family were not "primitive" or "lacking intelligence!" They (and their extended family which followed) were just *destitute* and had to start completely over, and there is a big difference between the two!

Today, we have many similar destitute people in big cities all over the world, "living on the street" in cardboard boxes, and having to start over. But that certainly doesn't mean they are "primitive" and can't read, write, or even speak an intelligent language. It was once (not too long ago) seriously thought by evolutionary minded scientists that the negro slaves of the colonial period or the "Aborigines" of New Zealand or the native American Indians, etc. were all somehow "less intelligent" and "less evolved" than the more civilized world which deemed them so at the time. However, even modern evolutionary minded scientists today would put this false notion on the same level with scientists once seriously believing the world was flat. Yet, modern evolutionary scientists and thinkers still adhere to the little different evolution theory that historic man had to be less intelligent when, in fact, there is absolutely no real *proof* for such a basic assumption!

> One must understand that just because the global flood and ice age both made the new civilization of man *look* pretty "primitive" for hundreds of years, doesn't at all mean they were.

In fact, according to biblical record, the very first man, Adam, himself was even more intelligent than we are today, knowing how to both read and write simply because Moses (who wrote Genesis) had to have gotten his record of happenings during the creation week from Godly men like Asa, Solomon, David, Joseph, Jacob, Abraham, Shem, Noah, Enoch, and Methuselah who all got them from Adam. And just to show its historical authenticity, the biblical record literally names every generation from Christ all the way back to the first man Adam (see Genesis chapter 5, 10, 11; Matthew 1:1–17). And many of the real historical people recorded in the genealogy records of the Bible all actually "check out" with other nonbiblical historical sources.

So what more could have been done by God who preserved our entire genealogy record through the Old Testament patriarchs? No other religion (or belief system) in the world even attempts to give us a complete record of every generation all the way back to man's beginning. But why would that be if they have the real truth? But if our one and only true creator was behind the one true faith, carefully recording all the generations from the very beginning would just make sense if God were to establish the trust of the human race he created. Just because us modern men didn't live all the way back in Adam's time doesn't at all prove that the biblical account is untrue, for at least the Bible is a very credible historical record.

However, much to the contrary, the Theory of Evolution (or any other belief system for that matter) does not even compete with the historical records of the Bible as they don't even give us a record of every generation within traceable human history. Again, they just want us to take their word for it without any historical records whatsoever to back them up.

Additionally, in Genesis 2:19–20, we are told (through the records Adam himself must have kept) that God let Adam name all the basic kinds of domestic animals, birds, and smaller wild animals which God had created on the fifth and sixth days of creation week. According to the account, creation scientists have estimated that Adam very possibly named 2,000–3,000 animals in the space of about five hours! And, of course, this certainly shows no lack of intelligence in Adam either. Not to mention Adam got married on the same day! However, the *assumption* that ancient man was less intelligent than man is today would have to be true, if one also started with the *biased assumption* that Darwinian evolution in general were true.

But is "true science" all about assumptions being built on just more assumptions which all require blind faith? If not, why would evolutionary thinkers believe their position is more scientific than biblical Christianity concerning the origins of man? To the contrary of the very basic blind assumptions of evolution, what does our entire historical/archaeological record truly reveal? Less intelligence back in history? No. And if it doesn't reveal *any* "less intelligence," what must that honestly say about the basic Theory of Evolution?

Again, I implore you to think for yourself and draw the only simple conclusion left standing—if man was not at all less intelligent as we go back in our recorded human history, this puts a large crack in the very foundation of Darwinian evolution, which must insist on the opposite.

While it is easily admitted by general historians and scientists alike that in the last 150 years or so the "knowledge base" from our modern technologies has exploded (mainly due to our discovery and employment of the fossil fuels), our full historical record does not at all seem to indicate that the basic "intelligence" of man increased in the last 150 years any more than it has shown that man's intelligence has basically evolved from the beginning. As we've already pointed out, if evolution's theory of "less intelligence the further back in history you go" is true, we would undoubtedly have discovered some even slight evidence of this in the earliest writings within recorded human history.

Are students in our school system today really more "intelligent" than the students were in the schools of ancient Egypt four thousand years ago? Probably not. In fact, if anything, historical records reveal that the Egyptians were just as intelligent. Modern archaeologists have discovered artifacts from ancient Egyptian ruins which have greatly surprised them with intelligence, and we still do not understand some real mysteries about their knowledge and way of life. Egyptian pyramids will continue to outlast anything we have built, and the Egyptians themselves certainly held world dominance longer than we have in the United States of America. No sign of less intelligence there!

Actually, we are still "in our diapers" compared to most "ancient" civilizations who held world dominance before us! In the ruins of ancient civilizations, archaeologists have discovered even things like batteries, complex computing machines, and even flying machines. Even the Romans knew how to create modern things like iron and cement to build their empire. Sometimes, archaeologists have uncovered more than one civilization on top of another. If evolution's theory of "less intelligence the further back in history you go" is true, then the lowest and oldest civilizations in such archaeological digs would undoubtedly reveal some evidence of this. However, this has not been the case either.

In other words, so far, all we have is evidence which reveals that ancient man was at least as intelligent as we are, even though they may not have had the compounded knowledge base that we have today which essentially developed from our modern fossil fuel technologies. As the population of the earth greatly grew in just the last three hundred years, our knowledge base compounded just because of that, and with the discovery of the fossil fuels, our capabilities literally skyrocketed, unlike in any other time before in the history of man. As it concerns our present knowledge base, it certainly must be admitted that scientifically, we are merely standing on the shoulders of men who in turn scientifically stood on the shoulders of men before them, etc. But, my friend, we must not confuse such a compounded knowledge base over time, population growth, and man's discovery of the fossil fuels with some kind of an evolutionary increase in man's basic intelligence!

The Average Life Span of Man

Also, if Darwinian evolution were true, one might even believe that the average life span of man would just increase over time, especially if those who live longer are more wise or "more intelligent." However, once again, all recorded human history does not at all reveal an overall shorter average life span of man the further back in history you go. In fact, of all reliable historical records we have, just the opposite is true.

For example, according to more than one Egyptian record, 110 years of age seemed to be the ideal Egyptian life span. And, of course, biblical record would even agree with these nonbiblical records, indicating that their average life spans equaled and surpassed ours today, even with all our modern medical technology. During the time of Egypt's rule, Joshua, who took the leadership of Israel after Moses in about 1300 BC, lived to be 110 years old (Joshua 24:29). Moses who, of course, lived contemporary with the Egyptians (around 1200 BC), lived to be 120 years old (Deuteronomy 34:7).

> We must not confuse such a compounded knowledge base over time, population growth, and man's discovery of the fossil fuels with some kind of an evolutionary increase in man's basic intelligence!

We've all had it drummed into our heads by our modern mainstream medical professionals that "because of modern medical sciences, man is living longer now than ever before." However, according to ancient recorded history my friend, this is simply not true! The average life span of man today is probably only about seventy-seven at the most, even with all our unnatural prescription drugs and surgeries desperately trying to sustain us. It may seem like the average life span of man has actually increased just because the sheer numbers of elderly have increased due to the baby boomer generation, but more elderly just due to post world war two families wanting to grow is quite different than the average life span of man increasing! It is still only about seventy-seven years old whether you are talking about baby boomers or not.

It may be true that our average life span admittedly surpasses those in our more recent history (such as during the middle ages when average life spans dropped to about fifty or so); however, any reputable historian would tell you that a more distant history tells quite a different story. For example, the Egyptians, Assyrians, Greeks, all lived as long if not longer than us. And, of course, biblical records indicate that going back in time before Moses, the average life span of man gradually increased to over 900 years old before the global flood (Genesis 5:27)! And that is simply because there is much evidence that pre-flood conditions would have been much more conducive to long life in general.

However, since the flood would have changed the oxygen levels, the ice canopy above the atmosphere, which the Bible describes, the top soil for growing, and other such things which determined the life span of man, it is easy to see just why the age of man radically decreased after the global flood of Noah's time.

Is There Any Evidence Other Than in the Bible that Ancient Man Even Believed in God?

Man's belief in monotheism can actually be traced back as far as our reliable historical records go, whether they be biblical or not. And this too is yet another reality which refuses to cooperate with Darwinian evolution. If Darwinian evolution were true, we would not reasonably expect any generation of man within our historical record to be *dominated* by man's belief in a monotheistic creator. Why would it? However, as it is, most every generation of man within our historical record is undeniably dominated by man's belief in a monotheistic creator.

One evidence among many others is that even our seven-day work week was ultimately patterned after the creation week as recorded in Genesis. Those who refuse to believe in the Bible may try to convince you that our seven-day week was *originally* patterned after the number of planets in our solar system by ancient civilizations. However, it was mainly just the godless empires and cultures (Romans, Greeks, Persian, and Babylon) which may have patterned their seven-day week after seven of our nearby planets (moon, Sun, Venus, Neptune, Jupiter, Mars, Saturn).

But for what *practical* reason did they do this considering the planet earth was an eighth planet which existed among all others which were visible in their day? So that doesn't make much sense either. Yes, our months and years are dependent upon the movement of our solar system. But our seven-day week is certainly not. So since our seven-day week really has absolutely nothing to do with the planets, why didn't they create a ten-day week based off of the number of their fingers or toes? We must understand that these ancient civilizations were steeped in astrology (their religion was based from the planetary bodies) characterized by even magic, which we all know has little to do with the natural sciences.

Historical records indicate that they not only studied the planets for their political reasons (all to please their king at the time) but also constantly studied the entrails of sacrificed animals for the very same purpose! Let's face it; many of the kings which ruled those empires were little different than dictator types who put tremendous life-threatening pressure on their "wise men" of the time to produce answers and guidance. So the bottom line is that these ancient godless civilizations often did resort to just the "signs" of planets, stars, and even animal guts to determine their political decisions and religious beliefs! Which, of course, points to the reasonable conclusion that our seven-day week actually came from a source which predated even these godless empires who knew neither God nor true science well enough to provide us with the original source of our seven-day week.

Since the Bible has now validated itself as the divinely inspired word of God over 2,000 times through its fulfilled prophecies and is actually one of our most reliable historical records, then it is only reasonable to believe it over any other godless source which has no such fulfilled prophecies to validate its authority for the *original source* of our seven-day week. Yes, the Romans, Greeks, and Babylonians may have patterned their seven-day weeks after the planets, etc. No one is disputing that. But this certainly does not prove that they based their seven-day week after the *original source* for our seven-day week.

But as everyone knows, according to the Bible, our seven-day week was directly patterned after the creation week in Genesis when God made everything in six literal days and then rested on the seventh day. But tell me one good reason why any godless nation who rejected the God of Israel would pattern their seven-day week after the Old Testament Hebrew scriptures, which they refused to believe in? Thus, they chose to pattern their seven-day week after the planets, even though it really made little sense considering eight planets total were in their field of observation.

But one must indeed wonder why their seven-day week was exactly the same number of days as the seven days of God's creation week, which the Hebrews patterned their week after before those empires were even around! Just a coincidence? I highly doubt it. And why didn't they even include Earth in their list of planets, making their week an eight-day week if eight was the total number of planets they were aware of? In fact, why did they even have a "week" at all?

As we've already mentioned, days, months, and years are determined by planetary movements, but "weeks" are not. So where did our seven-day week originally come from? Only the Bible gives us an answer which lines up with anything satisfactory and meaningful. Therefore if, in fact, our seven-day week was indeed patterned after God's creation week just as his inspired word teaches us (Genesis 2:3; Mark 2:27; Isaiah 66:23), then we must conclude that the very first man, Adam, and his wife, Eve (which means "mother of *all living*"— Genesis 3:20), definitely knew God and certainly were not some "ugha-bugha" cavemen who were just the product of the Theory of Evolution! But if, in fact, Satan wanted to deceive all mankind away from God and the eternal life he offers all mankind, then the Theory of Evolution begins to make some real sense.

Conclusion

Thus, there is actually perfect harmony with the biblical record of a massive global flood which literally destroyed all civilization on earth around 2348 BC and all modern archaeological efforts which have uncovered plenty of evidence for "cavemen" and "crude stone tools," etc. To automatically *blindly assume* those who lived in caves and used cruder tools when doing so were not intelligent and could not write or speak normally is an assumption which is simply not truly supported by the earliest records we have of historical mankind.

In the case of the Theory of Evolution, in order for "unintelligent" primitive mankind to go from grunting "ugha-bugha" to being intelligent man writing normally, we would expect to at least find some cave wall writings or pictures (or clay tablets) which would obviously indicate some lesser intelligence before historical man progressed! But no favors to evolution, all ancient historical pictures or writings on paper, clay, or stone have always indicated the full intelligence that man has today, which again lines up perfectly with just what the Bible has always taught.

But that is certainly not all the Bible has taught as it has also predicted the future and proven to be 100 percent accurate in those predictions roughly 2,000 times so far! Only about 500 more predictions which center around Christ's Second Coming still await their awesome fulfillments. And when Christ returns in our near future just after the seven-year tribulation of Revelation hits our world, it certainly should be plenty obvious to all evolution believers that they were greatly deceived by the enemy of their souls.

But even if you have been deceived into believing Darwin's Theory of Evolution, this does not have to happen to you! You can be ready for Christ's return and be right with God who is patiently waiting for the world to turn to him through Christ before he has to send even a worse judgment than Noah's flood upon the ungodly of this world (2 Peter 3:9). According to the plain teachings of the Bible, all those who believe in Christ will be supernaturally "raptured" off the earth *before* the seven-year tribulation of Revelation even hits (Luke 21:34–36). We have God's word on that.

To be right with God and be assured of his eternal life, I simply invite you to sincerely pray the prayer of salvation located at the end of this book. No matter what your past is like, God loves you and sincerely wants you to be a part of his awesome eternal kingdom!

Jesus said, "I am the resurrection and the life. He who believes in me, will live even though he dies; and whoever lives and believes in me will never die..." (John 11:25–26)

Note: Another good source for this topic is a book titled *Bones of Contention* by Marvin Lubenow.

OBJECTION 7

If the Global Flood of Noah's Day Was Real, Why Can't We Find the Ark Today?

Not only have archaeologists and creation scientists found overwhelming evidence for the biblical global flood during the time of Noah, but as we already mentioned in Objection 6, there are quite possibly as many as 500 different cultures in the world that have their own variations of the same basic global flood! Below is a list of just fifty of those many different cultures which all have specifically passed down historical record of a global flood which, in fact, are very similar to the Bible's account of Noah's flood (pg.3):[16]

In North America: Inuit, Tinneh, Kaska, Natchez, Nez Perce, Cheyenne
In Europe: Celtic, Scandinavian, Roman, Greek, Transylvanian Gypsy
In Asia: Samoyed, Altaic, Mongolia, Russian, Hindu, Tamil, Miao, Dusan
Near East: Sumerian, Egyptian, Assyrian, Chaldean, Zoroastrian
Australia: Gunwinggu, Manger, Andingari, Papa New Guinea, Maori
Africa: Masai, Cameroon, Mandingo, Pygmy, Kwaya, Yoruba, Ekoi
South America: Shuar, Chorote, Toba, Caraya, Ipurina, Yaruro, Muysca
Central America: Yacui, Totonac, Maya, Carib, Michoacan,
    Nahua, Toltec

---

[16] Hodge, Bodie & Welch, Laura. *The Flood of Noah*. Green Forest, Az. Master Books. 2014

And if Noah's flood was a real historical event, we would certainly expect most all these global flood legends to collectively share the exact same *basic* characteristics with that of the very unique biblical account of Noah's flood. And guess what? They do! Please consider the following unique shared characteristics of those many flood legends which line right up with the Bible's account of Noah's flood:

1. Man's growing evil brings divine judgment.
2. The divine judgment came in the form of a worldwide global flood.
3. A single favored family escaped the judgment in order for man to "start over."
4. Judgment was escaped by constructing a boat which survived the global flood.
5. Animals also survived by taking refuge in the boat.
6. Everything was destroyed by global flood.
7. Boat landed on mountain after the flood.
8. Birds sent out after the flood by surviving family to see if land was inhabitable.
9. Survivors worshiped God upon leaving boat and setting foot on land again.
10. Divine favor placed on the surviving family as they started their new lives.

Could all these hundreds of global flood legends which collectively share the same basic characteristics of the biblical global flood just be a mere coincidence? I highly doubt it! For if Noah's flood as recorded in the Bible did actually take place around 2348 BC, then these basically unified historical records from many different cultures around the world are exactly what we would expect, simply because they all find their same basis in a very real common historical event. And going as far back as the thirteenth century, this would also explain just why more than one of our ancient maps actually have a picture of Noah's ark on them as well! Please consider the following ancient world maps which all have a picture of Noah's ark right on them:

1. The "Ebstorfer" World Map—Thirteenth Century[17]
2. The "Ranulf Higden" World Map—Fourteenth Century[18]
3. The "Psalter" World Map—Thirteenth Century[19]
4. "Hereford Mappa Mundi"—Thirteenth Century[20]
5. "Tabula Asiae III"—Fifteenth Century[21]
6. "Georgie Armenie"—Seventeenth Century[22]

Could all these hundreds of global flood legends which collectively share the same basic characteristics of the biblical global flood just be a mere coincidence?

On the other hand, if Noah's flood was just some massive fairy tale concocted by a group of devious and sinister Hebrews, then all these many different ancient cultures and maps handing down historical record of the very same unique and unified global event really doesn't make much sense at all. If Noah's flood was just some fairy tale unique to the Hebrew culture, we would expect these many other cultures to just have their own very different fairy tales with almost no unification at all, simply because there would be no real event for any of them to be unified by and based from.

It is true that some of the details of Noah's flood may vary within different cultures (as none of them claim to be "the inspired word of God"), but since all the basics of Noah's flood have indeed been historically recorded in the many non-biased ancient cultures

---

[17] Thirteenth Century—wikipedia.org/wiki/Psalter_world_map (PD–Art)
[18] Fourteenth Century—wikipedia.org/wiki/Ranulf_Higden (PD–US)
[19] Thirteenth Century—wikipedia.org/wiki/Psalter_world_map (PD–US)
[20] Thirteenth Century—wikipedia.org/wiki/Hereford_Mappa_Mundi (PD–Art)
[21] Fifteenth Century—wikimedia.org/wiki/File:Armeniamap2 (PD–Art)
[22] Seventeenth Century—wikipedia.org/wiki/Alian_Manesson–Mallet (PD–Art)

around the world, then the honest historical evidence certainly favors the Bible's account of Noah's worldwide flood as being a very real event, which actually occurred in our human history.

It is basically true that when there are slight differences between different historical accounts of the same basic event, for accuracy of the event, historians would generally favor that historical account, which is longer and more detailed than all others, if there is one. And when studied and compared to all other historical accounts, the Genesis account of Noah's flood clearly gives much more overall detail, especially as it concerns the design and construction of the ark. This is one reason the Bible's flood account stands out as the accurate original account, which all the others were based from.

If Noah's Flood Was a Real Historical Event, Then Why Can't We Find the Ark Today?

Yes, some skeptics may ask this basic question. However, such a question automatically assumes that just because we have not been able to find Noah's Ark, then the ark couldn't have existed, and the whole global flood of Noah's time could not have been a real event.

While these fast assumptions may satisfy those who really may not want the global flood account of the Bible to be real for personal reasons, such quick unfounded conclusions have been shown to be rather hasty indeed in the field of archaeology. If we are honest, we all must technically admit that just because we can't find something yet that it doesn't ever automatically prove it doesn't exist or ever existed! Especially since reputable geologists have studied the mountains of "Ararat" region and concluded that Noah's ark could well have been ignited and covered by active volcano lava during the past millenniums.

According to creationist geologists, all mountains in general were either formed during Noah's flood by the massive water weight buckling the earth's crust or afterward by post-flood volcanoes continuing to erupt their lava layers. And geologists have actually determined that Mt. Ararat and the surrounding mountains of the area were at least in part formed from volcanoes of the region constantly erupting well after the flood. In fact, even our recent history bears witness of Mt. Ararat continuing to erupt as late as the 1800s.

Just what are we suggesting? It most certainly should not be ruled out that the ark has actually been burned up and covered over by the many eruptions of the volcano lava during past millenniums. Obviously, because hot lava would of course ignite and incinerate a wooden vessel covered with tar pitch of any size upon contact, it is certainly not out of the question that the ark could have been totally burned up and its ash covered over by erupting volcanoes of the area long ago. And aside from all this, Noah's flood happened over 4,000 years ago, and just the freezing and thawing of mountain snow covering a wooden vessel would certainly cause it to rot away to a real degree as well.

> It most certainly should not be ruled out that the ark has been long since burned up and covered over by the many eruptions of volcano lava during past millenniums.

As it concerns the fast assumption that the ark never ever existed, Bodie Hodge and Laura Welch in their book titled *The Flood of Noah* note that according to the oldest records we have which referred to the ark, the location of the ark itself was never even a mystery to the post flood world but was always well-known (pg. 2 of booklet on pg. 13)[23] And very reasonably, why wouldn't this famous ship be well-known to the generations following the flood who undoubtedly knew its exact location directly from Noah and his family?

There is not only good historical evidence that the location of the ark was well-known but that literally hundreds and hundreds of people visited the ark during the millenniums following the flood and often pulled off pieces of the ark to take home as souvenirs or even

---

[23] Hodge, Bodie & Welch, Laura. *The Flood of Noah.* Green Forest, Az. Master Books. 2014

objects of worship (pg. 2 of booklet on pg. 13).[24] After all, if they all knew that the human race was literally saved through this massive wooden vessel, it becomes easier to understand just why many men after the flood began using pieces of it as objects of worship.

But if the Ark never even existed, then why do we have such historical record of ancient man visiting it and taking home souvenirs from it? It just doesn't make sense. The following is a quote from the famous Jewish historian, Flavius Josephus (AD 90) in his book 1, chapter 3 of *Antiquities of the Jews*:

"Now all the writers of barbarian histories make mention of this flood, and of this ark; among whom is Berosus the Chaldean. For when he is describing the circumstances of the flood, he goes on thus: "It is said that there is still some part of this ship in Armenia, at the mountain of the Cordyaeans; and that some people carry off pieces of the bitumen, which they take away, and use chiefly as amulets for the averting of mischief's." Hieronymus the Egyptian also, who wrote the Phoenician Antiquities, and Mnaseas, and a great many more make mention of the same (pg. 3 of booklet on pg.13).[25]"

> But if the ark never even existed, then why do we have historical record of ancient man visiting it and taking home souvenirs from it?

This quote from a real man who lived in history not only confirms to the honest soul that Noah's Ark really did exist, but according to Berosus, the Chaldean, many ark artifacts and pieces were even carried away by travelers wanting to take them home. While there have been more than one party in recent decades that have claimed

---

[24] Hodge, Bodie & Welch, Laura. *The Flood of Noah*. Green Forest, Az. Master Books. 2014

[25] Hodge, Bodie & Welch, Laura. *The Flood of Noah*. Green Forest, Az. Master Books. 2014

to have sighted/visited the ark on Turkey's Mt. Ararat,[26] even if the ark has never been found by man in recent centuries, this certainly does not mean that:

1. The Ark never existed;
2. Post-flood man has never seen/visited Noah's ark (which would go against what historical records we have);
3. The global flood event as recorded in the Bible never took place.

The Local Flood Theory

Some who want to mix the theory of evolution with the Bible may refuse to believe that Noah's flood was global and insist that it was only a local flood of some kind. However, such a theory really creates more problems than it solves as one has to throw out a lot of plain scripture (as well as common sense) in order to believe the biblical flood of Noah was only "local." The following are just some of the unsolvable problems with the "local flood" theory:

1. Given the biblical dimensions of the ark (510 feet long, 85 feet wide, and 50 feet tall), it was simply too immense to make sense with any mere local flood.
2. If the flood was only local, God would have simply instructed Noah and his family to move where the flood was *not going to be.*
3. If the flood was only local, God would have just lead all the animal kinds to safe territory rather than into the ark.
4. If the flood was only local, let's be *honest*; there would have been no real need for Noah to build a boat at all.
5. The Bible clearly teaches that in Noah's flood, "*[a]ll flesh died that moved upon the earth, both of fowl, and of cattle, and of beast, and of every creeping thing that creepeth upon the*

---

[26] Documentary DVD—*Noah's Ark Revealed.* Mill Creek Entertainment, LLC. 2014

earth, and every man: all in whose nostrils was the breath of life, of all that was in the dry land, died. And every living substance was destroyed which was upon the face of the ground... And Noah only remained alive, and they that were with him in the ark" (Genesis 7:21–23). None of this passage makes any sense at all with a mere local flood.

6. The Bible clearly teaches that God was judging *all mankind* aside from Noah and his family, not just some men through a partial flood. It says the whole earth "was filled" with the violence of mankind (Genesis 6:13).

7. The Bible clearly teaches that during the flood, *"[t]he waters prevailed exceedingly upon the earth; and all the high hills, that were under the whole heaven, were covered. Fifteen cubits* (or about twenty-six feet) *upward did the waters prevail; and the mountains were covered"* (Genesis 7:19–20). Once again, let's be honest; this passage of scripture, of course, could not make any sense with a local flood either.

8. All the historical flood legends from different cultures around the world collectively describe a global event, not a local flood event.

9. And last, but not least, the entire account of Noah's flood in the Bible mentions absolutely nothing at all about the nature of the flood being only "partial" or "local!"

So as you can see, it would not only be quite absurd to believe that Noah's flood was only local (just like trying to make the Bible harmonious with Darwinian evolution), but one would have to be plainly *dishonest* with the entire account of Noah's flood as recorded in the Bible in order to make their local flood theory *seem* even plausible. If one is going to believe any part of the account of Noah's flood within the Bible at all (that there even was a flood), then it is only fair to believe all the details of that amazing account which the same author conveyed as well.

Who are we to pick and choose through any author's account of what they are claiming to be an actual event in history? Did we live back then? All in all, it is rather amazing that the local flood theory is even seriously believed by anyone claiming to believe in the Bible. Thus, by far, most of the "professing Church" totally rejects the local flood theory, simply because of the obvious evidence which we've just discussed.

Some of the Many Obvious Evidences for Noah's Worldwide Flood

Archaeologists have also uncovered what are called "poly-straight" fossils which alone should convince the honest soul of the worldwide flood which the Bible teaches. Typically, these fossils consist of a vertical petrified tree (turned to stone), which was catastrophically buried in many layers of rock strata. The problem is that evolutionists maintain that the layers of rock strata in which these trees are buried actually represent many thousands (or even millions) of years in time as they were laid down. And going by the many different rock strata layers in the earth's crust, because they believe each layer to represent millions of years, they then believe the earth to be well over four billion years old!

Not only have many poly-straight tree fossils been uncovered by archaeologists, but also petrified vertical large fish or whales have also been found buried in rock strata which evolutionists have assigned millions of years to. And we all know they would have rotted even quicker than any tree if, in fact, they were somehow buried slowly! Thus, just because they would rot at a normal rate, all such petrified "poly-straight" fossils had to have been quickly buried in their surrounding rock strata by some very large flood-like catastrophe and not buried slowly over millions of years as evolutionists may assume. And all this obvious "poly-straight" archaeological evidence not only defies the millions of years which evolutionists assign to the geological layers of the earth's crust (making the earth much younger) but also greatly confirms the biblical account of Noah's flood which could only account for such rapid burials of plants and animals all over the world.

Just because they would rot at a normal rate, all such petrified "poly-straight" tree fossils had to have been quickly buried in their surrounding rock strata by some very large flood-like catastrophe...

Dinosaur Fossils

Many other artifacts uncovered also validate the Bible's account of a worldwide flood as well. For example, many of the dinosaur fossils which have been unearthed give clear indication that they were buried quickly (like one would expect in a worldwide flood) and not slowly over time. Of course, if they were buried slowly over time, their flesh would have rotted long before they got a chance to fossilize. Not to mention, scavengers would have also picked them apart long before they could fossilize! And this is exactly why such fossils are, of course, not still forming today. Additionally, whole herds of dinosaurs around the world have been found buried together and fossilized as if they were suddenly trapped. Some dinosaur fossils which have been unearthed display two dinosaurs that seem to have been catastrophically buried in the midst of a fight to the death.

Whether or not they were actually fighting is rather irrelevant, because either way, they were obviously quickly buried! Other fossilized dinosaurs (and or fish) which have been unearthed display mothers giving birth while catastrophically buried right in the process! Many of the fish fossils still have their fins spread out in defense mode, which also indicate catastrophic rapid burial. Even fossilized seashells and clamshells have been discovered on the tops of many of the world's mountains. Just how did all these seashells scale all the mountains around the world without the help of something like a worldwide flood to bring them up there anyway? Of course, we would expect all these uncommon fossilized scenarios in the case of a worldwide flood, but such fossils are indeed a severe blow to the Theory of Evolution which flatly denies the Bible's account of a worldwide flood.

And just how did all these seashells scale all the mountains around the world without the help of something like a worldwide flood to bring them up there? Such fossils are indeed a severe blow to the Theory of Evolution.

The Grand Canyon

No disrespect to evolutionists, but it should be common sense to even teenagers that the Grand Canyon could never have been "carved out" by any normal river (including the small Colorado River, which exists today), even over millions of years. No matter if you assign billions of years to the carving out of the Grand Canyon (and other massive gorges all around the world), it would simply take a much more massive body of water to carve them out to such a massive width. Considering they are all basically U-shaped, being massively wide at the top and even continue to remain quite wide until the bottom, any smaller normal river to carve them out just doesn't make any sense at all.

It really shouldn't take a certified geologist to figure out that the body of water which started and pretty much finished its carving had to be at least as large and massive as the top of the Grand Canyon itself. My friend, this is just simple common sense. In addition, all the tall and abnormally isolated rock formations (out West and elsewhere) which are surrounded by massive plains can really only be explained by a massive amount of water moving through the whole area which could only leave the rather "naked" looking rock formations behind. Certainly, no small Colorado River carved them out over millions of years either!

All the tall and abnormally isolated rock formations (out West and elsewhere) which are surrounded by plains

can really only be explained by a massive amount of water moving through
the whole area...

In fact, if there was a global flood, just like the inspired word
of God plainly teaches us, how would the topographical surface of
the earth look any different than it does today? The truth is, the surface of our earth today with all its unusual formations and fossils fits
perfectly with the global flood, which was recorded for us in God's
word. It would seem evolutionists just don't want to believe the Bible
for their own personal reasons, which have little to do with real science, much less common sense. However, all such massive U-shaped
gorges around the world fit perfectly with Noah's flood, because as
the massive amount of flood water rapidly drained off into the large
oceans, which we now have, it is only reasonable to believe such large
canyons would have been carved in the process. Additionally, the
massive tonnage of sediment deposits all over the world can only be
explained by a worldwide flood moving very large amounts of water
fast. No slow-moving smaller river of water could accomplish this,
no matter how much time one assigns to it!

Conclusion

Most of the time, realizing the truth just requires the honesty of
a little child, and that is the point of our whole book series. We don't
at all have to be a super-intelligent scientist with some long degree.
We just have to be honest. And this is exactly why all men will be
accountable someday to our creator for believing the truth of God's
word. The honest evidence we could cite for Noah's flood (which also
defies Darwin's Theory of Evolution) could go on and on, but truly
sufficient is that evidence which we have already presented in our
objections thus far.

While modern man may never actually be able to find Noah's
Ark for the obvious and perfectly sensible reasons we gave, this certainly does not mean that it never existed. However, sufficient should
be the evidence which we gave for the worldwide flood, which in

turn should strongly validate the existence of Noah's Ark. For after all, not only the Bible but about 400-plus other historical accounts from many other cultures around the world testify that the two (the global flood and Noah's ark) went together. If there was a global flood without an ark, I would not be writing this book right now, because the entire human race would have been wiped out! Thus, if there was indeed a global flood, there had to have been an ark which would have been required to preserve record of the flood. This is just simple logic.

While God promised with the sign of the rainbow to never again destroy the earth's inhabitants with a global flood, he also promised one last future time of judgment upon the Christ rejecting world during the seven-year tribulation of Revelation which will probably be even worse than Noah's flood in many ways (Matthew 24:21–22; Jeremiah 30:7; Daniel 12:1; Joel 2:2).

Since God, our eternal creator, does have perfect foreknowledge of all the freewill choices mankind will make, he can therefore easily tell us the future in advance. And scripture collectively teaches us that as mankind's sins pile up, they actually reach a fullness, and God then has no choice but to judge our sin, simply because the violation of his perfect character has also reached its limit (Genesis 6:12–13, 15:16, 18:20–21; Matthew 23:32; 1 Thessalonians 2:16; Revelation 18:4–6). But just as in the case with Noah's flood, God also invites the whole world today to miss this future time of awful tribulation judgment which will probably leave only about 10 percent of the world's population left alive according to God's collective word (Isaiah 24:6, 13:12; Revelation chapters 6–19).

This, by the way, is not at all some scare tactic. I myself would have absolutely nothing to gain by trying to scare people with some fictitious fairy tale. What would be the point? It is simply the truth of God's word which has proven its divine inspiration throughout history over 2,000 times through fulfilled prophecy! And all the prophecies of God's Word were not given to mankind so we would be *scared*; they were just given to us way ahead of time so we would be *prepared*.

And there is a difference between the two as one is just unloving and emotional and the other is loving and practical. From scripture, we know that the world's inhabitants of Noah's day foolishly rejected God's continued call for repentance. Scripture indicates that men like Enoch, Noah, Methuselah, and others probably preached repentance for many years before the global flood even hit. And we also know from scripture that millions and millions of very wise souls will miss Revelation's terrible judgment through the rapture event of the Church, just because they will be wise enough to genuinely choose Christ.

If you don't yet know Christ, you too can choose to miss that terrible time of judgment. If you want to make sure *today* that you too are right with God and will miss this worst time of God's judgment upon man's sin, just begin your right relationship with God by sincerely praying the prayer of salvation located at the end of this book. No matter what your past is like, God loves you and sincerely wants you to be a part of his awesome eternal kingdom!

Jesus said, "I am the resurrection and the life. He who believes in me, will live even though he dies; and whoever lives and believes in me will never die..." (John 11:25–26)

OBJECTION 8

If God Is Loving and Just, Why Wasn't Noah's Ark Even Large Enough for Anyone Else of the Pre-Flood World Other Than Just Noah's Family?

What if many of the people in Noah's day decided to repent of their wickedness once the rain started falling? There wasn't enough room on the ark for a larger group of people, plus all that it already contained. Wasn't that a bit unfair of God? Not at all.

In Genesis 6:12, we read that before Noah was even instructed to build the ark, "*all flesh*" on earth (other than Noah and his family) *had already "corrupted their way.'"* The Hebrew word *shachath* for *corrupted* here basically means "spoiled" and essentially implies ruin beyond return. In Genesis 6:5, it says that "*God saw that the wickedness of man was great in the earth, and that every imagination of the thoughts of his heart was only evil continually.*" Undoubtedly, the very conscience of man was seared by this time.

And once man's conscience is seared, Scripture collectively indicates that it cannot be made normal again as it directly connects a man's seared conscience with his falling away from God and an inability to repent afterward (1 Timothy 4:1–2; Hebrews 6:4–6).

Nevertheless, because God was "playing fair," Scripture does indicate that men like Enoch, Noah, Methuselah, and others probably preached repentance to the pre-flood generations for many years before Noah was even instructed by God to build the ark. This belief is only reasonable as all throughout God's word, we see that God always had his prophets warn men of his judgment before he would actually bring it. And very logically, all warnings of God's judgments (ahead of time) throughout his Word would make absolutely no sense if those being warned could not actually avoid the judgment they were being warned of.

> In Genesis 6:12, we read that before Noah was even instructed to build the ark, "*all flesh*" on earth (other than Noah and his family) *had already* "corrupted their way."

Scripture teaches us that only Noah (and his family) were "*righteous*" (in right relationship with God) before the Lord and found God's "*grace*" (unearned favor) because of it (Genesis 6:8, 7:1). The Bible even says that Noah was "*perfect in his generations*" (Genesis 6:9). *Perfect* here in the Hebrew doesn't technically mean absolutely perfect like God is (otherwise Noah would be God) but rather morally "blameless" in a general sense compared to the rest of his generation.

Was it that God was being partial and favored Noah over the rest of mankind in an unfair sense? No. Noah simply made different freewill heart choices than the rest of his generation. In fact, because everyone else in his generation had clearly compromised their morals and conscience, it should, if anything, show us that the resolve of Noah and his family to follow God was by choice of *strong free will,* simply because they had to swim against the strong current of their entire corrupted generation to do it! Obviously, they had plenty of opportunities to compromise their morals like the rest of their generation chose to do. All throughout both the entire Old and New Testaments, we see that man's freewill choices have always determined whether or not he is "right with God" as God himself shows no partiality whatsoever (Romans 2:7–11).

If God had just randomly picked Noah and his family totally apart from their freewill choices, then God's judgment of all other men in the flood would have made no sense; not to mention it would have been immoral. A perfect God could never judge men for staying in their sin if he himself predetermined them to do so; such thinking makes no sense at all and is certainly not biblical. Therefore, because the wickedness of mankind had spread so much, only Noah and his family passed the tests of heart to be right with God and live for him. And because only Noah *"found grace in the eyes of the Lord"*—and because only Noah was *"righteous"* in God's sight within that entire wicked generation—then it becomes easier to understand that God only intended Noah and his family to be saved from the destruction of the flood by the time Noah was commanded to build the ark. It was simply too late for the rest of mankind who *"had* (already) *corrupted their way upon the earth"* (Genesis 6:12). Thus, a bigger ark (or more arks) was simply not needed to house the rest of corrupt humanity just before the flood.

God Gave the Whole Pre-Flood World a Chance for Repentance

As we've already mentioned, there is much indication in the Scriptures that God had his prophet, Enoch (and probably others like his son, Methuselah), preach repentance to the entire pre-flood world *long before* he instructed Noah to build the ark (Jude vs. 14–15). Since man lived to nearly 1,000 years back then, it is not at all unreasonable to believe that God's call to repentance through Enoch (and others) took place *for hundreds of years* before Noah was even instructed to build the ark. Enoch's son, *Methuselah*, lived the longest of any man recorded (969 years), and his name meant "when he dies, judgment." And since Enoch himself lived on earth 365 years and had his son Methuselah at age sixty-five (Genesis 5:21–23), this strongly indicates that the prophet Enoch likely received a prophecy of God concerning the coming flood judgment when Methuselah was born (or before) and was able to preach about it to the pre-flood world for about 300 years after he had received it from God.

> Since Enoch himself lived on earth 365 years and had his son Methuselah at age sixty-five, this strongly indicates that the prophet Enoch was able to preach about the coming flood judgment to the pre-flood world for roughly 300 years…

Additionally, the Bible indicates that it took Noah and his family (eight people) about 120 years to build the massive ark boat and prepare it with food and supplies for the one-year voyage they would have to ride out. During this time, the Bible really doesn't indicate that Noah and his sons were even preaching repentance anymore, because as we've already mentioned, before Noah was even commanded to build the ark, "*all flesh on earth had already corrupted their way*" (Genesis 6:12).

In both Genesis 6:11 and 6:13, it says that the earth was "*filled with violence.*" As it would seem, the pre-flood world was so bent on violence that they likely would have destroyed themselves over a short time anyway, even if the flood hadn't! Nevertheless, long before God instructed Noah to build the ark, he had his witness and call to repentance through Enoch and others, just as he does in every generation like even ours today. And as it plainly teaches in 2 Chronicles 16:9:

> **[t]he eyes of the Lord run to and fro throughout the whole earth, to show himself strong on behalf of them whose heart is perfect toward him.**

And this is because God never takes any pleasure at all in the "*death of the wicked,*" just as he says through his prophet Ezekiel in Ezekiel 18:23.

God Gives the Whole World Today a Very Fair Chance for Repentance

And now even in our generation, the Lord has foretold in the book of Revelation (and many other books of the Bible) of the coming seven-year tribulation period, which will also be a major judgment of God (like the flood of Noah's day) against sin. In Matthew 24:37–42, Jesus directly compares the coming tribulation judgment with Noah's flood. And just the same, God has provided all mankind a way out of that judgment through the "rapture" of his Church.

The "rapture" is simply when God will supernaturally catch his entire Church up to heaven and is similar to the ark of Noah's day in that it too provides a way of escape for the righteous from God's judgment. As we've already mentioned, very logically, all warnings of God's judgments (ahead of time) throughout his Word would make absolutely no sense if those being warned could not avoid the judgment they were being warned of. Not to mention, this just makes sense with a God who professes to be perfect love! Many verses within the Bible, like Luke 21:34–36, inform the Church (and the unsaved world) of the rapture event so we can escape the coming tribulation judgment of God, which will leave the earth with only a *"few men left"* (Isaiah 24:6).

> Many verses within the Bible, like Luke 21:34–36, inform the Church (and the unsaved world) of the rapture event so we can escape the coming tribulation judgment of God which will leave the earth with only a "few men left."

While according to Jesus, no man can know the day or hour of the rapture event (Matthew 24:36), we are actually commanded to know the basic season of the rapture and be ready for it (Matthew 24:32–34; Luke 21:34–36). The Apostle Paul speaks plainly of the rapture of the Church in 1 Thessalonians 4:16–18 and many other verses such as 1 Corinthians 15:51–52. 1 Thessalonians 4:16–18 says:

> **For the Lord himself shall descend from heaven with a shout, with the voice of the archangel, and with the trump of God: and the dead in Christ shall rise first: then we which are alive and remain shall be caught up together with them in the clouds, to meet the Lord in the air: and so shall we ever be with the Lord. Therefore, comfort one another with these words.**

The apostle Peter teaches us in 2 Peter 3:9 that God is today still patiently waiting for all those who would come to Christ before he raptures his Church and begins the seven-year tribulation judgment. It states:

> **The Lord is not slow in keeping his promise, as some understand slowness. He is patient with you, *not wanting anyone to perish*, but everyone to come to repentance (through believing in what Christ did for them on the cross and turning from their sin).**

In Matthew 24:40–42, Christ also encourages us all to be right with God so we will be raptured to heaven and escape the coming time of his judgment by saying:

> **Then shall two be in the field; the one shall be taken and the other left. Two women shall be grinding at the mill; the one shall be taken and the other left. Watch therefore, for you know not what hour your Lord will come.**

Additionally, in Luke 21:34–36, Christ also says to us:

> **Take heed to yourselves, unless at any time your hearts be overcharged (weighed down) with surfeiting (wasteful living) and drunkenness, and the cares of this life, so that day (of the tribulation—see vs. 7–33) come upon you unawares (when you are not ready). For as a snare it shall come upon all them that dwell on the face of the whole earth. Watch you therefore, and pray always, that you may be counted worthy to escape *all these things* (of Luke 21:7–33) that shall come to pass, and to stand before the son of man (Christ).**

Conclusion

Therefore, since God is now "playing just as fair" as he did in Noah's day before the global flood by warning us way ahead of time of his coming judgment upon sin, are you ready to escape this coming global seven-year tribulation judgment through the rapture, just as Noah escaped the flood judgment of his day through the ark? My friend, the reality is that this present Christ-rejecting world with all its pleasures will soon pass away, *"but those who do the will of God will abide forever"* in Christ's awesome eternal pain-free kingdom (1 John 2:17; Revelation 21:4)!

If you are one who knows in your heart that this present world is heading for trouble, and you wish to avoid God's coming judgment upon the ungodly as he has promised you can, I invite you to just take that first small step of faith by sincerely praying the prayer of salvation located at the end of this book. No matter what your past is like, God loves you, my friend, and sincerely wants you to be a part of his awesome eternal kingdom!

> **Jesus said, "I am the resurrection and the life. He who believes in me, will live even though he dies; and whoever lives and believes in me will never die..." (John 11:25–26)**

OBJECTION 9

How Can the Bible Even Be in Compliance with Science When It Is So Full of Fantastic Miracles?

Obviously, none of us are in danger of knowing too much about miracles. While our historical records (with more than one reliable witness) are quite littered with what we have come to call "miracles," mankind as a whole still knows very little about them. I guess that's what makes them a "miracle." When one just looks up the definition of a miracle on Dictionary.com, it reads:

> "A surprising and welcome event that is not explicable by natural or scientific laws and is therefore considered to be the work of a divine agency."

Very similarly, according to a Wikipedia encyclopedia, the definition of a miracle is:

> "A marvelous event not ascribable to human power or the operation of any natural force and therefore attributed to supernatural, esp. divine agency; especially an act (e.g. of healing) showing control over nature and used as evidence that the agent is either divine or divinely favored."

Since it is the Bible which is being addressed within the above question, it is therefore only reasonable to understand that the miracles, which we'll be discussing, are biblical miracles. Therefore, because the Bible teaches it clearly, we'll understand the "divine agency" in our dictionary definition to be the supreme God of the Bible and not some Greek god or evolutionary alien, etc. However, while the above objection question may have been sincerely asked by some, it may also blindly assume something which may not be true at all. And the grand assumption built into this question is, of course, that miracles themselves could have nothing at all to do with real science or even scientific laws for that matter.

While most creation scientists believe that miracles themselves *transcend* our natural scientific laws as the Wikipedia definition defines them, they cannot really be proven to be *unscientific* either. Especially if, in fact, they are just natural scientific laws that have been supernaturally manipulated by our eternal creator who is not necessarily limited by just the "*natural* scientific laws," which he has put in place for mankind during his "natural state." For a practical example, in *Luke 4:39*, when Christ instantly healed the disciple Peter's mother-in-law from a fever, we can clearly see that natural healing processes were just supernaturally accelerated.

> The grand assumption built into this question is of course that miracles themselves could have nothing at all to do with real science...

In other words, a miracle (whether it be great or small) could be more accurately viewed as just "a manipulation of natural scientific law by our creator for his own purposes." And while manipulated natural scientific laws transcend "natural science" as we know it, it nonetheless still remains "science" if it is just science supernaturally manipulated beyond our comprehension. In fact, "supernaturally manipulated natural science" could even be considered a "far higher science" than are just the "natural sciences," which we can observe.

However, to *assume* that the supernatural has nothing to do with true science, just because it leaves our comprehension, is to assume all things within even the natural sciences which we cannot yet understand are also divorced from true science as well. After all, a wild native Indian could consider our invention of the rocket that carries us to the moon to be a "supernatural miracle," just because the science behind it leaves his comprehension. In this false assumption, our limited ability to understand something can actually become the standard by which we measure all true science, which we know, of course, is absurd.

> To *assume* that the supernatural has nothing to do with true science, just because it leaves our comprehension, is to assume all things within even the natural sciences which we cannot yet understand are also divorced from true science as well.

For, if anything, mankind has found just the opposite to be true:

"It is not so much that our understanding is the measure of true science but rather that true science is more apt to measure our understanding."

In this sense, then, we who are imperfect must be careful not to "measure the yardstick by the cloth" when it comes to miracles we do not understand. Therefore, because natural science supernaturally manipulated may very well be considered a "higher science," it certainly should not be considered void of true science, simply because it is still science that is just supernaturally carried beyond our comprehension. An equal question to our objection question, which also relates to our discussion, could be asked as well: "Does the supernatural God of the Bible always make rational sense?" Or "Is God ever irrational?" Well, according to scripture, it is rather impossible for God, who is perfect and eternal, to be irrational, even though his "rational" does indeed go far beyond our comprehension. For example, it states in 1 Corinthians 14:33 that "*God is not a God of confusion.*"

Therefore, in so far as we know "irrational" to mean "unreasonable" or "meaningless," it is actually impossible for God (who is perfect) to be irrational in any way. In other words, God always makes perfect sense, even if we cannot yet *understand* his ways! Therefore, because our understanding is limited, it cannot really be used to judge or measure what we cannot yet understand. And even though God himself may go well beyond our reason with miracles, etc., this in no way proves he goes *against* our reason or even against true science for that matter.

Of course, ever since man's sin invaded God's perfect creation, the effect of that sin has definitely been "irrational" and might make God's creation *appear* irrational. But if, in fact, the effect of our sin is not truly representative of God's original perfect creation, then the "irrational" (or abnormal) we observe within nature is only a reflection of man's sin, not God or his character.

The Miracles Within the Bible

Within the Holy Bible, we actually find hundreds of miracles, some of which could be categorized as:

1. Creation of matter (Creation of the physical cosmos—Gen. 1:1)
2. Creation of energy, force, or power (Parting of the Red Sea—Ex. 14:29)
3. Creation of order, information, or complexity (Water into wine—Jn. 2:9–11)
4. Creation of biological life (Rod turned into a serpent—Ex. 4:2–4)
5. Creation of spiritual life, or spiritual renewal (Christ's virgin birth—Lk. 1:26–38)

6. Control of physical process rates or timing (Stilling of waves—Lk. 8:24)
7. Control of biological process rates or timing (Plague of flies—Ex. 8:24)
8. Acceleration of decay processes in the human body (Firstborn death—Ex. 12:29)
9. Acceleration of healing processes in the human body (Severed ear—Lk. 22:51)
10. The control of the demonic realm (Men in Gaderene tombs—Mt. 8:28–32)
11. Providential control and timing of events (Elijah fed by ravens—1 Kings 17:6)
12. Satanic and demonic miracles allowed by God (Giants—Gen. 6:4)

> Even though God himself may go well beyond our reason with miracles, etc., this in no way proves he goes against our reason or even against true science for that matter.

While all these miracle types do indeed go beyond human understanding, since it is quite obvious that many are natural scientific laws manipulated, we can also reasonably *lean* in the direction of believing all other miracle types have not forsaken rational reality either, even though, once again, they are definitely beyond human comprehension…not to mention human ability.

Miracles Are *Connected* to the Natural Sciences

Just to confirm that miracles themselves must be in some way connected to the natural sciences, many scientists have often observed that all of life sustained on planet earth is essentially one big miracle, simply because of all the natural laws of the universe and planet earth which must be *constantly "just right"* in order to sustain all delicate life on earth. For just a few examples:

1. If there was too much oxygen on earth, there would be constant flash fires which would threaten all life on earth. However, if there was not enough oxygen, all life would also of course cease to exist.
2. Additionally, if the sun was just 100 degrees hotter than what it is, it would threaten all life on earth as well…and if it was just 100 degrees cooler than what it is, all life on earth would also likely cease.
3. Likewise, if the sun, moon, and earth did not maintain their precise constant orbits and distances from each other, everything would also be thrown off, and all life on earth would be threatened. And on and on goes the list of all "natural law parameters," which must be "miraculously" just right in order to constantly sustain life on earth. You get the idea…

In other words, if all life and the universe itself is just the mere product of haphazard, random, reckless chance as Darwinian evolutionists insist, then all the natural laws which have been perfectly maintained in their narrow parameters in order to sustain all delicate life on earth really make no sense at all, simply because they are anything but "haphazard." And to top it off, not only do *scores* of these massive natural laws have to be just right themselves, but they also have had to be in complete harmony with one another in order to have sustained life on earth for at least the last 6,000-plus years!

Yes, especially from a scientific point of view, it would certainly seem that behind the scenes, someone very intelligent and loving is definitely controlling everything, just so life here on earth can exist. And in the case of evolution happening over millions of years, it is even a far greater bag of miracles that all these natural law parameters have been narrowly maintained in perfect harmony in order to sustain all delicate life on earth!

In this real sense, life on earth brought about and maintained by Darwinian evolution requires *even more faith in miracles* than does the biblical explanation. Nevertheless, both would have to be considered a miracle. However, since Darwinian evolutionists reject a personal God and creator who is intelligently and lovingly controlling all earth and universe parameters, they, unlike creation scientists, have no explanation for those even greater miracles which have sustained all life on earth for a much longer period of time. After all, how could the "impersonal random reckless, haphazard chance" of Darwinian evolution really account for the constant delicate and precise sustaining of all human and animal life on earth for millions of years? Darwinian evolution teaches "survival of the fittest," not the careful loving consistent sustaining of many natural science parameters which preserve life. However, a *constant intentional act of love by a personal creator* certainly makes much more sense, even if we may not at this time see our creator who is behind it all.

> In the case of evolution happening over millions of years, it is even a far greater bag of miracles that all these natural law parameters have been maintained in perfect harmony in order to sustain all delicate life on earth!

The Uniqueness of the Bible

Yes, many may find all the miracles within the Bible just too hard to believe and assume that their "fantastic" nature is somehow "proof" that the Bible was just written by men who made up such stories to get attention. And since mankind has had somewhat of a historical habit doing just that in many fantasy/fiction stories written *by just men*, it is easy to see why some may quickly assume that the miracles of the Bible are just proof that it was written by men.

However, the truth is that no fantasy/fiction stories which have been written by just men throughout history have even seriously claimed to be the inspired "Word of God" to all mankind. Nor do they contain any single figure who seriously claimed to be God in the flesh visiting his own creation for the purpose of mending a broken relationship between God and man. Nor do they prove to be the Word of God through what could only be hundreds of divinely fulfilled prophecies. Nor do they even claim to be a real record of history containing many miracles performed in front of many real and credible historical witnesses. Therefore, because of its extreme uniqueness in these awesome respects, it is quite difficult indeed to even attempt comparing the Holy Bible with any other book in the world, whether that book be spiritual or obvious fantasy/fiction in nature. And since:

1. Biblical Christianity is the largest unified religion in the world today;
2. And the Holy Bible holds the record for the most copies sold without ever getting outdated;
3. And Jesus Christ has had far more influence on the world than any one single historical figure;
4. And the world has been full of New Testament churches ever since Christ;

Then it only stands to simple reason that there had to be something or someone *very powerful* which began the New Testament Church. And only the obvious power of God demonstrated to man thoroughly through supernatural events would seem to even "fit the bill." In fact, most pastors, Church leaders, Bible scholars, and even most Christians would easily contest that without the miraculous hand of God clearly and thoroughly demonstrated through Christ and his apostles, the historical Church would never have been born! However, it's not just Bible-believing Christians who believe this, for even skeptics of the Bible who lean in the direction of Darwinian evolution would probably even admit that God simply could not clearly reveal himself to mankind unless he would supersede his natural laws in miraculous power many times over.

In other words, my friend, if, in fact, God is perfect, eternal, all-powerful, all-knowing, and created everything, and wanted to reveal himself to his own creation through that power and knowledge, then all the "hard to believe" miracles throughout the Bible would only make perfect sense, simply because they could not be mistaken for the acts of mere mortals. In fact, the bigger the miracle, the more it couldn't be misunderstood by man that God himself was plainly revealing himself to man! And because there would certainly be very good reason and purpose for our creator to reveal himself to us exactly in the miraculous manner which the Bible records, the only question then is, what does all the historical evidence that we have actually point to concerning these many miracles?

> If God is perfect, eternal, all-powerful, all-knowing, and created everything, and wanted to reveal himself to his own creation, then all the "hard to believe" miracles throughout the Bible would only make perfect sense.

Old Testament Miracles

Could the miracles of the Old Testament performed thousands of years ago even have any honest evidence today which backs them? The answer is, they most certainly do! In fact, much evidence that archaeologists have uncovered just confirms the major miracles within the Old Testament. For examples, please consider the following miracles or Bible recorded events affirmed by archaeology and historical records:

1. Sodom and Gomorrah destroyed by raining fire and brimstone—According to Dr. Lennart Moller, a Swedish scientist, in his book titled *The Exodus Case*, there is certainly plenty of honest evidence for this supernatural event recorded in the Bible

(pg. 37–47).[27] Dr. Moller compiled his book largely from the efforts of his late friend, Ron Wyatt, an amateur archaeologist from the US. This book is not only a wonderful source on the overall Exodus event but also gives much credibility to the Old Testament miracles in general through the genuine archaeological evidence which it presents.

According to Dr. Moller, in the plains surrounding Masada, where the cities of Sodom and Gomorrah are thought to have existed near the Dead Sea, there can be found an unusually heavy ash which encases much of the raised areas which actually outline the many shapes of city walls.

In addition, large quantities of unusual "sulfur balls" can also be found in the area as well. And after many scientific lab tests were accomplished, the whole area showed real signs of intense heat wherein the sulfur had actually melted into the limestone and minerals in the area. Not only can we find all the proper geological evidence which matches the Bible's account of Sodom and Gomorrah burning with fire and brimstone, but also the historian, Josephus (who had access to much older historical records which pertained to those cities before they fell), also testified that Sodom and Gomorrah (along with the three other cities of the plain) were indeed supernaturally overthrown with fire and brimstone just as the Bible records (pg.39).[28]

2. The ten plagues of Egypt—The Bible records that God supernaturally judged Egypt with ten different plagues so the Pharaoh would finally let the Israelites go from Egypt. They are as follows:

   1. The Nile River turned to blood when Moses struck it with his staff.
   2. Swarms of frogs came up from the Nile and covered Egypt.
   3. Lice (gnats or mosquitoes) covered Egypt.
   4. Flies cover Egypt.

---

27 Moller, Dr. Lennart. *The Exodus Case.* Copenhagen NV, Denmark: Scandinavia Publishing House. 2002

28 Moller, Dr. Lennart. *The Exodus Case.* Copenhagen NV, Denmark: Scandinavia Publishing House. 2002

5. Egypt's cattle and livestock destroyed by disease.
6. Both man and beasts of Egypt afflicted with boils.
7. Large hail fell which wiped out both crops and livestock.
8. Locusts covered Egypt and destroyed the crops and vegetation.
9. Thick darkness covered only Egypt for three days.
10. All the firstborn of Egypt die; even the firstborn of beasts.

And by their biblical descriptions, these plagues had to involve the divine manipulation of the natural sciences, not to mention each and every one instantly happened and then instantly disappeared at Moses's command in their exact chronological order. And not only did the plagues instantly come and go by the command of Moses, but they only effected the Egyptians, not the Hebrews in the nearby land of Goshen! But is there any real historical evidence that these biblical plagues actually brought the world's strongest empire to its knees? The answer is yes!

However, the reason there is probably *not an abundance* of Egyptian records available to us on this major ten-stage event, which would have happened at the end of the eighteenth dynasty (1446 BC) is for several good reasons. First of all, we simply do not have many preserved ancient documents which are 3,450 years old, no matter what the subject! That is a serious stretch of time for any ancient document to survive. Secondly, we must understand that the entire military of Egypt as well as the Pharaoh himself was wiped out in the Red Sea just after the ten plagues. And according to the records we do have, Egypt afterward was in complete chaos, lacking leadership, labor, animals, food, raw materials, medicine, etc. Historically, such a world power would have been greatly humbled (if not embarrassed) by this disaster and would not have even wanted it published for the world to know.

However, the records we do have do, in fact, indicate a significant but mysterious lull in prosperity at the end of the eighteenth dynasty. One such document dated around the beginning of the nineteenth dynasty does, in fact, describe what was very likely this whole ten-stage supernatural judgment of Egypt which the Bible records. It is called the "Ipuwer papyrus" (pg. 143–149).[29] In this ancient Egyptian document, we find quite a number of unique unnatural catastrophes that happened to Egypt, which line right up with the unique judgments of the biblical text. Most important of all is the fact that the "Ipuwer papyrus" dates at the exact time period (beginning of the nineteenth dynasty), which would fully cooperate with the biblical time of the Hebrew exodus (1446 BC). Consider the following statements in the Ipuwer papyrus, which fit perfectly with the biblical description of the time during the plagues and just prior to Israel's departure from Egypt:

1. "Foreigners have become people everywhere." Obviously, the Hebrews in the Land of Egypt as slaves were considered "foreigners" (Exodus Ch. 5). And according to the biblical text, the Hebrews increased in Egypt (Exodus 1:20, 5:5).

2. "Foreigners are skilled in the works of the Delta." According to biblical text, the Hebrews were not only foreigners but lived in the delta region and were put to work as slaves making bricks, etc. (Exodus Ch. 5).

3. "What the ancestors foretold has happened." Joseph, the one whom God used to bring the Hebrews to Egypt in the first place hundreds of years earlier, had also foreseen Israel's departure from Egypt as well (Genesis 50:24–26).

4. "We don't know what has happened in the land." Obviously, if the biblical text is true, the supernatural nature of these rapid judgments would have produced much confusion in Egypt, warranting such statements as these. Even the pharaoh's magicians chalked it all up to "the finger of God," because events defied natural scientific explanations (Exodus 8:19).

---

29 Moller, Dr. Lennart. *The Exodus Case.* Copenhagen NV, Denmark: Scandinavia Publishing House. 2002

5. "The river is blood." According to biblical text, the Nile and other waterways became actual blood, not just blood-colored (Exodus 7:20). And according to the Ipuwer papyrus, the whole Nile river was literally "blood" toward the end of the eighteenth dynasty, which could not have happened much in Egyptian history!

6. "There's blood everywhere, no shortage of death." Obviously, this statement could have referred to all the waterways turning to blood as well as the other "death" causing plagues (Exodus 9:6).

7. "Many dead are buried in the river." This comment would line up perfectly with the many Egyptians who undoubtedly died in the last plague of all Egypt's firstborn dying, so many so that they could not be buried in any normal manner but had to be thrown into the Nile (Exodus 12:30).

8. "The people of Egypt said, 'Let us go plunder;' the mayor of the city goes unescorted." In other words, Egypt had no military to control the people! And of course, this highly unique situation for any nation would line up perfectly with the fact that the entire Egyptian military was wiped out in the Red Sea just after the plagues (Exodus 14:28).

9. "Food is lacking;" "great hunger and suffering;" "Ladies say, 'We want to eat;'" "The storehouse is bare;" "Women are barren and none conceive;" "Their bodies suffer in rags." This overall condition of famine and lack of clothing after the departure of Israel would line up very well with the fact that the hail and locusts wiped out all Egyptian crops as well as the shortage of Hebrew slave labor to make clothing (Exodus 9:25).

10. "Exhausted are materials for every kind of craft;" "Lacking are grain, charcoal...brushwood;" "Trees are felled, branches stripped." These kind of statements too would fit perfectly with the sudden vacuum of labor that would have been characteristic of Egypt right after the plagues and sudden departure of Hebrew slaves.

11. "Scribes are slain, their writings are stolen." Obviously, the chaos ensued upon Egypt by the biblical plagues would have been a nasty blow to any culture. Evidently, the scribes of Egypt at the time were hunted down and slain to hide the shame of what Egyptian leadership was left. And more than likely, this is a good reason we do not have more ancient Egyptian documents about this major Hebrew exodus event. The art of writing in Egypt was a privilege of the few in unique positions, just like later European scribes in medieval castle times.

12. "See now, the land is deprived of kingship;" "See, all the ranks, they are not in their place, like a herd that roams without a herdsman." Not many nations in history have recorded such an amazing sudden vacuum of leadership. However, this would have been the case right after the entire Egyptian army was supernaturally destroyed by God in the Red Sea!

13. "One says 'woe' to the place of secrets;" "What shall we do about it? All is ruin!" "Gone is what yesterday was seen;" "If I knew where God, is I would serve him." Such amazing comments could only be explained by unique major disasters such as we observe in the biblical text just prior to Israel's departure from Egypt. Obviously, by the last statement, God got Egypt's attention to some degree. It is not unreasonable to believe that some Egyptians did believe in the God of Israel after this amazing string of miracles that were visited upon them by the hand of God.

3. The parting of the Red Sea in the exodus of Israel led by Moses—Also, according to Dr. Lennart Moller, in his book titled, *The Exodus Case*, many recent discoveries confirm the historical Exodus of Israel from Egypt. For example, in his book, Dr. Moller presents real photographs taken underwater at the bottom of the Red Sea bed in the region where Moses

and the Israelites likely crossed on a wide flat underwater land bridge between Nuweiba and Saudi Arabia (pg. 188–191).[30]

Even though the depth of the Red Sea over that underwater land bridge is still about 300 meters deep, they nonetheless found remarkable evidence at the seabed's bottom there that would certainly seem to confirm the Exodus account. Sea corals always tend to grow on something and eventually replace the very object they attach to. And there were not only more than a few corals found which were the exact shape of Egyptian chariot wheels but also piles of corals the exact shape of horse and even human bones which were found upon the floor of this natural underwater land bridge (pg. 208–216).[31]

According to biblical record, the pursing Egyptian army had over 600 chariots. And the historian Josephus mentions the very same number of chariots and also that there were 50,000 horsemen and 200,000 infantry. But according to Moller, there is, however, good reason to believe that much of the evidence (and many of the lighter objects) of the pursuing Egyptian army was actually swept off the raised underwater land bridge by the strong tidal currents and fell down into the greater depths of the Red Sea on either side which is approximately 1,900 meters deep (pg. 210)![32] And there is much more evidence for the entire Exodus in general which is discussed in this very powerful source by Dr. Moller containing over 570 photographs, tables, and graphic illustrations.

4. A massive river of water instantly flowed from a rock Moses struck with his staff—Again, according to Dr. Moller in his book titled *The Exodus Case*, there is, in fact, a very large prominent split rock at the base of Mt. Horeb which was likely the very rock Moses

---

[30] Moller, Dr. Lennart. *The Exodus Case.* Copenhagen NV, Denmark: Scandinavia Publishing House. 2002

[31] Moller, Dr. Lennart. *The Exodus Case.* Copenhagen NV, Denmark: Scandinavia Publishing House. 2002

[32] Moller, Dr. Lennart. *The Exodus Case.* Copenhagen NV, Denmark: Scandinavia Publishing House. 2002

struck with his staff at the command of God (pg. 243).[33] Pictures are shown of this famous rock in Moller's book, and as Moller discusses, not only do many other historical factors tie in to locate this biblical rock, but the obvious major water erosion patterns at the base of this unusual rock (which is basically located in a dry desert region) can still be seen today.

The list of Old Testament miracles with their archaeological and historical backing just continues. For one more example, according to the Bible, the destruction of the city of Jericho was definitely divine as the timing of its sudden collapse occurred precisely when the Israelites encircled the city seven times, blowing their trumpets (Joshua 6:20). Archaeologists have located the ruins of the ancient city of Jericho some time ago, and more than one documentary exposes unusual characteristics of the ruins which, in fact, cooperate fully with the miraculous biblical account of just how the city fell. In fact, most all ruins for the prominent cities mentioned in the Bible have been located in the world, just where the Bible indicates them to be. Coincidence? I highly doubt it!

Archaeologists may not be able to find all the evidence they want to find, but all the evidence we have found so far gives solid credibility to the Bible, and even many of the miracles it records. And considering we do have much evidence which solidly confirms many Old Testament miracles, it is then even reasonable to believe in those Old Testament miracles and events which we cannot even have historical evidence for, simply because in most cases, both kinds of miracles were wrought through the very same men of God.

> In fact, most all ruins for the prominent cities mentioned in the Bible have been located in the world just where the Bible indicates them to be. Coincidence? I think not.

[33] Moller, Dr. Lennart. *The Exodus Case.* Copenhagen NV, Denmark: Scandinavia Publishing House. 2002

It Doesn't Make Much Sense to "Pick and Choose" Through the Miracles of God's Word

Some skeptics may choose to believe in Christ and his apostles and the many divine miracles they did on earth but at the same time find it just too hard to believe in other Old Testament miraculous accounts such as Noah's flood, Daniel in the lion's den, or Jonah being swallowed by a fish. However, once again, if one believes in Christ and what his apostles taught, they must also believe in the Old Testament miracles as well, simply because Christ and his apostles not only "put their stamp of approval" on each other as genuine men of God whom God worked through but also confirmed many times that all the Old Testament men of God were not only real, but the miracles God performed through them were also quite real as well. For example, Christ completely affirmed the reality of Noah's flood in Matthew 24:37–39 when he said:

> **But as the days of Noah were, so shall the coming of the Son of man be. For as in the days that were before the flood they were eating and drinking, marrying and giving in marriage, until the day Noah entered the ark, and knew not until the flood came and took them all away; so shall the coming of the Son of man be.**

Similarly, the Apostle Peter also confirmed the reality of Noah's flood (see 2 Pet. 2:5). Christ also completely confirmed Jonah's hard to believe experience of being swallowed by a fish for three days and three nights and living afterward to preach repentance to Nineveh. In Matthew 12:40–41 he states:

> **For as Jonah was three days and 3 nights in the whale's belly, so shall the Son of man be three days and three nights in the heart of the earth. The men of Nineveh shall arise in judgment with this generation, and shall condemn**

it, because they repented at the preaching of Jonah; and behold, a greater than Jonah is here.

Additionally, Christ also confirmed Daniel as a genuine prophet of God with not one mention that anything in the book of Daniel was false or made up by men (see Mt. 24:15; Mark 13:14). And because Christ's recorded statements about Daniel are both in the books written through Matthew and Mark, we can also believe that both Matthew and Mark believed Daniel to be a genuine prophet of God who would have recorded nothing false within the book of Daniel, including the account of when Daniel was thrown into a lion's den and lived.

In Hebrews 11:33, the Apostle Paul also confirms that the account of Daniel in the lion's den was real. James, the half-brother of Jesus also confirmed that the story of Job was completely true when in James 5:10–11, he states:

Take, my brethren, the prophets, who have spoke in the name of the Lord, for an example of suffering affliction, and of patience. Behold, we count them happy which endure. You have heard of the patience of Job, and have seen the end of the Lord; that the Lord is very pitiful, and tender of mercy.

The Apostle Peter confirms the real account of Sodom and Gomorrah being supernaturally and instantly burnt to ashes in 2 Peter 2:6–9. The Apostle Peter also affirms all the New Testament writings of the Apostle Paul in 2 Peter 3:15–17. In Hebrews chapter 11, the Apostle Paul confirms all the Old Testament accounts of Cain and Abel, Enoch (who was supernaturally translated to heaven), Noah, Abraham, Isaac, Jacob, Joseph, Moses, walls of Jericho, Gideon, Barak, Samson, King David, and Samuel as being completely real accounts.

Essentially, the Apostle Paul also confirms the entire Old Testament in Hebrews chapter 11 as he includes all "the Old Testament prophets" in verse 32. And since the Apostle Peter also affirmed all the Apostle Paul's writings in 2 Peter 3:15–17, we must also conclude that he shared the Apostle Paul's same convictions of the realness of entire Old Testament as recorded in Hebrews chapter 11.

The list of "cross confirmations" of real biblical accounts, of course, continues within scripture. Therefore, one who is familiar at all with the historical records of the Bible must inevitability conclude that all the miracles within scripture must be real if one should accept any of them at all! This is simply because most all men of God within scripture completely confirmed each other *with absolutely no indications to the contrary*. Therefore, in order to believe the Bible was just written by men or that its many recorded miracles were just made up stories, one would essentially have to believe all "men of God" within the Holy Bible were a *collaborate* band of deceiving liars.

Or perhaps they all collectively suffered from the exact same very detailed case of insanity, even though they all lived sane godly lives throughout a time period of about 1,500 years in all different parts of the Middle East? I don't think so, my friend. I don't think so. And for one to believe all men of God within the Bible to be a collaborate band of deceiving liars, one would also have to do so completely contrary to the honest godly lives they lived in front of many historical witnesses. And since no historian has discovered any historical proof that Christ or any of his followers were, in fact, deceitful, dishonest, or insane, then it would only follow that those who would *dogmatically insist on it* are themselves the ones being dishonest and deceitful, not to mention unloving, simply because even any civil court of law would maintain that the character of any man (even in history) is innocent until proven guilty.

In order to believe the Bible was just written by men, or that it's many recorded miracles were just made up stories, one would have to believe all "men of God" within the Holy Bible were a collaborate band of deceiving liars.

The truth, my friend, is that the many demonstrations of God's miraculous power within the scriptures of the Holy Bible are only confirmed by credible historical witnesses and the many findings of archaeologists. And since the obvious purpose of miracles within the Bible are easily explained by our personal creator revealing himself to mankind in a way we cannot deny, then the "burden of proof" that the miracles within the Holy Bible are fabricated by a band of deceiving liars would fall squarely upon the shoulders of those would insist upon it. And not only have archaeologists uncovered much evidence which confirms many of the miracles within the Bible, but it is only reasonable to also rely on the very real combined historical testimonies of those many men in the Bible who lived back then more than we would rely on the mere opinions of skeptics today *who did not live back then.*

Besides, where is any honest proof that all the miracles within the Bible did not happen? Skeptics can produce nothing but their mere opinions. With just their *opinions*, these skeptics can provide no honest proof that the miracles recorded in the Bible did not happen, simply because they did not live back then. All credible historical records we possess favor that they did happen. So unless the very character of those in the Bible who did live back then could also be proven deceitful through historical record of some kind, then it would only be reasonable to believe those who did live back then over those who did not.

It is only reasonable to rely on the very real combined historical testimonies of those many men in the Bible *who lived back then* more than the mere opinions of skeptics today *who did not live back then.*

However, if we are to just *blindly* believe that all men in the Bible who God wrought large miracles through were just a collaborate band of deceiving liars, then we might as well believe the very same about all men which manifest in our overall historical record, simply because the historical record of the Bible is even far more "reliable" in the sight of historians than most all other historical writings!

Biblical Christianity a Massive Collaborated Spiritual Hoax?

Aside from the fact that some mass deception or a collaborated spiritual hoax over a 1,500-year period of time by the authors of the Bible would have indeed been quite unlikely, it wouldn't have even been remotely possible. For instance, if all the spiritual truths taught by the human authors of the Bible were all just part of a massive collaborated spiritual hoax, then all miracles within the Bible, which God wrought through these many men, would also have to have been either:

1.   Fabricated made up stories; or
2.   Faked miracles by the hand of many very talented magicians.

If they were all just fabricated made up stories with absolutely no substance, then most certainly, there would have been some real comments by more than one historian to this very deceitful effect. But once again, we cannot find any such major refutations made by men in any of the historical writings we possess. One can even go to Israel today and see firsthand the places where Christ went and even did many of his miracles. So many real places in Israel also line right up with the historical record of the events in the New Testament.

Additionally, the Church would never have been born if the miracles were not real nor would the early church fathers of the second, third, and fourth centuries have even taken them and their writings within the Bible seriously if it was all just made-up stories. It is simply far too big of a lie for anyone group of people to successfully pull off without being exposed by many witnesses and historians.

Additionally, one would have to explain how all 2,000 prophecies within both the Old and New Testaments were fulfilled if God was not actually speaking through the apostles and prophets of the Bible who also did miracles. And to make matters worse for skeptics, "faked magician-type miracles" would have required even more talent than the major preplanned cooperate lying required in fabricating stories for all the New Testament miracles. In fact, in most all cases, mere magician tricks masquerading as all the miracles of the New and Old Testaments would have been completely impossible, especially with the many unbiased witnesses involved.

For one of many examples we could cite, as recorded in Acts 3:1–16, God healed a forty-year-old crippled man through the Apostles Peter and John. Just how could such a miracle be fabricated when all the witnesses around them personally knew the crippled man who was "*laid daily at the gate of the temple (Acts 3:2)?*"

Considering many such miracles were often done through the apostles in front of many unbiased witnesses who all knew the one being miraculously healed, they would have been quite impossible to fabricate. Not only our history bears no such records of anyone accusing the apostles of just performing mere magician tricks while claiming they were miracles from God, but not even the best of magicians could even come close to performing the many public miracles which were wrought through Christ, his apostles, and the Old Testament prophets.

For example, how does a mere magician feed well over 5,000 people with a few fishes and loaves of bread? And then do it again with another crowd of well over 4,000? The notion is, of course, absurd. Magicians throughout history would have done things like that a long time ago and made big money doing it if it were even remotely possible.

> When God healed a forty-year-old crippled man in Acts 3:1–16, just how could such a miracle be fabricated when all the witnesses around them person-

ally knew the crippled man who was "laid daily at the gate of the temple?"

Or how does a mere magician instantly control the weather as Christ did more than once? The only reasonable explanation, my friend, for such New Testament miracles is that Christ was just who he claimed to be, and the Bible is the inspired word of God to all mankind! The only question is: Will we believe in our very own creator? Or will we rebel against him?

Conclusion

The Bible clearly teaches us that all things which exist were not only created through Christ, but they continue to be held together by him as well (Colossians 1:16–17). Creation scientists know that any "constant" (especially one which is narrowly maintained to sustain delicate life for a long period of time) is the very opposite of haphazard, random, reckless chance. They also know that there must be an intelligent loving God who is actually controlling all the awesome and delicate parameters of the universe to all be in perfect harmony with one another in order to sustain all life on earth.

Therefore, since we know that all life on earth (which is permitted by all natural scientific laws being supernaturally controlled) is one big complex miracle, it also shows us that natural scientific law and miracles must indeed have some rational relationship with each other by the hand of an intelligent and loving source. Throughout the scriptures, God does not just irrationally sprinkle miracles upon his creation for his own amusement as we would sprinkle decorations on a cake. As is evident throughout the scriptures, every single miracle which God worked in human history was not only *necessary* but was ultimately an *act of love* for the overall spiritual well-being of humanity.

Yes, all miracles of God may have transcended our *natural* sciences, but that doesn't mean they were irrational or even unscientific for that matter. Nor does it mean they were unloving in any way. Because all scientists pretty much agree that there is more than three dimensions, the resurrected eternal state of man will undoubtedly operate in some of those additional dimensions, which we can know very little about at this time.

Jesus walking through walls in his resurrected state is just one example of what I'm referring to (John 20:26). Because God himself is always *rational*, such things just employ a rational science which is beyond our present natural sciences. Thus, it's not so much that God, heaven, invisible angels, or even things like miracles are all unscientific; it's just that they all employ a "higher science" beyond our comprehension which we certainly can look forward to understanding more about if indeed we choose to be with Christ throughout eternity.

If you'd like to know for certain that you too are right with God and have his awesome eternal life, I invite you to just take that first small step of faith by sincerely praying the prayer of salvation located at the end of this book. No matter what your past is like, God loves you and sincerely wants you to be a part of his awesome eternal kingdom!

Jesus said, "I am the resurrection and the life. He who believes in me, will live even though he dies; and whoever lives and believes in me will never die..." (John 11:25–26)

OBJECTION 10

I Believe All Life Came from Aliens

Yes, undoubtedly, there are many honest evidences for "supernatural" or "superhuman" things which have happened in the world around us which simply cannot be denied. Whether they be strange intelligent circular patterns left in crop fields or other superhuman phenomena like how the Egyptian pyramids were built, it seems pretty obvious they were not accomplished by the *normal* human race. But are evolutionary outer space "aliens" themselves really a reasonable explanation for these supernatural phenomena around the world? Or does the idea of them doing these things really leave us with more questions than answers?

For example, if outer space aliens did, in fact, help the Egyptians to build their pyramids, why is there not some very obvious large written record of such fantastic events left by the Egyptians themselves? Since the Egyptians themselves claimed to have built their own pyramids according to historical records, one would reasonably believe that if outer space aliens aided them at all, the Egyptians most certainly would have had to communicate with them during the process (unless the aliens helped them by night, keeping perfectly quiet as they moved the massive stones into place). But the truth is that the obvious written records which we would fully expect from such a unique and powerful phenomenon simply cannot be found anywhere within Egyptian archaeological artifacts!

Most of all, we still have to answer the basic question: If outer space aliens are, in fact, real, where did they come from? And this brings us right back again to our choice between creation or evolution, which are really the only two main "world views" that man can choose to ultimately base his beliefs from. If "life came from aliens," are aliens then God-created intelligent beings or intelligent beings that evolved completely on their own over billions or trillions of years as Darwinian evolution would assume?

If outer space aliens are indeed created by the God of the Bible, then why indeed are they not even mentioned once in the Bible along with all else God created? And assuming the Theory of Darwinian Evolution were true, and aliens evolved before we did, then aliens themselves would still just be a another "middleman" in the supposed chain of evolutionary life around us and really do not provide a satisfactory explanation of where "life" itself *originally came from*.

Even if they evolved over trillions of years (the time involved is rather irrelevant), they would have had to of originally evolved from water, dirt, heat, explosion, light, or some microorganism over those supposed trillions of years. And then the question must be asked, where did the water, dirt, heat, explosion, light, or microorganisms come from? Again, many evolutionists try to assert that ultimately, "everything came from nothing." But such a belief could not be more unscientific since man has never observed (as the scientific method requires) anything coming from absolutely nothing.

> Aliens themselves would still just be another "middleman" in the supposed chain of evolutionary life around us and really do not provide a satisfactory explanation of where "life" itself *originally came from*.

Nobody (no God) times nothing simply could not equal everything! It is probably the *most unscientific notion* that has ever been entertained by man, and yet many still fall for it. And if everything did not come from nothing according to some evolutionist believers, just where did all the water, dirt, heat, explosion, light, or microorganisms come from which supposedly began life? And yet other evolutionary thinkers will actually try to convince us that "everything always existed."

However, as we've already mentioned in an earlier objection, this basic assumption would also contradict the basic laws of science as well as all nature/creation, which man can observe is definitely in a process of deterioration, which means it must have had a beginning when it was new. Nevertheless, any way one would look at it, aliens themselves would be just another "middleman" and not a sufficient explanation of where "life" itself *originally* came from.

Also, if super intelligent outer space aliens were real through-out the thousands of years of man's recorded history, it seems rather unthinkable that all we have to work with today for any real honest proof of it is Hollywood and hearsay! Especially, if they, in fact, were superior to us in intelligence and not afraid of us, controlling uni-verses, etc., one would most definitely think they would have inter-acted with us and revealed themselves plainly to us by now! It would be just like if we never interacted with the animal kingdom after having lived on the same planet together for thousands of years—the notion seems rather absurd indeed.

Even according to the biblical view, our own creator has plainly interacted with us many times. Some extraterrestrial believers may insist that alien beings have not fully revealed themselves to mankind (and remained hidden) simply because as a "superior race," they've been very careful not to "prematurely alter" our "primitive" natural course and thus cause us harm by doing so.

However, ironically, many of these same alien believers also believe that alien beings have indeed been clearly cited, and revealed themselves to mankind (and that's why they, in fact, believe in alien beings) and have interacted with us on our planet in some way or another. But then in such cases (if they were real alien "encounters"), would they not also "prematurely alter" our natural course and thus cause us harm by revealing themselves to us? The truth is that both of these theories greatly conflict with each other, and reasonably, one simply cannot have it both ways. If aliens can't reveal themselves to us, then they could not have interacted with the human race at all at the risk of altering our natural course. If they have revealed themselves to us at all, then they have interacted with the human race and have actually altered our natural course. Either way, the theory that aliens can't reveal themselves to us at all because they would somehow alter our natural course just doesn't make much sense.

> Either way, the theory that aliens can't reveal themselves to us at all because they would somehow alter our natural course just doesn't make much sense.

Additionally, it makes little sense that superior alien beings would remain hidden from us, just because they might alter our "natural course" and cause us "harm." If they are truly "superior" to us because they "evolved" first (as the theory of evolution might assume), then why would they ever cause us harm by interacting with us? So far, man's "natural course" has brought the human race to the brink of extinction. Today, we've not only caused great harm to our planet through pollution, etc., but after two major world wars, we wonder just who's going to push the nuclear war buttons first. So what would be so harmful about superior beings altering our "natural course" if, in fact, they were superior to us and our natural course is clearly heading for disaster? And if they were *inferior* to us, looking at the reckless human race, why would they care about their influence upon us? Undoubtedly, they would have tried to take us over by now through inferior means! Either way, if evolutionary aliens were real, why wouldn't they have followed the evolutionary "survival of the fittest" way of life and fully engaged the human race on earth a long time ago instead of staying completely hidden? Again, "hidden aliens" really make very little sense.

Angelic Beings

However, the Bible gives us a far more reasonable explanation for the supernatural and or superhuman phenomena which litters human history. The Bible refers to them as "angels." According to the Bible, before God created the *first man*, Adam (1 Corinthians

15:45), he created millions and millions of invisible angelic beings *to "minister" to us* and are no less real than we are (Hebrews 1:13–14). And quite unlike the theory of evolution aliens, the invisible angelic beings which God created have indeed interacted with and revealed themselves plainly to mankind on many different occasions within recorded human history. Not only have many men and women of sound character within the Holy Bible plainly testified of their real interactions with angelic beings made visible, but many other historical men and women of sound character have also testified of the same.

> The Bible gives us a far more reasonable explanation for the supernatural and or superhuman phenomena which litters human history. The Bible refers to them as "angels."

Could Biblical Angels Pretend to be Evolutionary Aliens?

But for what possible purpose would an any angel then pretend to be an alien by making an intelligent circular design in some crop field, etc.? To answer this, we must realize another whole part of the Bible's creation account before the first man, Adam, was created. Before Adam was created, the Bible tells of how one-third of the angels which God created chose to rebel against God. One of those angels called "Lucifer" was, in fact, God's most beautifully created angel and actually worshiped God with musical instruments built right into his body (Ezekiel 28:12–19)!

But according to the Bible, Lucifer soon became proud (Isaiah 14:12–14) and convinced one-third of the angels to rebel against God along with him (Revelation 12:4). Yes, like us, angels too were given a "free will." And because one third of these angels chose to rebel against their own creator, God then "cursed" these angels who rebelled against him, and they became "demons" because they would no longer "minister" good to mankind (as in God's original purpose for angels) but were rather bent on destroying mankind, just because we were created by God and in his image. Ever since Lucifer rebelled against God and was cursed, the Bible refers to him from that point on as "*Satan*" or the "*Devil*" who is now bent on destroying mankind both physically and spiritually. As 1 Peter 5:8 plainly teaches us:

> **Be self-controlled and alert. Your enemy the devil prowls around like a roaring lion looking for someone to devour. Resist him standing firm in the faith...**

So back to our question: For what possible purpose would any angel pretend to be an evolutionary alien by making an intelligent circular design in some crop field, etc.? According to the Bible, all the good ministering angels (two-thirds of them) would really have no purpose to do so. However, also according to the Bible, the one-third demonic fallen angels are fiercely bent on deceiving all mankind away from God whom they despise. And according to the Bible, they are not only far more intelligent than us in the crafts of evil and deception, but according to the Bible, they actually have created most all false doctrines, religions, and theories which may appeal to men in order to deceive mankind away from the truth of God (1 Timothy 4:1–2). But why on earth would they do this?

Again, according to the Bible, we must understand that at least now in God's prophetic program, all mankind (as God's loved creation) is rather caught in the middle of Satan's "cross war" against God, and the demonic realm will do most anything to deceive men away from the truth of God, which would lead them to God's eternal salvation. And as the Bible teaches, this gives us some good insight into exactly why there are so many conflicting religions out there in the world which obviously cannot all be right (1 Tim. 4:1)!

We are in the middle of Satan's war against God, and if the demonic realm has hatched all manner of lies and false doctrines to try to keep men out of God's eternal kingdom, then all the conflicting false religions of the world begin to make some real sense, Darwinian evolution included.

But if evolution is true, then all the different religions in the world which pursue God make little sense indeed. Of course, the demonic realm cannot make any man believe their deceptive lies, but it can make those lies and false doctrines very appealing to men *who may really not want the truth*. Am I then suggesting that it actually has been fallen angels of the demonic realm who have very cunningly performed certain supernatural phenomena in man's history with the sole purpose to deceive men into believing in outer space aliens, which would just fuel the Theory of Evolution and pull mankind away from their true creator? Absolutely!

You see, according to scripture, Satan knows all about his own eternal fate in the lake of fire when Christ returns to set up his eternal kingdom on earth. And he just wants to pull as many men into that same lake of fire with him as possible, just because we are created in God's image, and he hates God! But then one might ask, if God really loves mankind, why doesn't he just stop Satan and his war of deceptive lies from having any influence upon man at all? Well, even though our objections 18 and 23 will cover much of this, we'll explain just a couple of basic biblical realities, which will help answer this age old question.

1. First of all, *all the world's evil and suffering* ultimately comes from the lack of spiritual good in the freewill heart choices of men (and angels). And since it would not be "love" for God to control our freewill choices, God himself really has no choice but to let us make our choices, even though many of them grieve him and cause other people harm. God simply cannot go against his own perfect loving character *in any way* and control the freewill choices of his own creation.

2. Second of all, according to the Bible, *the demonic realm cannot do anything to man without God's permission, which severely limits them* (see Job chapters 1–2). I say "severely *limits*" because if it were up to Satan, his demonic host would have just killed off all mankind a long time ago (John 10:10)! But the truth is (which really fit's the strange spiritual battle we see lingering on and on throughout all human history), God has a very

accurate restraint put on Satan and his demonic hosts, which is overseen and enforced by the two-thirds of God's good angels (who are actually stronger than the fallen angels because they were not "cursed" by God). This is why the Bible says that not even a sparrow *"falls to the ground without the Father's will"* and even the *"very hairs of your head are all numbered"* (Matthew 10:29–31).

So in this real biblical sense, there really are no such thing as "accidents," and God is perfectly sovereign and in complete control of all his creation down to the subatomic world, and *all calamities* are very accurately limited according to God's specific will. So even though God cannot control the freewill choices of men without going against his perfect character, according to the Bible, he does indeed "put a cap" on our evil choices if they should threaten the spiritual well-being of the human race too much. Evidently there is a limit put on our collective sinful choices when God does stop the Hitlers of the world and or brings a blanket judgment upon our spreading sin as in the case of the global flood of Noah's time. And on a smaller scale, God will even limit the amount of testing you will go through in a given day, and all of these things are ultimately his perfect love in operation, simply because he won't let the human race destroy itself, nor will he let the demonic realm destroy mankind either.

3. Thirdly, according to the Bible, even though sin entered God's creation totally against his original "perfect will," once it did enter, he had to allow it through his "permissive will" just for a season within his overall prophetic program for man. One reason is because we (meaning all mankind) had to experience the awful effects of our own disobedience to permanently learn that sin (or the breaking of God's moral laws) simply could not give us the true life, happiness, or fulfillment we needed, which can only come from our perfect eternal creator (Proverbs 14:12).

Once sin entered God's perfect creation, it corrupted the very heart of man and broke man's relationship with God. And the Bible teaches us that ever since sin corrupted the heart of man (Job 5:7; Jeremiah 17:9; Romans 3:10–20) that it has been absolutely necessary for God *to ultimately "test" our heart's love for him* before he is able to share his eternal life and kingdom with us (James 1:12; Jeremiah 17:10).

Am I suggesting that demonic beings have actually performed supernatural phenomena with the sole purpose to deceive men into believing in evolutionary outer space aliens and pull them away from their true creator? Absolutely!

And obscurely enough, according to the Bible, this "testing process" of man definitely includes Satan and his demonic hosts who are very willing participants, just because of their hatred toward God (Job chapter 1–2). And although God may "allow" demonic fallen angels to ultimately test our hearts with false doctrines, physical hardships, financial hardships, etc., it is critical to understand that it is not God who is doing the actual evil, which he allows Satan to test us with (see James 1:13–14)!

We must remember that all evil and suffering ultimately comes from only the lack of spiritual good in the freewill heart choices of men (and angels). It is also important to understand that according to the Bible, when God allows the hearts of men to be tested, not only is the test limited by his power but also that God allows it in his love, really desiring us to ultimately pass the tests of our heart so we can spend eternity with him (see Genesis 4:6–7; 2 Peter 3:9; 1 Corinthians 2:9)! This is very different from Satan's evil motives, which are always hoping we will not pass the tests of our heart and go to the lake of fire with him!

And so, all in all, even though we may never understand everything about them in this life, the millions of angelic beings which the Bible clearly teaches us about do, in fact, give us a much more believable explanation for the supernatural phenomena which man has encountered throughout his recorded history. Angels are not only more believable than evolutionary outer space aliens because of the many human eyewitnesses with sound character who have communicated directly with them in recorded human history, but also because outer space aliens have really never communicated with man in any way which has ever been recorded in our history books.

If one goes back just to the colonial days, children definitely learned about the Bible and angelic beings in their history classes in school. However, they never learned about evolutionary outer space aliens simply because the real documents of our recorded history completely lack any such alien encounters with mankind! Similarly, the renaissance painters and writers always portrayed and wrote of both good and demonic angels, but you will be hard-pressed to find any evolutionary aliens in their historical art or written records. And why is that if aliens were just as real back then as they are now?

According to our historical record, evolutionary aliens have basically only been in the thoughts of mankind for the last 100 years or so. Why? Simply because they are just another attempt to deceive all mankind away from God and his eternal salvation, which has only been late in the game of human history. But angels can be found in the records throughout all of our traceable human history!

> Children in school during the colonial days learned about the Bible and angelic beings but never about evolutionary outer space aliens, simply because our recorded history completely lacks any such alien encounters with mankind!

It is true that some people (more in our very recent history) may have claimed to have personally encountered aliens, but again, the many more recorded historical encounters with angels would strongly suggest that these "personal alien encounters" were really just encounters with demonic beings who cunningly posed as "outer space aliens" in order to deceive those men away from God.

According to the Bible, it is even possible for demonic fallen angels to "*transform*" themselves into the appearance of the good "*angels of light*" in order to deceive men (2 Cor. 11:14). Also similarly, many have claimed to have communicated with their dead relatives. However, once again, according to the Bible, this is not only impossible because all dead men are immediately confined to heaven or hell in the center of the earth, but also, Satan and his demonic host can perfectly "transform" themselves and actually imitate the exact appearance, voice, and even smell of the "familiar spirits" of one's dead relatives in order to deceive men away from God and into "necromancy" (talking with the dead, which are really only demons).

You see, God's word has always clearly taught that intentional persistent "necromancy" (which is really communicating with demons posing to be dead relatives) is an abomination to the Lord and actually disqualifies one from God's eternal salvation if not repented from (please see Deuteronomy 18:10–12 and Revelation 21:8). And Satan and his demonic host know this and try to rope as many people into it as they can just to destroy their opportunity for a right relationship with God and his eternal life.

Therefore, even though there has undoubtedly been many more recent sightings of "alien beings" by men (because Satan knows it fuels the more recent theory of evolution), in biblical reality, they are only fallen demonic angels which have "*transformed*" themselves into the appearance of evolutionary outer space alien beings in order to deceive men away from God and into the false theory of Darwinian evolution, which again also destroys one's chance for eternal salvation if sincerely believed without a creator.

> God's word has always clearly taught that "necromancy" disqualifies one from God's eternal salvation if not repented from. And Satan and his demonic host know this and try to rope as many people into it as they can.

"Nephilim" or "Giants of Old"

However, even though fallen angels themselves do give us a very reasonable explanation for much of the superhuman phenomena encountered in the history of the world, they really do not seem to answer some other questions which would be better explained by what the Bible refers to as the "Nephilim" or the *"giants of old"* who had strength which superseded normal human strength. Just what are "Nephilim" or the *"giants of old"* as recorded in the Bible? Hold onto your hat, for strangely enough, according to God's Word, they were actually the inconceivable cross between a human woman and a demonic fallen angel (see Genesis 6:2–4)!

According to Genesis 6:2–4, these original "Nephilim" (before and after Noah's flood hit) could have been beyond fifteen feet tall, simply because they were the strange cross between a human woman and a demonic fallen angel.

But how could an invisible demonic fallen angel actually mate with a human woman and produce larger than normal human offspring? Well, first of all, angels throughout scripture were always able to also take on human form if allowed by God (Gen. 18:22; Heb. 13:2). We don't and won't probably know just how it happened, but we can glean enough from the scriptures to know it would have been possible. Also, according to the Bible, angels have always been much taller or larger than humans with super strength (2 Samuel 24:15–16). And throughout the Scriptures, they have always been given masculine names, never feminine names (Rev. 12:7). Thus, we can just ignore any painting where some ignorant artists have actually depicted angels as women or baby cupids, because they are just not biblical.

Why would God even allow a demonic fallen angel to mate with a human woman? No doubt, these pre-flood human women were willing participants delving into the "occult" demonic realm long before their relationship with these demonic fallen angels who took on human form. God probably allowed it to once again test the hearts of men, seeing men back then were so bent on delving into the demonic realm. The Bible does say that the *"thoughts of man's heart* (before Noah's flood) *were only evil continually,*" and that's exactly why God had to send the flood (Genesis 6:5).

What Kinds of Phenomena Were the "Nephilim" or "Giants of Old" a Part Of?

Of course, it is rather doubtful that invisible fallen demonic angelic beings helped the Egyptians build their pyramids, simply because this explanation has the same difficulties as does outer space alien aid. Like alien aid, it simply cannot be found in Egyptian historical records that demonic (or even good) angelic beings helped them build their pyramids. And again, the Egyptians no doubt would have basically recorded such amazing events. However, this is not necessarily so with the "Nephilim" or giants of old, simply because they were well-known throughout the land and considered "human," and there is little reason for the Egyptians to make special note of them if they were just human slaves and well-known among the human populace after Noah's flood.

These larger than normal humans could have just been among the other slaves helping to build the Egyptian pyramids. In fact, to believe the Egyptians used them for slave labor to some degree is not at all unbelievable. In fact, the construction of things like the Egyptian pyramids, Incan Indian stone temples, and even Stonehenge in Ireland may not be sufficiently explained by the mere physical ability of normal-sized men and are all strong evidence for these "giant" men who had their real place in history.

But why would demonic fallen angels even want to propagate with humans in the first place? As mentioned earlier, we must understand the basic war between the demonic realm and God. Evidently, before and even after Noah's flood, one of Satan's strategies to corrupt mankind and hurt God was to propagate with human mothers in their attempt to destroy the genetic bloodline leading to Christ, the Son of God, who Satan knew would be the Savior of the world. However, the Bible teaches us that God somehow protected that bloodline through Noah's son, Shem, who was his son that the Jewish nation and savior of the world genetically came from. But what real evidence is there that these "Nephilim" giant offspring were even real?

Actually, there is much historical and archaeological evidence pointing to the fact that there were indeed many larger than normal human "giants" who once inhabited our planet with normal human beings. Technically, according to the Bible, they were not fully human, so I'll just refer to them as "giants." Obviously, all the original "Nephilim" giants were destroyed by Noah's flood. However, since much post-flood historical and archaeological evidence for these giants can be found today, we must conclude that either the genetic bloodline of the giants was carried through one of Noah's sons or demonic fallen angels once again propagated with human women after the flood.

However, the latter is far more likely, simply because both Noah's ancestors were godly men and did not delve into the demonic realm. But again, what real proof do we have of these "Nephilim" giants which were much bigger than normal men?

As a reliable historical document, not only is the Bible laced with numerous mentions of these giants and their interactions with men (such as the biblical account of King David slaying "Goliath of Gath" who was over ten feet tall), but also many other nonbiblical records of man's history mention these "giants" as well. "Giants" are kind of like "dragons;" there are far too many different cultures around the world, which have a *basically* united historical record of them for them to be completely imaginary and have no basis of truth whatsoever. This, of course, does not mean that many historical "giant" legends have not been "fancifully embellished" by man (as in the case of dragon legends), but it certainly doesn't mean all historical giant legends do not have a real basis of truth to them. And not only does written history bear witness to these giants being very real, but according to Dr. Kent Hovind, in his *Garden of Eden* DVD, archaeologists have also plainly uncovered much evidence for them as well.[34]

---

[34] Hovind, Dr. Kent. *The Garden of Eden*. CSE Ministry. 2006

The truth is that there are some archaeological artifacts which can only make sense with these "giants." For example, archaeologists have found thirty-nine-pound stone hammerheads. If just the stone head is thirty-nine pounds, who's swinging a forty-plus pound stone hammer? Certainly not a six-foot man for any length of time!

> There are some archaeological arti-
> facts which can only make sense with
> "giants." For example, archaeologists
> have found thirty-nine-pound stone
> hammerheads.

If all this is true, then why haven't these giants been clearly exposed to the public? Well, they have. In fact, right now, you can Google "Nephilim" or "giants," and you can see for yourself firsthand some of their skeletons uncovered by archaeologists. Who can argue with many giant/human skeletons, which range anywhere from ten to thirteen feet tall?[35] However, one must also be aware that mixed into such a website are obvious hoaxes which are not real, but photos which have been doctored up by those who are afraid of this basic truth. In fact, mainstream evolutionary scientists, historians, etc., many times try to cover up or explain away these many very real honest proofs for "giants," simply because they not only verify the truth of the Bible, but because they also go against Darwinian evolution, which basically teaches that man is always evolving into more strength and intelligence, not less.

Additionally, it should not be impossible for anyone to believe in the "giants" recorded within the Bible since even our very recent history has record of more than one man enjoying heights of about nine feet tall. For example, Robert Wadlow is one such very large

---

[35] Hovind, Dr. Kent. *The Garden of Eden.* CSE Ministry. 2006

man who reached the height of almost nine feet tall before he died in 1940.

> It should not be impossible for any-one to believe in the "giants" recorded within the Bible since even our recent history has record of more than one man enjoying heights of about nine feet tall.

Could such tall men of our recent history be genetic descendants of biblical giants? Since all the more modern "giant" men that we know of certainly got their genes from somewhere, I don't think we can genetically rule that possibility out! Obviously, they did not get their genes from smaller men. Of course, religions like Greek mythology and historical storytellers alike may have grossly exaggerated the true stature of biblical giants, making them out to be fifty-foot-tall one-eyed Cyclops, but this is often done with most hard to believe *facts* of history. Thus, myths are born. Nevertheless, even the "giant" myths almost certainly spring from these very real giants in history who have left behind much evidence for the honest soul to ponder.

The Biblical Future "Rapture" Event and Aliens

While on the subject of aliens, it should be also noted that the demonic realm is certainly not done deceiving mankind with the concept of outer space aliens. Along with the amazing reality of fallen angelic beings and "Nephilim" giants, the Bible also teaches us about a unique one-time future event which will be no less real called the "Rapture (or catching up) of the Church." According to the Bible, just before the future seven-year tribulation judgment hits the earth, the true "Church" (those who believe that Christ had to die for all their sins on the cross and are truly living for him) will be supernaturally caught up to heaven by the power of God.

While this may indeed seem too fantastic to our rational think-ing, it is certainly no less fantastic than all the other divinely inspired accounts of miracles within the Bible or even outer space aliens, for that matter! Even if one chooses to believe in "nothing," this is the most fantastic belief system of all! So any way one chooses to look at it, all we have for choices are "supernatural fantastic" options. It's just which *"fantastic"* belief system will you adopt for yourself based on the real historical evidence we have?

In fact, the Bible records several other "raptures," which have already taken place in human history. The first one recorded was the prophet Enoch who was taken alive up to heaven by the power of God, because he *"walked with God"* (Genesis 5:24). The second one recorded was the Godly prophet, Elijah, who was "raptured" up to heaven by a *"whirlwind"* (2 Kings 2:1–11). Also the Apostle Paul of the New Testament was *"caught up"* to heaven, although he was not sure whether or not it was a bodily translation (2 Cor. 12:2–4). Even other New Testament saints were supernaturally translated by the power of God, like the Apostle Phillip who was just supernaturally translated from one city to another instantly (Acts 8:39–40). The interesting thing is that all the apostles and prophets of both the Old and New Testaments (all showing themselves to be honest men of sound character) confirm such records with absolutely no objections to these other *"catching up"* of men to heaven by the power of God.

In this obvious sense, they all put their "stamp of approval" upon such amazing events recorded in Scripture, even though they are certainly hard for our rational minds to conceive. But just like the future seven-year tribulation period could be likened to Noah's flood, this future "Rapture" event, which the Bible describes, could be lik-ened to Noah's Ark which saved the righteous from God's judgment on the unrighteous. We are not told by scripture just exactly the *"day or hour"* when the rapture event will take place, simply because God wants his Church to always be spiritually ready for it at all times.

But there is one verse (and only one verse that I know of) in the entire Bible which *could* pin down a *basic time frame* for its occur-rence. In Matthew 24:23–34, many Bible scholars believe Jesus may be telling us that the Rapture will occur within a *"generation"* of

Israel becoming a nation again. And if Israel became a nation again in 1948, and seventy years has already passed since, then the rapture could not be too far away. Just what Jesus defined as a generation would be the critical information we lack. However, whether one deems a "generation" to be seventy or even 100 years in length, it should be rather obvious that the "*generation*" Christ referred to is quickly coming to an end! Additionally, most Bible scholars believe that the biblical rapture event will take place in the very near future, simply because the prophetic stage is now completely set (like never before) for Revelation's tribulation period to occur.

When the Rapture does take place, most likely, the seven-year tribulation period, which the book of Revelation describes in great detail, will begin within only months of it. Since right after the Rapture, only unbelievers (those who do not believe in Christ and the Bible) will be left on earth, the world will be rather ripe for non-biblical deception. While many millions will undoubtedly come to Christ right after the Rapture and believe in the Bible because of the obvious rapture event it teaches, many more, who will still refuse to believe in the Bible will more than likely be deceived into believing that it was really "outer space aliens" who took all the Bible-believing Christians off the earth and not God through the Rapture.

> [m]ost Bible scholars believe that the biblical rapture event will take place in the very near future simply because the prophetic stage is now completely set for Revelation's tribulation period to occur.

Maybe it will be said that aliens took all Bible-believing Christians off the earth simply because the true Bible-believing Christians could not be "team players" in the "New World Order," which will be offered to the world through the Antichrist. Who knows? But because the rapture event will also remove *all* small children and babies as well, such an explanation should certainly not satisfy those who have any sense! Nevertheless, there will undoubtedly be some deceptive explanations hatched by the demonic realm which will appeal to those who refuse to believe the Bible's clear teaching on the Rapture (see 1 Thessalonians 4:13–18; 1 Corinthians 15:51–53).

> While many millions will undoubtedly come to Christ right after the Rapture… many more will likely be deceived into believing that it was really outer space aliens who took all the Bible-believing Christians off the earth.

However, the fact that every detailed tribulation period event described clearly in the book of Revelation will take place in its exact chronological order right after the Rapture should indeed settle the issue for any *honest* soul and awaken many evolutionary thinkers out of their unbelief! It will definitely be an "A-ha" moment for many as they will be forced to say, "A-ha! The Bible was right after all!"

> However, the fact that every detailed tribulation period event described in the book of Revelation will take place in its exact chronological order right after the Rapture should settle the issue for any *honest* soul!

Conclusion

As we've already exposed, prior to the last eighty years or so when the Theory of Evolution was popularized, there is very little to no written historical testimonies of men encountering outer space "aliens." And why would that be if they were just as real prior to seventy years ago as they supposedly are now? However, on the contrary, prior to that, there is much more written historical testimonies of men encountering the biblical angelic world. And since, according to the Bible, it would be well within the character of demonic angelic beings to fuel the Theory of Evolution in order to pull men away from the eternal salvation of God, the millions of demonic angelic beings posing as aliens would be a much better explanation of "extra-terrestrial" phenomena observed by recent man. However, as we've already discussed, real outer space aliens just give us more questions than answers and certainly cannot even explain to us where life *originally* came from.

However, on the other hand, the Bible's clear teaching that all life originally came from our one and only creator who must be both perfect and eternal makes much more sense than the evolutionary theory that "everything came from nothing," which somehow, against all observable science, gave birth to outer space aliens.

According to God's Word, which has proven itself over and over again through miraculously fulfilled prophecy, the demonic realm just wants to harm all men and deceive you away from the one true God and his eternal salvation. But the one thing the demonic realm cannot control is your freewill choices, which your loving creator has so wisely given you. If you'd like to be connected to the greatest power in the universe and know for certain that you too are right with God and have his eternal life, I invite you to just take that first small step of faith by sincerely praying the prayer of salvation located at the end of this book. No matter what your past is like, God loves you and sincerely wants you to be a part of his awesome eternal kingdom!

Jesus said, "I am the resurrection and the life. He who believes in me, will live even though he dies; and whoever lives and believes in me will never die..." (John 11:25–26)

OBJECTION 11

I Already Believe in God

While it is certainly good to believe in God, amazingly enough, the Bible teaches us that *just* believing that God really exists is not at all good enough to get anyone to heaven. Why? Simply because it teaches that since all mankind is born into sin, our main problem isn't that we don't believe our creator exists; it is that our relationship with him is broken due to our sin, and we are eternally separated from him as a result.

As we already pointed out in our Objection 3, even professing "atheists" technically believe God exists (that's why they take his name in vain). But they are just either unaware that they really do believe he exists in their heart or are just unwilling to admit it. As the Bible points out the obvious—even the demonic world believes God is real and shudder with fear because of it (James 2:19).

But obviously, they are not "right with God," which is the real issue when it comes to obtaining God's eternal life. Therefore, it is certainly good that you are honest enough with yourself to admit that our creator is real (you have a one-up on the evolutionists), but you just need to take the next step of faith if you want to be right with him and have his eternal life. And according to God's Word, the only way man can be right with God and obtain his eternal life is by simply believing Jesus, God's Son, took the punishment for all our sins when he died on the cross.

And the reason that is so critical is because according to God's perfect justice, all sin must be punished. And if we do not want to take our own just punishment for all our sins (all the times we've broken God's perfect moral standards), then God very graciously just requires that we believe that God's Son, Jesus, took our punishment for us when he died on the cross. But if we reject the fact that God himself graciously took the punishment for our sins when Jesus died a brutal death on the cross, then God has no other choice but to have us take our own punishment.

> According to God's word, the only way man can be right with God and obtain his eternal life is by simply believing Jesus, God's Son, took the punishment for all our sins when he died on the cross.

Either way, though, God's perfect justice must be satisfied. Would we respect a civil court judge who constantly let the guilty go free? Certainly not, especially if you were the one who was wronged by the guilty party. And if a very imperfect civil court judge would never knowingly let the guilty go free, how much more could our absolutely perfect creator in heaven never let the guilty go unpunished?

In fact, if he did, he'd compromise his own perfect character and immediately cease to be an eternal being because of it. But according to the Bible, since he is absolutely perfect, it is absolutely impossible for God to compromise his own character in any way (Titus 1:2; Hebrews 6:18). Thus we can be sure that the just punishment for all sin must be administered upon those who finally reject what Christ did for them on the cross.

However, if we truly believe that Jesus, God's Son, actually took the punishment for our sins on the cross, we have the sure promise of God's own Word that we will be put in "right relationship" with him through that faith, and we will not have to undergo the just eternal punishment for our own sins. Many different verses of God's Word clearly teach us that *only through believing in what Christ did for us* can we obtain God's eternal salvation:

> However, if we truly believe that Jesus, God's Son, actually took the punishment for our sins on the cross…we will not have to undergo the just eternal punishment for our own sins.

> **Jesus answered, "I am the way and the truth and the life. No one comes to the Father except through me." (John 14:6)**

> **For God so loved the world that he gave his one and only Son, that whoever believes in him shall not perish but have eternal life. (John 3:16)**

> **[i]f you confess with your mouth, "Jesus is Lord," and believe in your heart that God raised him from the dead, you will be saved. For it is with your heart that you believe and are justified, and it is with your mouth that you confess and are saved. (Romans 10:9–10)**

> **Salvation is found in no one else, for there is no other name under heaven given to men, by which we must be saved. (Acts 4:12)**

Conclusion

Because God does not wish that any man should perish (by receiving their just punishment of eternal torment—2 Peter 3:9), this is exactly why he so graciously sent his Son, Jesus, to take our punishment for us on the cross. In other words, God gave us all "a way out" of our punishment, just by believing Jesus, God's Son, took it for us on the cross. Thus, it's not that any man actually *deserves* or can somehow even *earn* God's free gift of eternal life, but God loves us because of who he is, and his perfect justice is satisfied if we just believe that Jesus took our punishment for us on the cross. And that, my friend, is exactly why the Gospel message of salvation (what Christ did for us on the cross) is such good news!

But scripture makes it clear that just believing God exists is not enough. God, your creator, loves you and wants a right relationship with you. If you do not yet know for certain that you too are right with God and have his eternal life, I invite you to just take that first small step of faith by sincerely praying the prayer of salvation located at the end of this book. No matter what your past is like, God loves you and sincerely wants you to be a part of his awesome eternal kingdom!

> **Jesus said, "I am the resurrection and the life. He who believes in me, will live even though he dies; and whoever lives and believes in me will never die..." (John 11:25–26)**

OBJECTION 12

I Don't believe in Just one God (Monotheism); I believe in Many Gods (Polytheism)

It is understandable just why some would want to *lean* in the direction of "Polytheism;" because after all, how could just one God be in control of everything? From our limited weak human perspective, the job simply seems too immense for only one God to manage. Surely it must require the help of many gods! Thus, religions like Greek Mythology, the Viking's folk religions, the religion of the Egyptians, and the native American Indian religions may all certainly have some appeal.

However, while all the different gods of all these polytheistic religions may be entertaining to the mind of some, it would seem by far that most of the world who are not polytheistic have concluded that polytheism as a belief system actually creates more problems than it solves and gives us more questions than answers. Typically, polytheism religions portray their "gods" to be disunited with each other or even fighting each other at times. And of course, this is because they are not of one substance and are completely different beings from one another, each *having their own wills*. And it's this disunity problem among the "gods" of a given polytheistic religion which poses an obvious problem for "polytheism" as a whole as is evident from the following questions:

1. If the "gods" of typical polytheism religions are not perfectly united with each other, how then could they be absolutely morally perfect?

2. And if they are not absolutely morally perfect in every way, how then could they possibly be eternal?

3. And if they are not eternal, then what existed before them, what will exist after them, and who even brought them into existence?

4. If they somehow evolved on their own, then aren't we really talking about Darwinian evolution atheism and not polytheism?

5. If they were all created by a singular perfect eternal being who existed before them, then aren't we really talking about monotheism which holds that there is a single supreme being behind everything else?

6. If there are many different gods, which are all in control of different things like the sea, mountains, deserts, animals, earth, weather, Hades, the cosmos, etc., then who decided which gods are in control of what (and for how long), if they did not come from a monotheistic God or if they are not all of the same substance?

7. If there is a god among many who is more superior (like Zeus in Greek mythology), how could he be superior to the others and in control of them and their roles if he is not absolutely perfect, eternal, or monotheistic himself or ultimately from a perfect eternal monotheistic God?

8. Much unlike Christ of the Holy Bible, there are no human historical witnesses who have claimed to see, touch, hear, and walk with the mythical so-called "gods" of Greek mythology, Egypt, Viking folk religions, or even the native American Indian religion. However, all the apostles (and many more) did testify to have witnessed Christ firsthand

and actually saw his miraculous divinity displayed. But who actually walked with Zeus? Or the Viking folk religion gods? Or the Native American Indian gods? Even in the Old Testament, Moses and many other saints spoke with God of the Bible who proved his divinity over and over by miraculously interacting with the human race many times.

According to the Pew Research Center online, world religion statistics were roughly as follows as of September of 2016:

84 percent of the world is religious.

16 percent of the world is unaffiliated with any religion.

And of the religious (84 percent): Monotheists make up 55 percent, Reincarnationists make up 22 percent, and Folk religionists make up 6 percent.

And of the Monotheists (55 percent): Christians make up 32 percent, and Muslims make up 23 percent.

And of the Reincarnationists (22 percent): Hinduism makes up 15 percent, and Buddhists make up 7 percent.

And of the unaffiliated (16 percent): Agnostics make up 11 percent, and Atheists and free thinkers make up about 3 percent.

If 84 percent of the world is religious (which believes in God or gods), and 55 percent is monotheistic (believing in only one supreme being), and 22% are reincarnationists, then that would mean only about 6% believe in polytheistic "Folk religions" (believing in many gods). Perhaps the unsolvable *problems* for the "gods" within polytheism (which we've just listed) is one major reason why most of the world has rejected polytheism as a belief system.

Biblical Christianity a Polytheistic Religion?

It is sometimes claimed that biblical Christianity is not truly monotheistic because of the Bible's clear teaching on the trinity (three persons in one God). However, the central doctrine of biblical

Christianity is that only one God exists in three persons *who are of the very same substance or essence because they share only one will.* And because each "person" of the trinity (or Godhead) is indeed just an expression of the very same God which only has one will, the God within the Bible would definitely be considered monotheistic. The biblical "trinity" is a concept which, of course, clearly goes beyond our human reason, but not necessarily against it. In other words, according to the Bible, there are not three different individuals in the Godhead who are alongside of and separate from each other with their own wills, but only three different personal self-distinctions or expressions within one single divine supreme being who only has one will.

> Perhaps the unsolvable *problems (which we've just listed)* for the "gods" within polytheism is one major reason why most of the world has rejected polytheism as a belief system.

Within those holding to monotheism in the world today, biblical Christianity is the largest religion (32 percent of the 55 percent which is monotheistic). While Muslim numbers are climbing, they are only about 23 percent of the 55 percent monotheistic. Today, biblical Christianity is still by far the largest unified religion in the world with the Bible itself continuing to be the most sold book in the world on an average. According to more than one online source, there are roughly about twenty different *major* religions in the world (which in turn all eventually subdivide into about 4,300 different smaller religions). And obviously and logically, all twenty major religions within the world (which all have conflicting basic doctrines) cannot all be right.

In fact, if there are truly twenty different basic religions in the world (polytheism being one of them) which all conflict with each other in their basic doctrines, then shall we not *honestly* conclude that at least nineteen of those twenty religions must inevitably be incorrect and a false explanation of the origin of life around us?

> There are not three different individuals in the Godhead who are alongside of, and separate from each other with their own wills, but only three different personal self-expressions within one single divine supreme being who only has one will.

Though the unity dilemma among the gods of polytheism is a real problem, perhaps another reason some may still hold to polytheism is the same reason many may hold to most of the other eighteen major religions in the world, which must be false by simple reasoning. Perhaps they are genuinely deceived because they were just born into it, and their whole family believes it, being handed down from the previous generation. And perhaps they really don't know why they even believe what they believe and have never even wrestled with our above questions. Or perhaps they just cling to a belief system (which they know is made of only myths) for emotional reasons, because they are consciously or unconsciously rebelling against the one and only true God who created them.

Martyrdom for Mere Fairy Tales?

It is interesting indeed to also note that those who may consider the Bible to be just a bunch of myths or fairy tales are often seriously threatened by its teachings. Often throughout the history of the church age we live in (all the way back to Christ), those who *professed to not believe* in the Bible actually went out of their way to persecute those who did, because they were obviously threatened by them.

During the days of Rome, especially Bible-believing Christians were often persecuted to death for their faith in Christ. In fact, probably more than in any other religion in the world, biblical Christianity has the largest history of martyrdom within the last 2,000 years, even though it has probably been the largest religion in the world ever since Christ. "Martyrdom" itself is specifically the murder of someone because of their spiritual beliefs, which would not really include all historical "wars" over lands, money, or material things. Not only were Christ's apostles murdered/martyred for their faith, but so were countless other individual followers of Christ throughout the entire "Church age" we live in. But one must ask the sincere honest question: If biblical Christianity is not really believed by those who are so threatened by it, why on earth would they be so threatened by it to the point of murder?

Especially to the point of martyring peace-loving Christians who were certainly no physical threat? If the Bible is truly false in their heart and mind and just a bunch of fairy tales, why would anyone murder others over mere fairy tales? They might think you foolish or even mock you to have fun with you, but murder you just because of your adherence to your personal beliefs in the Bible, which calls all men to love each other? It simply makes no sense to the honest soul. The only basic reasonable explanation concerning this question is that they really do (or did) believe the Bible to be true in their heart (contrary to what they may have verbally admitted) and were very threatened by that truth with its very real implications upon their own life and eternal destiny. After all, who would be so afraid of a book full of fairy tales if they truly believed them to be fairy tales? Kids believe in fairy tales all the time, but no one goes around murdering them for it!

> If biblical Christianity is not really believed by those who are so threatened by it, why on earth would they be so threatened by it?

After all, how could a mere fairy tale even be a threat? It couldn't if it truly wasn't connected to reality, *but of course the God-given truth with its personal implications could.* And that is exactly why many murderers kill—because they are sincerely threatened by something which they know to be true which will affect them personally. If something really has no substance to it, which registers in the conscience of man, then it certainly shouldn't make anyone uncomfortable. For after all, why be threatened by something which is simply non-reality? However, if it is the truth which is shared, and that truth registers in the conscience of men, then we can expect to see the hearts of men greatly tested by it. And if we reject the truth when tested by it, the reaction of even murder can be the result! But if we fail our tests of heart when encountering the truth, then certainly it is only ourselves we cheat, for then we forfeit our present opportunity to gain the life and freedom which only the truth can give us.

Thus, just considering this, we could reasonably conclude that many more people in the world who are threatened by biblical Christianity may very well believe in the truths of Bible, even though they are (or were) quite unwilling to admit it or surrender to its reality. When one considers that religious persecution and martyrdom would reasonably surround the true faith the most, just because evil men are threatened the most by the truth, then one can also understand why one seldom hears about anyone being martyred for believing in any of the gods which polytheism religions imagine. After all, when is the last time you heard of anyone ever being martyred *just for believing in* the Greek god, Zeus, the Viking god, Thor, the Egyptian sun god, Ra, or the Native American gods such as the eagle, bear, or lion? Hmm...I wonder why that is? Probably because it is not the truth and therefore cannot be a threat.

However, the martyrdom of Bible-believing Christians is still taking place around the world today in Third World countries. The ministry, The Voice of the Martyrs, is a Christian ministry which actually keeps basic track of Christian martyrdom which still persists in our world today. Nevertheless, if those polytheistic gods are not representative of reality, then why would even 6 percent of the world's population today adhere to polytheism? In the case when anything is not representative of reality, but yet man clings to it, I would simply suggest that it is because they wish to *escape* from reality for their own personal or emotional reasons.

When is the last time you heard of anyone ever being martyred *just for believing in* the Greek god, Zeus, the Viking god, Thor, the Egyptian sun god, Ra, or the Native American Indian gods such as the eagle, bear, or lion?

The Importance of Real Historical Eyewitnesses

Aside from other evidences which can confirm a given religion, real historical eyewitnesses are also vital to confirm the validity of the one true faith. For example, biblical Christianity has many real historical people who actually lived in both the Old and New Testaments and actually witnessed the events recorded within the Bible. They not only witnessed the events, but also God himself who caused those events! For example, Christ's disciples and many others testified in historical record that they personally walked with and were actual eyewitnesses of the divine Christ and the miracles he did on earth over a three-year period of time (1 John 1:1–3; 2 Peter 1:16–18). In fact, many also personally witnessed Christ after he had risen from the dead in his resurrected body (Luke 24:39; 1 Corinthians 15:6; Acts 1:1–3).

Additionally, men like Moses and Abraham even saw Christ incarnate in Old Testament times (Genesis chapter 18; Exodus 33:23); not to mention most Old Testament patriarchs actually testified to communicating directly with God or were given dreams and visions directly from him. And as we further discuss in Objection 35, even prominent non-Christian eyewitnesses testified to the reality of Christ in their own day, telling us plainly that he "wrought surprising feats."

However, if any religion simply has no real historical eyewitnesses to confirm its divine source, then it is indeed much more difficult to confirm that faith as even connected to reality. And this is just one more unique aspect where biblical Christianity stands quite alone from among all the religions of the world with, of course, the exception of Judaism which shares the same God because it is actually New Testament biblical Christianity *incomplete.*

> If any religion simply has no real historical eyewitnesses to confirm its divine source, then it is much more difficult to confirm that faith as even connected to reality.

The Deity of Polytheistic Religions Lack Any Real Eyewitnesses

The reality is that no one in recorded history has ever actually physically seen, touched, and talked with any other so called "god" on earth, other than Jesus Christ! It cannot be historically confirmed by any reliable historical records/witnesses that the Viking god, Thor, ever physically came down to earth and was personally seen and experienced by mankind. Nor has any historical eyewitness ever seen Zeus or any other polytheistic god ever visiting mankind and walking among men, demonstrating their sinless deity for any length of time!

Jesus Christ is truly unique in this respect which, of course, should beg the question, why? I guess when you think reasonably about it, it only makes sense that our true creator would obviously introduce himself to his own creation for the purpose of relationship (as we already discussed in Objection 1); otherwise, the whole point of creating man would certainly lack meaningful purpose.

Most Greeks probably viewed the unnatural creatures of Greek mythology as just what they were—myths made up in the imaginations of men, just for the purpose to convey some "lessons in life." For no reliable historical eye witness has ever really personally seen Medusa, a Centaur, a Pegasus, a multiple-headed Hydra dragon, a giant one-eyed Cyclops, or the three old hags who all share an eyeball. Nor has any real historical figure ever verified that the many fantastic stories of Greek mythology which involve such imaginary creatures actually happened in our real history.

While some of the unnatural creatures of Greek mythology may have had their origin with real dinosaurs or Nephilim giants which once walked the earth, we can all be reasonably sure that the actual very unnatural creatures of Greek mythology themselves are quite fictional. And while all the fantastic stories of Greek mythology may have some truths to convey, we can be reasonably sure that such stories were never part of our real history.

But strangely enough, even though there are certainly no real historical eyewitnesses which confirm the real existence of the Greek mythology gods, many of the ancient Greeks themselves (depending upon the time period were talking about) really did believe that Zeus, Poseidon, or Hades were real gods who had sway over the earth and the affairs of men! And the following is a reasonable explanation as to why they did, even though they completely lacked any real historical eyewitnesses.

When one understands that the gods of Greek mythology were the very basis for social and political authority in the Greek culture, then it becomes easier to understand just why these imaginary gods were taken seriously.

Political and social leaders often actually used the gods of Greek mythology to make their decisions to rule the people of their culture. For example, if a natural disaster occurred, then they were inclined to draw spiritual/political conclusions from it, such as Zeus punishing them for going to war with the Romans, etc. And as in most folk religions, the Greeks also believed there had to be many gods, most likely because there were so many aspects of nature to control. Zeus controlled the thunder and lightning, and Poseidon controlled the oceans, and Hades controlled the underworld, etc. And because their social and political actions were directly tied into what they believed were the very actions of the gods of mythology, their society taught them from infancy to take "the gods" of Greek mythology very seriously with no tolerance for doubt.

However, when one sees the assumed relationship between social and political affairs of Greek society and the gods of Greek mythology which completely lacked any real eyewitnesses, then one essentially concludes that any other "god" imagined in the minds of men could have worked within Greek society in order for it to function as it did. Instead of Zeus, they could have called him Thor, and it wouldn't have made any difference, for both would have equally served their social and political agendas. In fact, all the different gods of the polytheistic folk religions pretty much confirm this as they pretty much operate the same way politically and socially with just different names to the "gods" which sway their actions and decisions.

However, once again, since no one in recorded history has ever actually physically seen, touched, and talked with any so-called polytheistic "god" on earth, then any civil court judge would most certainly conclude that it is more difficult to confirm that any such "gods" were even connected to reality, much less weather and wars!

And to top it off, not only do all the gods of the polytheistic religions lack reliable historical eyewitnesses, but they also seriously lack obvious divine power plainly demonstrated to mankind on earth in the form of miracles or fulfilled prophecies. Yes, the Greeks may have claimed that Zeus caused a certain natural disaster and there may have even been Greeks who foresaw the disaster coming, but these are not the kind of sure "miraculous proofs" which Christ and his apostles demonstrated over and over again.

First of all, it's pretty tough to prove that a natural disaster is nothing more than a natural disaster, and Christ or the apostles certainly did not rely on natural disasters for their display of divine power. Second of all, many imminent natural disasters are reasonably easy to predict if they are going to happen in the very near future. The prophecies we are talking about are those that predict a detailed event in the future hundreds or even thousands of years in advance that really couldn't be anything else other than the supernatural fulfillment of a divine prophecy. And what we are talking about are scores of divine miracles which could not be anything else, because they clearly supersede the laws of our natural sciences. And these two awesome displays of divine power (real miracles and fulfilled prophecy) are the reasonable evidences, which all polytheistic religions seriously lack. And not only polytheistic religions, but all other belief systems in the world other than biblical Christianity!

Conclusion

When one considers:

1. The unsolvable unity problems among the gods of any polytheistic religion;
2. And that those gods greatly lack any real historical eyewitnesses;
3. And that they were just largely used to sway the social and political actions of a given society;
4. And that they seriously lack any divine power displayed through either prophecies or miracles;

Then it certainly becomes rather difficult to confirm that any such polytheistic religions are even connected to reality.

The bottom line is that the one true faith must display real divine power beyond that which mere humans could contrive. Also, it must have its basis in reality, and real historical eyewitnesses of divine power greatly secure our confirmation of that! And if our real creator wanted us to discover him without any doubt for the purpose of meaningful loving relationship, it becomes easier to understand just why he would physically introduce himself to his own creation in a way we simply could not honestly deny.

The life of Christ on earth from beginning to end is such a miraculous introduction. As we discuss in Objection 36, Jesus was the only one in human history who not only claimed to be God visiting his own creation but also openly demonstrated his divinity over and over again in front of many historical eyewitnesses by doing hundreds of miracles before he finally died and rose from the dead to prove his divinity.

Since *all polytheistic religions* have unsolvable unity problems, lack real historical eyewitnesses, were largely just used to sway the social and political actions of their society, and lack any

real divine power, then why should we
believe that they are even connected
to reality?

Among all the religions of the world, biblical Christianity
stands alone in its display of real divine power. And as we also discuss
in Objection 28, unlike any other so-called "holy book" in the world,
the Holy Bible proves its divine authorship through thousands of
fulfilled predictions of the future. Yes, there are many different conflicting man-made religions out there in the world which claim to
have the truth and the way of eternal life. But the Bible teaches us
plainly that *only through Christ*, who actually proved his divinity to
the world, can we obtain God's eternal life.

**Jesus answered, "I am the way and the truth
and the life. No one comes to the Father except
through me." (John 14:6)**

Perhaps you are one who has believed in the gods of polytheism
but also know in your heart there is no real evidence for their actual
existence. If you are unwilling to trade reality for the mere traditional
myths of men, and you would like to know the one and only true
God who created you and be assured of your place in his eternal
kingdom, then I invite you to just take that first small step of faith
by sincerely praying the prayer of salvation located at the end of this
book. No matter what your past is like, God loves you and sincerely
wants you to be a part of his awesome eternal kingdom!

**Jesus said, "I am the resurrection and the life.
He who believes in me, will live even though
he dies; and whoever lives and believes in me
will never die..." (John 11:25–26)**

OBJECTION 13

If God Is Real, Why Doesn't He Just Show Himself Plainly to the World?

Many may have wondered, "If God wants the whole world to believe in him, why doesn't He just show himself plainly to the whole world, and then no one could possibly doubt his existence?" Yes, such a question seems reasonable—for why the big game of "hide and go seek?" According to the Bible, there are some very good reasons as to why God does not just jump down out of heaven and show himself plainly to the world in his true state of being. Please consider the following basic biblical realities:

1. First of all, if God the Father did show himself plainly to the world in his true state of being, all men on earth would perish instantly in his presence (2 Thessalonians 2:8). The Bible says that God himself is eternal Spirit and that He shines above the brightness of the sun, dwelling in unapproachable light (Acts 26:13–14; 1 John 1:5; 1 Timothy 6:16; John 1:18). The Bible teaches very plainly that no man can even look upon God and live.

    As God said to Moses in Exodus 33:20–23—"*Thou cannot see my face: for no man shall see me and live.*" One must understand that in our present sinful condition, if we stood in God's presence, his justice would spill over and execute us immediately for all our crimes against his perfect moral laws. Those who ask this ignorant question may simply fail to comprehend just how sinful we are and just how perfect our eternal creator truly is.

Any evil simply cannot dwell in the presence of God for even one moment (Psalm 5:4). Therefore, some of the main ways God has chosen to *safely* reveal himself to us is not only through his creation, but also through his Word which was given to us through his prophets who were supernaturally inspired by the Spirit of God as they wrote the Bible (2 Peter 1:21).

2. Secondly, God did show himself plainly to the world through his Son, Jesus Christ, who actually did come down to earth and displayed all the divine attributes we would reasonably expect of our all-powerful creator. By actually becoming one of us, God did have an amazing way to actually live among us and reveal himself closely to his own creation without destroying us in the process!

Jesus Christ, the third person of the trinity actually remained 100 percent God when he became 100 percent man at the same time. He was supernaturally born from the virgin Mary who was fathered by the Holy Spirit (Luke 1:30–35). As you know, anyone in history claiming to be God in the flesh would be thoroughly examined and cross-examined for any sin proving them wrong!

But not one single person in recorded history who lived with him stepped forward with any such evidence, not even his close family members such as his mother or half-brothers, Jude and James, who wrote their books in the Bible. If anyone, James and Jude would have been the ones to expose their elder half-brother, Jesus, as a fraud plagued with sin simply because they grew up with him. But as it is, they both became full believers that Christ was indeed the Son of God, Fathered by the Holy Spirit, and wrote their books in the Bible to help others believe it too! Even all his disciples testified that he was absolutely sinless in all he said and did (1 Peter 2:22). And even to his enemies, Christ openly challenged them by asking, "*Can any of you prove me guilty of sin* (John 8:46)?" My friend, no other figure in human history or in any other religion in the world has this very powerful and unique divine attribute, which only Christ displayed!

If anyone, James and Jude would have been the ones to expose their elder half-brother, Jesus, as a fraud plagued with sin simply because they grew up with him.

Christ Clearly Revealed Himself as God to the World Through His Many Miracles

All throughout the historical accounts of the New Testament, all the apostles testify that they witnessed firsthand the many divine miracles of Christ. In 1 John 1:1–3, the apostle John stated:

That which was from the beginning, we have heard, which we have seen with our eyes, which we have looked upon and touched with our hands, concerning the word of life—the life was made manifest among us and we saw it, and testify to it, and proclaim to you the eternal life which was with the Father which was made manifest to us—that which we have seen and heard we proclaim also to you so that you may have fellowship with us; and our fellowship is with the Father and with his Son Jesus Christ.

Obviously, Christ did not just reveal his divine attributes to his apostles only, but mostly to the unbelieving world as well. In fact, that's exactly why he performed miracles, so unbelievers would believe after seeing the miraculous power, which could only come from God. In fact, without miracles, even his disciples would have never believed he was who he claimed to be!

One of Christ's most powerful miracles, which he did in front of unbelievers, was when he raised Lazarus from the dead four days after he had died (John Chapter 11). But Christ also did many other miracles in front of unbelievers so that they would believe—and thousands did! The following are just a small number of those many miracles Christ openly performed in front of those who did not yet believe in him:

1. He instantly turned water into wine at the wedding of Cana in Galilee (John 2:1–11).
2. He instantly healed the man at Bethesda pool who had been crippled for 38 years (John 5:1–9).
3. He fed both a multitude of 5000 and 4000 with fishes and loaves on two different occasions (John 6:1–14).
4. He instantly healed the Centurion's servant (Luke 7:1–10).
5. He instantly healed two blind men (Matthew 9:29–30).
6. He instantly healed a man's withered hand (Luke 6:5–11).
7. He healed a blind and mute man who was also possessed (Luke 11:14).
8. He healed another two blind men at Jericho (Matthew 20:30–34).
9. He instantly healed 10 leapers at once (Luke 17:12–14).
10. He healed a nobleman's son who was sick at the point of death (John 4:46–52).
11. He restored the sight of a man born blind (John 9:17).
12. He raised a mother's dead son from the dead (Luke 7:11–16).
13. He raised Jairus's daughter from the dead (Matthew 9:25).

And of course, not last and not least, Christ raised himself from the dead and was seen afterward by over 500 witnesses (1 Corinthians 15:3–8). Nevertheless, even though God showed himself plainly to the world through Christ, as John 1:10 says: *"He was in the world, and the world was made by Him, and the world knew him not."* Actually, one must ask the reasonable question: What more could Christ have actually done to reveal his divinity to the world than what he did?

3. Thirdly, God must test the hearts of all men through *faith*. Evidently, one of the biggest demonstrations of our love for God during this natural state of our existence is that we believe in him, even though we do not see him. In other words, to God, even our reasonable faith in his existence is all part of our love for him. As we've already discussed in Objection 11, this doesn't necessarily give us eternal life, but it is certainly a prerequisite to being right with God and obtaining his eternal life.

However, just because we may not be able to see God right now doesn't at all mean he hasn't ever shown himself openly to mankind or that there isn't plenty of honest evidence for his existence in his own awesome creation around us. Therefore, God is not asking us to have a "blind faith" in him but only a reasonable faith in him! That is why Christ said to his disciple, Thomas, who struggled with doubt of Christ's resurrection: *"[b]lessed are they who have not seen and yet believe"* (John 20:25–29). It has been said that the most unloving thing anyone can do to someone isn't to just believe wrong or bad things about them, but is to actually doubt or ignore their very real obvious existence! And evidently, God himself feels the same way. In 1 Peter 1:7–8, we read:

> **[T]he trial of your faith, being much more precious than gold (to God) that perishes, though it be tried with fire (trials and hardships), might be found unto praise and honor and glory at the appearing of Jesus Christ. Without having seen him you love him. Though you do not even now see him, you believe in him with inexpressible triumphant heavenly joy.**

In a sense then, God has also determined to play a bit of "hide and go seek" with us to a reasonable degree in order to test our basic love for him. This whole hide and go seek drama between God and man is also evident throughout the scriptures of God's word. That's why in Mathew 7:7, Christ says *"Ask, and it shall be given to you; seek and you shall find; knock and the door shall be opened unto you...."* Additionally, Proverbs 25:2, it states:

It is the glory of God to conceal (or hide) a thing, but the honor of kings is to search out a matter.

In Colossians 2:2–3, it also plainly teaches us that *"all the treasures of wisdom and knowledge are hid"* in God. However, because in many other verses of the Bible, man is encouraged to grow in the *"knowledge"* of God, we know God would have us actually seek him so that we can "know" him (Proverbs 1:20–2:10; 2 Peter 3:18). The root word of *knowledge* is *know*, because we can actually come to know our creator through the "knowledge" of his own word to us. Additionally, Jesus many times spoke in parables to also test the hearts of men to see just how much they really wanted to know God and his truth (Matthew 13:10–15). In other words, God himself is deliberately playing a bit of "hide and go seek" with us, but the whole while, he wants us to find him!

All down through the ages, pagan philosophers and intellectuals alike have asked: "What is the meaning of life?" And their answers are often conflicting and remain unsatisfactory. But as Christians, we know the answer is, "To know the author of life," which only makes good sense when you think about it. But if those who reject Christ cannot know God, it explains why they cannot answer that basic question. Nevertheless, God plainly says to us through his prophet Jeremiah that if we seek him with all of our heart (not just half-heartedly), then we will certainly find him (Jeremiah 29:13). The real problem as to why many men do not know God is that they fail to sincerely seek him *with all their hearts*. However, just the fact that you are reading this book would lead me to believe you are sincerely seeking God. So if you don't yet know him, don't give up, because he wants you to know him! And he not only wants a real and right relationship with you, he wants you to also know just *why* you believe in him.

> The real problem as to why many men do not know God is that they fail to sincerely seek him *with all their hearts.*

Conclusion

The truth is, God desires that we not only believe he exists, but also that we believe in who He really is—good, perfectly loving, merciful, full of truth, and the creator of all things (1 John 4:8; John 1:14,17; Colossians 1:13–17). Not only because it is true but because it is, of course, necessary for a right relationship with him. This only makes sense when you think about the fact that even in all our human relationships with friends and family, part of our basic love for one another is "believing the good truth about each other."

Even in a court of law, concerning strangers, we at least believe the best of our fellow man unless we have sound evidence to the contrary. Why are all men considered innocent until proven guilty? Just because that is the law? No. Because it is love! In fact, love itself is what's behind most all civil laws, which should essentially protect the well-being and respect of our fellow man. Therefore, God requires that the very first loving step which man takes in knowing him is that of "good" faith. If we step out in good faith and seek him sincerely with all our hearts, God has promised to reveal himself to us just as it says in Deuteronomy 4:29:

> **[i]f from there (now on) you seek the Lord your God, you will find him if you look for him with all your heart and with all your soul.**

If you don't yet know Christ personally, but you'd like to be right with God and be assured of your place in his awesome eternal kingdom, I invite you to just take that first small step of faith by sincerely praying the prayer of salvation located at the end of this book. No matter what your past is like, God loves you and sincerely wants you to be a part of his awesome eternal kingdom!

> **Jesus said, "I am the resurrection and the life. He who believes in me, will live even though he dies; and whoever lives and believes in me will never die..." (John 11:25–26)**

OBJECTION 14

I Was A Bible-believing Christian for Many Years...But Now I'm an Atheist

If a woman had a genuine diamond in her ring and then replaced it with a fake diamond because she lost the real one out of her ring, would her fake diamond at all negate the fact that genuine diamonds still exist in the world? Of course not, especially since most women do not lose their real diamonds and replace them with a fake one.

In other words, the private personal experience of a given person does not *necessarily* define reality for everyone else. According to the Bible itself, it is quite possible for true Bible-believing Christians to fall away from their faith in Christ. Please consider the following verses which plainly teach this (Galatians 6:7–8; Romans 8:13–14; Hebrews 10:26–27; 2 Peter 2:20–21; Hebrews 6:4–6; 1 Timothy 5:12; Hebrews 3:12–14; Colossians 1:22–23; 2 Timothy 4:10).

However, if the Bible is true, and men fall away from its truth, then that reality, while it is a sad one, wouldn't necessarily make the Bible false, especially if most Bible-believing Christians actually stay with Christ throughout their whole natural lives!

> In other words, the private personal experience of a given person does not *necessarily* define reality for everyone else.

Many People "Meet the Wrong Jesus"

However, another whole scenario is that unfortunately, many in this life do not actually even meet the real biblical Jesus, even though they think they have because "a certain religious group" may have told them they did. But we must remember that it is the "Word of God" (or the Bible) which tells us who Christ really is, not any certain religious group! Yes, many Churches can reflect the true Christ and do. But ultimately, we all must take personal responsibility by weighing everything we are taught *in any church* against what the Bible really teaches.

If you happen to be one who is a hardened atheist, just because you may have had a bad experience with some religious group who professed Christ, you must realize that the devil is truly the enemy of our soul, and that's why he's tried so hard to stain the true reputation of the biblical Christ in this world and cause people to rebel against Him. But sadly, in such cases, when people do rebel against Christ, just because of poor examples in the *"professing"* Church, all their rebellion is really just against a lie or a false portrayal of the true Christ.

> But ultimately, we all must take personal responsibility by weighing everything we are taught in any church against what the Bible really teaches.

Let me explain. Even if you've been in rebellion against God for years, what if it is not the real biblical Christ which you have been really rebelling against but rather just a false portrayal of Christ which you were shown through very imperfect men? But just like we'll also cover in Objection 35, there are two basic realities to be aware of in such cases:

1. First of all, there are actually *false* Christians in the world who may claim to live for Christ, but in reality do not because they live in a lifestyle of sin (see 1 Corinthians 6:9–10). But why let another person's hypocrisy deceive

you away from the true biblical Jesus and rob you of eternal life? Trust me, because God is all-knowing and perfect, they won't get away with anything. The Bible clearly teaches us that the hearts of all men are *"open and laid bare to the eyes of Him with whom we have to do"* (Hebrews 4:13).

2.   Secondly, even the Apostle Paul, one of the most spiritual men who walked the earth, said that it was the perfect Christ which he was preaching, not himself, because he himself was still very imperfect and need Christ's forgiveness. And if you were to honestly search your own soul, you'd have to admit that you too are also very imperfect. So if you were to reject the perfect biblical Christ just because of the many imperfections you've seen in other *true* Christians, then you'd be falling into major hypocrisy and robbing yourself of the true perfect Christ because of it.

In truth, the only way you are going to get to know the true biblical Christ is to take some responsibility yourself by reading the New Testament yourself and meeting the perfect Christ who would never hurt you in any way. If you have never sincerely sought to know the true Christ by prayerfully reading the whole New Testament, I would strongly encourage you to do so. Then, if you still reject Christ, at least you will be rejecting the perfect biblical Christ and not just some false portrayal of Him created by the demonic world or fallible men. You see, the devil knows that Jesus Christ is your only source of real truth and eternal life, simply because he is, in fact, your creator. And if you just give the real biblical Jesus a chance, he will prove that to you!

The Religious-Legalistic Jesus

Some may have just met a "religious-legalistic Jesus" who is always angry and never really pleased with the lives of men. Unfortunately, some may get their angry impression of Christ from phony preachers or even parents who may portray that image of Christ, because they don't even really know him. And if such preachers are always angry when preaching, undoubtedly, they will also put you under the law in some way by insisting you do many religious good works in order to have salvation! And yet the New Testament has taught the opposite. And it has always plainly taught us that Christ is loving, kind, very patient with us, slow to anger, and does not ever heap big legalistic burdens upon us which we simply cannot carry (Ephesians 5:2; 1 John 3:16; Galatians 5:22–23). As Christ gently invited us all in Matthew 11:28–30:

Come to me, all who labor and are heavy laden, and I will give you rest. Take my yoke upon you, and learn from me; for I am gentle and lowly in heart, and you will find rest for your souls.

In addition to that, the Bible has always clearly taught that it is actually impossible for any man to please God with good works of any kind, simply because man cannot keep God's perfect moral standards (Ephesians 2:8–9; Romans 3:20). And because none of us can actually keep all of God's perfect moral standards (even when attempting to do good works), the Bible also clearly teaches us that it is only faith in Christ (not our works) which actually pleases God (Hebrews 11:6; Romans 1:17; Galatians 2:20).

Yes, it is true that our works can show our genuine faith in Christ once we are already right with God through faith, but it is only our faith in Christ which pleases God and makes us right with him—not our works. Thus, our good works can never be a means to obtain God's eternal life or even please God, simply because they are always imperfect in some way. One must understand just how perfect our eternal creator is! Yes, once we are saved by having faith in Christ, good works can be a genuine *result* of that saving faith in Christ. But good works themselves can never be the *cause* of our salvation nor even the avenue through which we please God (Romans 3:20, 28, 5:1; Hebrews 11:6; Romans 8:8).

Once we are saved by having faith in Christ, good works should be a genuine *result* of that saving faith in Christ. But good works themselves can never be the *cause* of our salvation nor even the avenue through which we please God.

God is just pleased with men having faith in his Son and what He did for them on the cross, which they couldn't do for themselves. And when men really believe in Christ, they will just be inspired of God to do good works, because they love God and are dependent upon God when doing them. So how does one know if they are just doing good works in some legalistic attempt to please God? Well, when you fail to meet God's standards (or even your own) when doing good works (which by the way is quite often for all of us), do you get really angry, depressed, or feel guilty? If you do, then undoubtedly, you are "under the law," trying to please God through your own good works instead of just having faith in Christ in a dependence upon him. And this just means "you've met the wrong Jesus."

> When you fail to meet God's standards…do you get angry, depressed, or feel guilty? If you do, then undoubtedly, you are "under the law" trying to please God through your own good works.

If we fail in any way to keep God's perfect moral standards while sincerely trying to follow him, then according to the Bible, we should know that God's grace and love covers us completely and that there is no guilt or condemnation for us at all (Romans 8:1–2). It's no different than a Circus trapeze man knowing there is a safety net under him at all times if he should mess up! Ultimately, God loves us all not because of any good works which we attempt or even do, but because of *who He is*. And this is exactly why his love for us never changes or fails (Hebrews 13:8; 1 Corinthians 13:8; Romans 8:35–39). In fact, Christ died on the cross for the sole purpose of removing our guilt, so if we are constantly living in guilt, then we've just met the wrong "religious legalistic Jesus" not the real Jesus.

So when they (who have only met a religious/legalistic Jesus) find that they simply cannot keep all the moral standards and laws of God's word, then they become disillusioned, bitter, and then fall away from, not the true faith, but just the man-made under the law gospel which was handed to them from other fake Christians who were really just living under the law without a genuine relationship with Christ themselves. But just because they think it was the real faith which they fell away from, then it, of course, stains their image of the real faith in Christ which they never really experienced. And while they might continue to reject true Christianity with great fervor, it is because they are always believing the lie that they really had the true faith at one time, when actually, they did not!

"The Prosperity Jesus"

Others may have just "met the prosperity Jesus." And just like the "religious-legalistic Jesus," the "prosperity Jesus" is just not the true biblical Jesus. Unfortunately, when one is introduced to the "prosperity Jesus," they also encounter a nonbiblical fake gospel as well which says, "If you come to Christ asking forgiveness for your sins, he will give you salvation, joy, peace, and love, all the money and material things you want, and you won't have any more problems!"

However, this is called the "prosperity gospel," and it has never been biblical. The real biblical gospel does teach us that when we come to Christ, we will certainly have his joy, peace, and love, but it also teaches us that there is also a cost to following Christ and that we will certainly not get everything *we want* in this life, having to endure many hardships, etc. (see Acts 14:22; 1 Peter 4:1; Psalm 34:19; 2 Timothy 3:12). And ultimately this is because God must test our hearts with hardships at times to expose that we basically love him more than money or anything else in this world, which is only reasonable if he is to share his eternal life with us!

So then, when what they (those who just receive a prosperity gospel) think is true Christianity doesn't deliver the promised goods, they become disillusioned, bitter, and then fall away from, not the true faith, but just the man-made fake gospel which was handed to them from other fake Christians who were really just living for money and materialism and not God. But just because they think it was the real faith which they fell away from, then it of course stains their image of the real faith in Christ which they never really experienced. And while they might continue to reject true Christianity with great fervor, it is because they are always believing the lie that they really had the true faith at one time, when actually they did not. Can you see just how clever Satan is with his false doctrines to deceive men away from the true faith (1 Timothy 4:1–2)?

The bottom line is that if people are handed the wrong gospel to begin with, then they may not have put their trust in Christ as much as they did themselves or other things like money. And if they did not really put their trust in Christ, then according to the Bible, they could not have come into a right relationship with God. And if they did not come into a right relationship with God, according to the Bible, the Holy Spirit did not come and live inside them (see Romans 8:1–11). And if the Holy Spirit did not ever come to live inside them, then they were not really saved and never even experienced the true Christian faith.

> And while they might continue to reject true Christianity with great fervor, it is because they are always believing the lie that they really had the true faith at one time, when actually they did not.

The Real Jesus

Will the real Jesus please stand up? The answer to this question is, "Yes," because he already did 2,000 years ago on the cross, demonstrating his awesome love for us (1 John 3:16)! God is both "love" (1 John 4:8), and "truth" (John 14:6), and that's how we know the real Jesus! So ultimately, we must all remember that the Holy Bible itself is our only trustworthy standard by which we can "meet the real Jesus." And probably far more often than not, many have met the real biblical Jesus and have been happy in his love and truth ever since. But please know that many cults will use just the "Holy Spirit" to confirm the truth of what they are teaching their "followers," because then there is really no way to confirm that what they are teaching is, in fact, the truth of God.

But that's exactly one main reason why the Holy Bible was written for the true Church—so we couldn't be deceived. It acts as our "spiritual compass." If a Church leader talks all about the Holy Spirit but will never back up what he's teaching with God's word (or insists that the Holy Spirit over rides the Bible), then there's something very wrong, because it was, in fact, the Holy Spirit who wrote the Bible! The two (the Holy Spirit and the word of God) will never contradict each other as the Trinity Godhead is in perfect unity with himself.

Surrendering to the Real Biblical Jesus

However, even if men meet the real biblical Jesus, this is not necessarily a guarantee they will believe in him or live for him. Sometimes the problem is that men may just be unwilling to surrender to their own creator, because life's hardships may have hardened their hearts against him. Or maybe the real issue is that they actually love the things in this passing world more than their creator who made it. The parable of the sower which Jesus told goes into these additional scenarios (Matthew Chapter 13). So if one really did meet the real biblical Jesus and were a true Bible-believing Christian, and they just fell away from him because they just couldn't live with him for their own personal reasons, then they still admit there is a God, and a contradicting atheist stance afterward would make no sense at all.

On the other hand, if one says that they "just thought" God was real for many years as a professing Christian…then according to the Bible itself, they probably "met the wrong Jesus" and thus could not have even known the Lord or experienced the true faith. Therefore, just to summarize:

1. If one claims to have really had the true Christian faith, they can't even logically hold to atheism afterward, because they admit there is a God. They just personally could not live with him for their own personal reasons. And this, of course, is a different matter altogether.

2. And if they never had a right relationship with Christ to begin with because they "met the wrong Jesus" or were "handed the wrong gospel," then they certainly do not have the grounds to say biblical Christianity can't be the truth, because they never really met the real Jesus or experienced the true Christian faith according to God's word in the first place. So either way, "atheists" who *claim* to have been a Bible-believing Christian simply do not have the grounds to insist that there is no God—or that biblical Christianity cannot be the one true faith. And all this is true, especially in light of the fact that there is really no such thing as a true atheist as we covered in our Objection 3.

The bottom line is that if you haven't met the real Jesus within the New Testament, and you want to, I would encourage you to just pray to God and ask him to reveal the real biblical Jesus to you as you quietly read the New Testament for yourself without any other outside influences or distractions—just you and God. If you pray and ask the Holy Spirit for help, he can reveal the real Jesus to you and help you understand God's Word.

If, in fact, there's the possibility you've believed lies about Christ and the Bible because of outside influences, pray to God that they would be exposed. The book of John and the other Gospels are good books to start with. If you've been tangled up in any false teachings, please remember that the authority of God's Word is far greater than the authority of any man. One day, Jesus will judge us by his own word (John 12:48), but he won't judge us by the words or teachings of any man. I would also encourage you to also find a Church which does teach the truth of God's word. Pray to God and ask him for help to find the right one for you. He wants us to ask him for help in all such things.

If you have met the real Jesus but have just been unwilling to surrender to his Lordship in your life because of hardships that may have hardened your heart, then I would encourage you to ask God in prayer to once again reveal his great and awesome eternal love for you and expose any lies you may be believing. Obviously, Jesus loves you more than you know if you drifted away from him. A common mistake we can all make as Christians is to unconsciously measure God's love for us by our hardships. But according to God's Word, those two things are *completely unrelated* to each other! Please consider Romans 8:35–39:

> **Who shall separate us from the love of Christ? Shall trouble or hardship or persecution or famine or nakedness or danger or sword? As it is written: For your sake we face death all day long… No, in all these things we are more than conquerors through him who loved us. For I am convinced that neither death nor life, neither angels or demons, neither the present nor the future, nor any powers, neither height nor depth, nor anything else in all creation, will be able to separate us from the love of God that is in Christ Jesus our Lord.**

Or if you have met the real biblical Jesus but have just drifted away from him because the things of this passing world have gotten a hold on you, please just remember the far bigger eternal picture and the awesome far better eternal future God has for you. Truly, nothing in this passing world is worth the price of our place in God's eternal kingdom. As Jesus said, even if one should gain the *"whole world,"* it would be nothing at all compared to the value of their eternal soul:

> **For what shall it profit a man, if he shall gain the whole world, and forfeit his life in the eter-**

> **nal kingdom of God? For what can a man give
> as an exchange (a compensation, a ransom) in
> return for his blessed life in the eternal king-
> dom of God? (Mark 8:36–37)**

Whoever you are, if you've drifted from Christ, please just know that his great love for you is far greater than any of your problems or attachments. If God is calling you back to him right now and you hear his voice, that means you are his, just as Jesus plainly teaches us that his sheep hear his voice (John 10:27). Jesus, who is the great shepherd of his Church, also said:

> **If a man owns a hundred sheep, and one of
> them wanders away, will he not leave the nine-
> ty-nine on the hills and go look for the one
> that wandered off? And if he finds it, I tell you
> the truth, he is happier about that one sheep
> than about the ninety-nine that did not wan-
> der off... (Matthew 18:12–13)**

Conclusion

Sometimes when people encounter false Christians and a false Christ portrayed by them, it can really be a test of their hearts. And that's undoubtedly why God allows that at times, even though he himself is not behind the deception. If you happen to be one of those who has undergone some spiritual abuse from those who you know really are not living for Christ, please just know God sees it all and is really hoping you will pass those tests of heart and will not throw him away, just because of the sins of some who hurt you.

If you truly want to sincerely give your life back to Christ, because you've drifted away from him, please know that the enemy of your soul cannot *in any way stop you*. Or if you at all think it is a possibility that you may not have even met the real biblical Jesus, to begin a new or restored relationship with the real loving God of the

Bible, I simply invite you to just take that first small step of faith by sincerely praying the prayer of salvation located at the end of this book. No matter what your past is like, God loves you and sincerely wants you to be a part of his awesome eternal kingdom!

> **Jesus said, "I am the resurrection and the life. He who believes in me, will live even though he dies; and whoever lives and believes in me will never die..." (John 11:25–26)**

OBJECTION 15
I'm an Agnostic

While there are admittedly many things we cannot be certain of in this life, the simple truth is that most people can also be *absolutely certain* about many things in life. For example, most would admit that they can be absolutely certain that they have five fingers on each hand (providing they actually do). They can walk up to a tree and easily admit that they are absolutely certain that they are looking at a tree and not a lion or a circus clown. Most sane people of society can be absolutely certain about who their son, daughter, mother, father, brother, or sister is (especially through blood tests). We also can be certain that the sun always gets up in the East and sets in the West. In fact, when you stop and think about it, most sane people of society (in all generations of our past, present, and future) have been, can be, and will be *absolutely certain* about many things in this life.

Strict Agnosticism

According to a modern dictionary, a typical "agnostic" is generally defined as someone who believes they cannot be sure about the existence of God or of really *anything beyond the "material world."* This we will refer to as just *"standard agnosticism."* However, if one is a "fully loyal" or a *"strict agnostic,"* they really must carry their strict "prove it" belief system into even the material world as well. After all, is it not rather inconsistent to just doubt nonmaterial things when really even material things cannot be absolutely proven to those who would actually doubt even their five senses and conscience? And this is why some "pure" or "strict" agnostics even technically doubt every aspect of the material world as well.

When it comes right down to it, to the strict agnostic, even basic science, mathematics, and the meaning of languages, etc. cannot be technically proven to be trustworthy instruments which define reality. In fact, the pure agnostic not only believes that he himself cannot be absolutely sure about anything, but he also believes that no one else can be absolutely sure about anything either, simply because man is "imperfect" and therefore has "imperfect judgment."

For example, a "strict agnostic" father cannot even be absolutely sure that his son is really his son. Therefore, quite reasonably, the strict agnostic cannot even believe that anyone else can be sure of their own family members either. Birth certificates can be forged, witnesses can lie, and even our five senses can deceive us. Literally, *everything* is "up in the air" and open to speculation.

The strict agnostic may believe in many "tentative" (or uncertain) truths but never "certain truths." The strict agnostic cannot even be absolutely sure that he has five fingers on each hand when, in fact, he does. Our system of mathematics could be flawed, or once again, our five senses may not be "perfectly" reliable to lead us to this "certain" truth. Ironically, strict agnostics may accept and trust honest evidence based on the unanimous conclusions of the five senses and conscience of man to pronounce an accurate verdict beyond a reasonable doubt in our civil courts, especially if they are the ones who have been violated. But at the very same time, they may reject and distrust the very same to pronounce an accurate verdict beyond reasonable doubt upon spiritual truth. Hmm…it would seem something is rather inconsistent there, would it not?

> Ironically, agnostics may trust their five senses and conscience to pronounce an accurate verdict in our civil courts. But at the same time they may distrust the very same to pronounce an accurate verdict upon spiritual truth.

But why would the strict agnostic trust the conscience and five senses of man to arrive at the basic life-giving truth with civil matters but not spiritual matters when, in fact, the honest evidence for basic life-giving truth is just as attainable in either case? Shouldn't one be consistent and treat our search for civil court truth the very same way we would our search for spiritual truth?

At some point in all this "strict agnostic doubt," which picks and chooses just when the five senses and conscience of man are reliable and when they are not, it seems at some point that sincere doubt must turn into *plain dishonesty* in the heart and conscience of the strict agnostic. Not only because the strict agnostic tends to be "inconsistent" and actually denies the unanimous conclusions of man's five senses, but because they also tend to be "inconsistent" and actually deny the unanimous conclusions of mankind's conscience as well. And this is exactly why our civil court system would pronounce someone either "dishonest" or "insane" if they disregarded the unanimous conclusions of man's five senses or the unanimous conclusions of man's conscience. And I do not say this with any disrespect or the lack of love toward the strict agnostic; I just say it as a matter of civil court fact. Why, even our saying, "Have you taken leave of your senses?" links insanity to some degree with the abandonment of our five senses.

Once a young Christian man inquired of his father's spiritual beliefs hoping for unity with him.

The son asked, "Father, there's stronger evidence for Christ and the Christian faith than there is for all other world religions put together. Do you believe in Christ?"

The father replied, "Well, son, because man is imperfect, I don't believe he can even recognize perfect or absolute truth. Therefore, I believe only in 'tentative' truth (truth not definite)."

The son then asked, "Are you absolutely sure you do not believe in absolute truth?"

Then the father replied, "No, I just tentatively believe we cannot recognize the absolute truth."

Then the son asked, "So you're not even absolutely sure I'm your son or that you have five fingers on each hand?"

Then the father replied, "No, I don't believe I can be absolutely sure about anything."

At that moment, the son realized that it wasn't at all a *truth problem* which his father had but an *honesty problem*, and that he had most likely chosen his extreme agnostic beliefs for the purely emotional reason *to hide from the truth* so he could stay in control of his own life without any interference from Christ his creator.

My friend, the honest truth is that without *basic honesty*, not even obvious reality itself can be verified or agreed upon by anyone! And that is exactly why the Bible even teaches us that basic honesty must be the heart of the New Testament Church (Luke 8:15; 2 Corinthians 4:2; Philippians 4:8; 1 Timothy 4:1–2; Hebrews 13:18). As it reasonably teaches us in Proverbs 12:17:

> **He who speaks the truth provides *honest* evidence, but a false witness utters deceit...**

To further illustrate the wayward condition of the strict agnostic, try absolutely proving that a tree is a tree to one who dishonestly denies reality. They can just say that a tree is a tree with uncertainty and that no one else can be absolutely sure a tree is a tree. Or they can just say that to them it is a circus clown or a wild Indian. All they have to say is that "all reality is relative to one's own perspective" and that it is just your opinion that a "tree" is a "tree" based from your own "imperfect" perspective and use of language. They can just claim our language system to define reality is flawed, and thus a "tree" could have been wrongly named. Well, I guess a tree could have been called something else in the English language, but for the sake of sane meaningful discussion (which ultimately revolves around love of our fellow man), the English speaking world had to *agree on some word* for a "tree," did they not? But no matter what word was chosen for the tree, the strict agnostic could doubt and dispute that the word chosen is flawed!

The bottom line is that without *basic honesty,* not even obvious reality itself can be verified or agreed upon by anyone!

Using an analogy, it's kind of like when one tired boxer just "holds" his better opponent because he knows he can't really outbox him. At that point, it is not effective boxing which the tired boxer is even after; it's just "holding," which isn't boxing at all, and that's why the referee has to blow his whistle and break them up every time.

In the same way, when trying to agree on reality with a strict agnostic, you may quickly find out that it really isn't the "certain life-giving truth" of reality they are even after. It may be that they are, in fact, doing just the opposite and "running from the truth," using their extreme dishonest agnostic beliefs just to "hold" you until the bell rings (which in their case could be physical death).

However, once again, the whole problem with this whole "strict agnostic" approach to life is that it must at some point require some real basic dishonesty which goes against the five senses and conscience of man. And this in turn will certainly effect relationships and leave a wake of disunity in the life of the strict agnostic. But if the strict agnostic really did have the truth (which is that no one can really know any truth), then honestly, why would their strict agnostic beliefs leave such a wake of destruction behind them in their personal relationships? Again, let's be honest: such a belief system could only lead to disunity, because *a very tiny percentage* of the human race (probably only about three percent) would agree with the strict agnostic!

Does Man Really Have to Be Perfect in Order to Discover Certain Truth?

One of the main smoke screens the strict agnostic may use is they may assert that man would have to be absolutely "perfect" in order to recognize certain truth. But does man really have to be perfect in order to discover certain basic life-giving truth? Once I knew a strict agnostic who insisted that he could not arrive at any certain truth, simply because he did not have "immaculate perception." But strangely enough, as I got to know him over the years, I learned he was quite unteachable and closed-minded no matter what the subject. And this of course troubled me, because even though on one hand he claimed to not have "immaculate perception," on the other hand, he really had all the answers, simply because he was so unteachable! And obviously, one cannot have it both ways.

You see, sometimes it is just our own pride or sin nature which keeps us from receiving the truth, even though we can honestly see the truth. Thus, rejecting the truth and honestly seeing it can be two very different things. The Bible teaches us that because God himself is perfect (or perfect truth), he does indeed have the ability to reveal himself clearly without confusion to his own fallen creation, even though we do have a sin nature and are very "imperfect." Why?

Because a sin nature (which was never God's will in the first place) is not all we have! God also gave man the ability to reason with his five senses and make freewill moral choices with a *conscience* to tell right from wrong and truth from error. This means we have been created and designed to be "responsible" beings and that someday, we will all be accountable to our own creator for how we listened to the conscience which he gave us. The fact that all men have the same unified conscience which basically agrees on what is right and what is wrong in our civil court systems is not exactly a feather in the cap of those who are strict agnostics or those who reject an intelligent creator behind it all.

Remember from Objections 4 and 5, the very process of evolution must be random, reckless, and haphazard by nature, not consistent with a consistent life-giving meaningful purpose. So if the Theory of Evolution were true, then why has all mankind collectively and consistently agreed in their consciences on what's right and what's wrong within past civil governments?

> This means we have been created and designed to be "responsible" beings and that someday we will all be accountable to our own creator for how we listened to the conscience which he gave us.

In fact, most people on the planet have even agreed on spiritual truth as well, like the Golden Rule or the Ten Commandments. The only reasonable explanation is that our one and only mutual creator created us all with His moral standards written into our consciences, and that's exactly what the Bible says (2 Corinthians 4:2; Romans 2:14–15). But really, when you think about it at all, how does a "conscience" even make any sense with the random reckless chance of evolution, which would have no need for it? Truly, the same conscience in every man only makes sense with a single mutual creator who put it there as a compass to determine right from wrong and truth from error. But he also wisely gave us free will along with our conscience so our love for him would be voluntary and not something forced. For our creator knows that "forced love" would really be no love at all.

So in the case of a strict agnostic who flatly denies a reality which can be easily confirmed by the five senses and conscience of the entire human race, is it that he is honestly unable to recognize the simple truth with certainty? Or is it that he is *dishonestly* going against his conscience and five senses which his creator gave him? If you ask the strict agnostic, he'll say he's unable to recognize certain truth. But what if he's not being honest when he says that? You see, if you ask a practicing alcoholic if he has a problem, he'll probably say "no" every time!

It is probably true in this life that we may never fully understand man's conscience or free will for that matter. But just because we may not fully understand something superior to our own intellects should not mean that we "throw it out" or disregard it altogether! A little boy standing beside his car mechanic father working under the hood of a car should not start pulling out wires and tubes in frustration, just because he doesn't fully understand them. It should be enough for him to know that his father does understand what he doesn't, and this is the same simple life-giving reasonable "faith" that God in the Bible calls all men to whenever biblical Christianity goes beyond our reason. However, strict agnosticism itself is really the opposite of faith as it "*doubts*" literally everything.

In fact, if strict agnosticism is reasonably "carried through" to its logical end, the strict agnostic must even doubt his own doubt, and then doubt even that doubt, and then doubt even that doubt—and so on throughout all eternity! And perhaps that is, in fact, exactly what the strict agnostic will do, which of course would be insane. And if he did just that, it truly reveals that any "honest evidence" really has no meaningful purpose within his belief system, which must therefore be completely disconnected from reality itself. And if one lives in such a constant "strict agnostic" state of being disconnected from reality, then they are not only dishonestly "living in denial" like the worst alcoholic but also technically "insane" by any standard dictionary definition of the term, just because they are, in fact, "disconnected from reality." And again, I say that not with any disrespect but rather just as a matter of fact.

> If strict agnosticism is "carried through" to its logical end, the strict agnostic must even doubt his own doubt, and then doubt even that doubt—and so on throughout all eternity!

The fact that the society of mankind as a whole has always had opposing opinions on every side of all issues of truth may not only point to the reality that man does not really follow his conscience like he should (except for that small place for genuine ignorance and genuine deception), but it also reasonably points to the fact that *truth itself could not have originated with man* and comes from a source *outside of man himself.* And of course, this basic realization fully cooperates with the biblical reality that all "truth" originates within the person of our eternal God who, as creator, is technically separate from his creation. And because according to the Bible, truth did not originate with mankind and is completely separate from him, imperfect man can at least recognize the basic life-giving truth, simply because God our creator gave us the adequate tools of our conscience and five senses to do so, which our civil court systems have also long recognized.

A simple example would be that our civil courts have always held that murder was morally wrong, because it violates the very basics of love, which always gives man life and not death. Since the entire civilized human race has *basically* always agreed upon this, it points to the fact that all men have the very same unanimous moral conscience which tells us right from wrong and truth from error. But in the case of those in the minority who do believe in murder, they are just being *dishonest* with themselves and "searing" their own God-given conscience. And that is exactly what the strict agnostic must do when they too cannot be absolutely certain murder is morally wrong. However, if someone actually attempted to murder a strict agnostic, and it went to court, then all of a sudden, that strict agnostic would believe the five senses and conscience of man were plenty reliable enough to pronounce an accurate verdict upon his perpetrator.

Typically, the strict agnostic will claim that even our senses and conscience are too imperfect to be trusted to pronounce any certain religion, "true" or "false," based on all available honest evidence, beyond reasonable doubt. However, to *a basic inconsistent degree*, they at the same time typically acknowledge our civil court system's basic ability to pronounce an "innocent" or "capital punishment" verdict beyond a reasonable doubt based on all available honest evidence. Especially when it comes to them being the victim of some crime! But again, why this basic inconsistency when plentiful honest evidence can be gathered for or against any religion in the world (just as we discuss more thoroughly in Objection 41)?

The truth is that most people on the planet (as well as the world's court systems) would say our conscience and five senses are certainly not too imperfect to be trusted to lead men to the *basic life-giving truth* and away from destructive deception, whether one is talking about civil court matters or spiritual belief systems. But the strict agnostic looking for a smoke screen will dogmatically assert that man's heart, mind, conscience, and five senses must be "absolutely perfect;" otherwise, they are not *really* reliable to give man the basic life-giving truth he needs. But does a civil court judge have to be absolutely perfect in order to pronounce an accurate verdict? Certainly not. The notion is, of course, absurd.

Does a doctor have to be absolutely "perfect" in order to save the life of his patient? Certainly not. Again, the notion is insanely absurd. Does a fireman have to be absolutely perfect in order to put out a fire and save a whole family from physical destruction? No. Nor does anyone in any profession have to be "perfect" in order to minister *basic life-giving aid* to their fellow man! Does a minister or pastor have to be perfect in order to preach the truth and help people find basic salvation through the one and only true creator? No, simply because it is not himself who he is preaching; he's preaching his perfect creator and is still able to steer men to him, even though he himself is very imperfect! Yes, we are all undeniably imperfect. But does one have to be perfect to demonstrate basic love to their spouse and have a healthy marriage? Absolutely not. Otherwise, we'd all be in the doghouse!

But all imperfect man has to have in this life is the *basic* ability (not the perfect ability) to love and recognize the basic truths which give men life and not harm. Then our human mission is essentially accomplished, simply because that is "life-giving" love. To say we must be perfect in order to even recognize *certain basic truth* is essentially to say the love of a marriage couple has to be perfect in order to have a basically healthy marriage. My friend, such thinking is obviously flawed.

Our Civil Court Systems and Strict Agnosticism

And this is exactly why any court of law does recognize languages (agreed upon by the human race) as well as basic science, history, mathematics, man's conscience, and the five senses, etc., and defines reality by them whenever they apply to a case. Again, anyone in a court of law who would consistently deny all these basic tools and their intended meanings would be immediately placed by the judge in either a "dishonest" category or an "insane" category. Though obviously, all aspects of reality may not be able to be discovered by man; obviously, general sane society does agree that we can all recognize the basic aspects of reality needed to love our fellow man.

> To say we must be perfect in order to even recognize *certain basic truth* is essentially to say the love of a marriage couple has to be perfect in order to have a basically healthy marriage; such thinking is obviously flawed.

Again, strict agnostics may insist that man himself would have to be absolutely perfect in order to recognize God (or perfect truth). But that would be as silly as saying just because you have barbecue sauce all over your white shirt, it automatically means you cannot recognize anyone else with an unstained white shirt on! This simple notion is not only unreasonable, but the very opposite would seem true, simply because the more imperfect your shirt was, the more you should actually be able to recognize an unstained white shirt because you would just have more of the opposite to compare it to.

Even if you got some of the barbecue sauce in your eyes, you could probably still see an unstained white shirt! And this is why the Bible basically teaches that the more a person can see their own sin (like the dishonesty of strict agnosticism), the easier they can discover our perfect creator and obtain a "right relationship" with him. However, what hope is there if the strict agnostic will not even be honest about their dishonesty?

But back to our white shirt analogy, the strict agnostic might argue that no shirt is absolutely perfectly white. True enough; but no shirt has to be absolutely perfectly white to be considered an "unstained" brand-new white T-shirt! You see, the strict agnostic who has to push everything to the absolute "perfect" extreme is not really after the essential basic life-giving truth which man needs but is most likely looking for a smoke screen which continues to keep him safely away from his own perfect creator who in turn holds him accountable.

But if all truth is really embodied in the very person of God who is also our creator, then this is exactly why the truth itself is always our friend and not our enemy. Because if you reasonably think about it, if our creator is real, who would love us more than he? But unfortunately, this is exactly what the strict agnostic may fail to understand—that God their creator really loves them far more than anyone else has!

If indeed there is a God, why on earth would he be basically against his very own creation? That would be similar to a parent being basically against their own child! It simply doesn't make sense, especially considering God himself must be absolutely perfect and far more loving than any human parent in order to be a *morally flawless eternal being*. The Bible tells us that Christ came down from his comfortable residence in heaven to become one of us and die a horrible death on the cross, just so he could take the just punishment for all our sins upon himself. And he did this all to demonstrate his awesome eternal love for us and make the only way possible for us to be with him for all eternity!

My friend, if you happen to be a strict agnostic, God loves you far more than you have ever realized! And it is the realization of his love that will open your eyes to the certain truth of his existence. Yes, in his perfect love, God must certainly allow mankind the loving freedom to make our own choices and sometimes experience the awful results, but this does not mean he's at all against his own creation! The Bible plainly teaches us that he wants all men to be right with him and have his awesome eternal life (2 Peter 3:9; 1 Timothy 2:4).

> When one reasonably thinks about it, who would love us more than our very own creator? But this is exactly what the strict agnostic may fail to understand.

There Is Such a Thing as "Healthy Surrender"

Though the "truth of God" may reasonably require man to "surrender" to his own creator, this does not at all mean that such a reasonable surrender is "bad" for us! No, history itself has shown us that all "surrender" does not automatically mean something bad. It all depends on who or what we are surrendering to, does it not? In fact, if an eternal God himself really is our creator and "perfect love," then our surrender to him is not only very reasonable but also the most "healing" and "normal" thing we could do, just as millions of Bible-believing Christians would attest to. We must understand that man is perfectly safe surrendering to perfect love! Biblical surrender to God in what we believe and the way we live is never "bad," because God (who is perfect and eternal) always has our highest good in mind as our loving creator.

Him calling us to surrender to his reasonable authority is no different than a father insisting that his kids not play in the street because they could get hit by a car! In fact, if our perfect loving creator happens to know that he himself is actually the very best thing for his own creation, then reasonably, our surrender to him would be the most healing and loving thing he could ask of us!

> If our perfect loving creator happens to know that he himself is actually the very best thing for his own creation, then reasonably our surrender to him would be the most healing and loving thing he could ask of us!

Is All Reality Really Relative to One's Own Perspective?

With many things, man can have differing viewpoints without moral disintegration. However, there certainly are many other things which man must agree on if morality and love of our fellow man is to be maintained. To list such obvious examples which are tied into the very honest conscience of all men is almost an insult to man's basic intelligence and dignity, but nevertheless, we will list a few of them just the same in order to make our basic point. Most moral issues of *certain truth,* which man must agree upon if he is to avoid self destruction, merely ride on the back of the golden rule which Christ clearly taught:

Whatsoever you wish that men would do to you, do so to them, for this is the fulfillment of the law and prophets of God. (Matthew 7:12)

1. Murder is wrong.
2. Stealing is wrong.
3. Gossip is wrong.
4. Adultery is wrong.
5. Lying is wrong.
6. Insincerity of serious matters is wrong.
7. Willfully deceiving is wrong.

If the wife of a strict agnostic was murdered, and the murderer was also a strict agnostic who told the judge that he was not absolutely 100 percent sure murder was wrong (he was only 99 percent sure and he was just experimenting with the 1 percent of his uncertainty), what do you think would be the reaction of the other strict agnostic whose wife was murdered? If he wasn't deeply hurt and very enraged, there would probably be something very wrong.

If the strict agnostic cannot even be absolutely sure about the above moral issues of truth (which they technically cannot be), is strict agnosticism really a belief system which promotes the basic love of his fellow man? And if it isn't love to be uncertain about all the certain truths which give men life, is the belief system of the strict agnostic really being "part of man's solutions or part of his problems?" Again, the answer should be obvious to the honest soul.

The Truth Is Always Married to Love

But the strict agnostic may contend that lying is not always wrong, and that may be true in very rare instances when it is actually "love" to lie. For example, when Corrie ten Boom was confronted by the Nazis as to whether or not Jews lived in her house, she lied, and it was probably credited to her account in heaven when she did so. However, we all must admit these are rare exceptions in which love for our fellow man is maintained, not abandoned. You see, ultimately, "truth" is all about love; otherwise, it has no meaningful purpose. And this is exactly why the Bible teaches us that true "*love*" always "*rejoices in the truth*" (1 Corinthians 13:6).

But how can the strict agnostic really "*rejoice in the truth*" if he does not believe even the basic life-giving truth is really attainable with any certainty? And if he does not believe the basic life-giving truth is really attainable, then how can he really love? One must finally understand that the two (love and truth), even for the strict agnostic, are always "married" or connected. You see, if we really love someone, we'll tell them the truth. And if we really want someone to know the truth, we'll love them. There is nothing more truthful than love, and there is nothing more loving than the truth.

Ultimately, "truth" is all about love; otherwise, it has no meaningful purpose.

Like the strict agnostic, if everyone in the world literally believed that no one could be absolutely sure of anything, then we would have a good idea of just where true agnosticism really leads. Because if it really is the correct belief system which one man should live by, then it should equally be good for everyone. But the simple truth, which also exposes it as a false belief system is that if everyone in the world were a strict agnostic, it would lead to absolute confusion and destruction, simply because nobody could agree on anything for sure. If everyone was a strict agnostic, no one could even agree on everyone's doubts! And unfortunately, in the case of serious human survival, man needs to be 100 percent sure about a lot of things. For some more ridiculously obvious examples:

1. Everyone needs to be 100 percent sure that when it comes to traffic lights, green means go and red means stop. If people were only 99 percent sure, people would get killed over the 1 percent of uncertainty, and that's not love, which again goes against the conscience of man.

2. Men and women must be 100 percent sure of who their spouse is. If people were only 99 percent sure, they would get involved with other people's spouses, which would immediately induce hurt, rage, and murder, which again is not love and, of course, goes against the conscience of man. If you are a strict agnostic, and you told your spouse that you were not 100 percent sure she was your wife, how do you think that would affect your relationship? Not in any good way, I imagine.

As you can see, the list of destruction caused by strict agnostic doubt in all situations pertaining to man's well-being and survival could go on and on. In fact, it is easy to see that mankind would quickly self-destruct if nobody could agree on anything for certain. In this real sense, strict agnosticism as a belief system can be easily seen as a false belief system just by the dishonest unloving fruit it consistently produces as it goes against the unanimous conscience and five senses of all men.

Standard Agnosticism (with Just the Nonmaterial World)

Technically, a "strict" agnostic is just being loyal to his belief system by reasonably carrying it into all of life. But many so-called "standard agnostics" are probably just "poor" or hypocritical agnostics who are not so "loyal" or "consistent" with their own belief system, because their main objective is just to deny the certainty of an unseen God, and after that, they don't as much care about being agnostic with the rest of life. But because we can plainly see the quick destruction of the human race when we apply "strict" agnosticism to it within the visible material world, this also gives us some insight into how destructive standard agnosticism is when it is consistently applied to the unseen world as well. In fact, it may well be even far more destructive!

For example, if, in fact, the Bible is true and man's eternal destiny hinges upon what man chooses to believe spiritually, then according to the Bible, the violated spiritual realm has far greater ramifications than does the violated material world, which according to the Bible was actually created by the spiritual world (see Hebrews 11:3).

The Inconsistency of "Standard Agnosticism"

Though most "standard agnostics" just deny the basic certainty of an intelligent creator (because they cannot see him), they do not generally deny the basic certainty of "love" in their marriage, even though neither God nor love in the heart of man are material things which can be seen. But if the married agnostic who denies the basic certainty of an intelligent creator was consistent with his beliefs and also denied the basic certainty of love in the heart of his spouse, just because "love" itself is not something seen in the material world, then his marriage would, of course, be stressed with the constant uncertainty of his spouse's love. And if everyone in the world consistently doubted every nonmaterial reality, everyone's marriage would be also stressed simply, because no one could believe in the basic certainty that their spouse really loved them; that is, before they actually had the chance to express it.

However, since everyone knows in their conscience that it is morally wrong to doubt the love of someone before they actually have the opportunity to show you (they are not "innocent until proven guilty"), we must once again conclude then that even standard agnosticism within the unseen spiritual realm is destructive and damaging to relationships. And this is just one example of many, which would ultimately serve to harm humanity if even standard agnosticism was loyally and literally applied to every aspect of the nonmaterial world! Not only love would be doubted, but also faith, hope, peace, confessed thoughts, and intentions of others, or any other aspects of the spiritual heart of man. And this, of course, does not even include all other spiritual realities which are inevitably doubted by standard agnosticism, such as God himself or angelic beings, which have even historically manifested themselves to mankind on many occasions.

Therefore, all in all, it would seem both strict and standard agnosticism as belief systems are quite destructive when applied literally and faithfully to both the material and nonmaterial world. However, since many standard agnostics (who just doubt the existence of God) do believe in love, trust, peace, and many other unseen things in the nonmaterial world, it would seem most "standard agnostics" certainly do not *consistently* apply their beliefs of doubt within the whole nonmaterial world.

Some may call it "inconsistency." Others may call it "hypocrisy." But why the inconsistency/hypocrisy of doubt if neither God nor love are a part of the material world? I submit it is simply because man is fully capable of *dishonestly* picking and choosing through reality, depending upon which aspects of it make him uncomfortable and which do not! Like the strict agnostic, even though the standard agnostic may start out with sincere doubts, his inconsistent picking and choosing through reality must eventually turn his original "insecure doubts" into plain dishonesty.

> Since many agnostics do believe in love, trust, peace, and many other unseen things in the nonmaterial world, it would seem they do not consistently apply their beliefs of doubt within the whole nonmaterial world.

Therefore, not only is agnosticism destructive to mankind *when consistently applied* to the material and nonmaterial world, but it is also destructive to mankind when *inconsistently applied* to both the material and nonmaterial world as well. In fact, this is exactly why the Bible has always taught that "*God is love*" (1 John 4:8) and that both "doubt" and "dishonesty" are not of God, simply because they ultimately cause harm and destruction to mankind.

Typically, those who are agnostic with Christ and the Bible may be trying to "ride the picket fence," because they may also believe they are still on "safe ground" with God by doing so. But the problem with "riding the picket fence" on most issues is that the "points of learning" are just too painful to stay there!

According to a true story, one man during the Civil War once thought he was on safe ground by compromising two opposing truths. So right before a battle, he put on half of a union uniform and half of a confederate uniform, trying to make a statement of peace, which attempted to appease the moral/political beliefs of both sides (kind of like the "coexist" bumper stickers you see on some cars). But since there is no "peace" with the compromise of truth (or even indecision), both sides opened fire upon him, and he probably died much faster than he otherwise would have!

Similarly, some agnostics may simply believe as long as they remain uncertain, they are not really accountable to surrender their lives to their own creator during this life and come into a right relationship with him. However, if a man is dating a woman who really loves him (and has demonstrated her love) and he constantly tells her that he is not "certain" about his relationship with her (or even her existence), he will no doubt seriously offend her, and his relationship with her would be broken instantly!

In this real way, our constant uncertainty of God despite the overwhelming honest evidence for him is truly a reflection of our love for him! Spiritually, even if someone chooses to believe in "nothing," then they still have chosen a "belief system," which ultimately reflects their love for God if, in fact, he has plainly revealed himself and his love to all mankind through his Son with plenty of honest evidence.

If a man told his sweetheart that he believes in "nothing" when it came to her love for him, even though she plainly demonstrated it many times to him, there would probably not be a wedding, and she would probably give him "nothing" in return. And according to the Bible, this is exactly the way God himself views it when man denies the certainty of his existence, even though he has plainly revealed himself and his love to all mankind throughout history many times! Jesus not only died on the cross to prove his love to us (by taking our just punishment upon himself), but he also lived a sinless life in front of many witnesses, did many miracles, and fulfilled many prophecies as well!

As we already discussed in Objections 4 and 5, even nature has God's obvious intelligent fingerprints all over it. In other words, if the agnostic is bent on believing in "nothing" and insists on remaining independent of God in this life, then throughout all eternity, God must also give him just what he really wants—nothing and isolation! Wow, that can't be too much fun! I sure am glad I'm not an agnostic.

Do You Even *Want* to Look for the Honest Evidence for Christ?

If you are a self-proclaimed agnostic, please ask yourself the honest question: "Do you even *want* to look for the honest evidence for Christ?" Even though millions and millions have discovered that the sound honest evidence for Christ is overwhelming, the interesting thing is that the goal of many agnostics isn't at all to even find the real truth about Christ by carefully combing through the honest evidence. It is actually to completely avoid any evidence for Christ and to purposely remain in their state of "indecision," just so they can stay in control their own lives. It has been said that the worst and most unloving thing anyone can do to another is just ignore them on purpose. And that is why Christ said, "*He who is not for me is against me*" (Matthew 12:30). In Luke 12:8–9, Jesus also said:

> **[w]hosoever shall confess me before men, him shall the son of man also confess before the angels of God: but he that denies me before men shall be denied before the angels of God.**

And if the agnostic refuses to even carefully look at any honest evidence for Christ with an open heart, then it would certainly seem there is something more going on in the heart of that agnostic than mere intellectual doubt; maybe some real hatred toward God, which even God himself can see (Hebrews 4:13)?

Ultimately then, giving our creator a fair and decent chance to reveal himself is really a love issue to him. When people won't even look at the honest evidence for the truth, it generally means their present beliefs are only based in mere emotion, because they are really afraid of the truth for just personal reasons. Or perhaps underneath it all, many agnostics are just angry with God and will not admit to his existence because of it. Maybe they are not even all that conscious of it.

But nevertheless, when such underlying anger cuts one off from their very source of life, it is much like an angry person kicking against a board which has nails sticking out of it! The person they are hurting the most is only themselves! Perhaps many agnostics are actually believing lies about God and the Bible, which actually fuel their hatred toward him. Only when such people look for such lies, they might be believing, and leave the realm of emotion and start objectively looking at the honest evidence, can they ever even hope to find the spiritual truth which leads to the life and inner healing they need. But that, of course, is a personal choice we must all make if we hope to find the spiritual truth. For God in his Word only promises all men that if they seek the truth *with all their heart* (not half-heartedly) that they will find it (see Jeremiah 29:13; Matthew 7:7–8). But some agnostics may still ask, "How could anyone know for sure they are going to heaven?"

When people won't even look at the honest evidence for the truth, it generally means their present beliefs are only based in mere emotion.

We really couldn't unless God himself came down to earth, fully proved his divinity among men, and then told us just how to be right with God and go to heaven. And that, my friend, is exactly what Christ did so that there would be absolutely no doubt in the heart and mind of the honest soul! And when you honestly think about it, what more could Christ have done? And all of Christ's apostles who personally walked with him for over three years testified that he did indeed prove to be the Son of God hundreds of times over through supernatural miracles, which they all witnessed firsthand (see 1 John 1:1–4). And because only Christ is the only historical figure which proved himself to be our creator through the very power of God, which he openly displayed in our human history, we can fully trust him when he said:

> **I am the way, the truth, and the life. No one can come to the Father except through me. (John 14:6)**

> **For God so loved the world that whosoever believes in him should not perish, *but have everlasting life*. (John 3:16)**

All his apostles were so sure of who Christ was that they fully backed what Christ taught with their very lives as they were all willingly martyred for their faith! And the Apostle John, the only apostle who was not martyred, plainly testified in 1 John 5:13 that:

> **These things have I written unto you that believe on the name of the Son of God: *that you may know that you have eternal life...***

Eternal Life Insurance

Of course, another gross inconsistency with probably most agnostics who continuously reject the honest evidence for Christ is that even though they may be unsure of many other things in life, they still won't take any chances and will most always err on the wise side of caution with them. For example, they don't really know if they will ever get into a car accident, but they still have auto insurance, simply because they know it is the wise and responsible thing to do. They don't really know if they will outlive their spouse, but they still have life insurance, simply because they know it is the wise and responsible thing to do. They don't really know if they will have any health problems which could devastate them financially, but they still have health insurance, simply because they know it is the wise and responsible thing to do. They don't really know what the daily weather will be like, but they often prepare for the worst, simply because they know it is the wise and responsible thing to do.

And very similarly, the agnostic may *claim* that they cannot know if Christ is really their God and creator who alone gives them eternal life, but strangely enough, they refuse to come to Christ and get the simple eternal life insurance he freely offers all humanity! Even though it is far more important than any other protective insurance they already have, they inconsistently take such an eternal risk. And so it would seem that this just further confirms that their rejection of Christ isn't so much about the lack of honest evidence for Christ as it is for only emotional reasons of their own. *Some* agnostics may even take pride in the fact that they do not gamble at all in the casinos. But if they gamble every day with their eternal salvation by rejecting Christ and all the honest evidence for him, then are they not being far more careless and irresponsible than casino gamblers who just have mere money to lose?

Conclusion

My friend, if you claim to be an agnostic in your spiritual beliefs and are both wise and responsible, having *insurance* with many other things in this temporary life which you simply cannot be sure of, then why not also be wise and responsible and "play it safe" with that which is most important of all—your eternal destiny? If you are going to be inconsistent, why be inconsistent with *that which is most important of all?* Clearly, obtaining eternal life through Christ is the wisest decision one can make in their life. Nevertheless, God's eternal life isn't just some insurance policy. When Christ died on the cross, he fully demonstrated God's real love for you, because your creator wants to spend all eternity with you in meaningful relationship!

Many professing agnostics say they cannot be sure of much. But they all know that genuine "love" is real and welcome it, because they've all experienced it to some degree. And what they may not realize is that ultimately, that love comes from our creator who is the source of all true love and all that is truly good in this world. In fact, from the very beginning, before man messed up God's perfect creation, all God ever wanted was a loving relationship with us for all eternity! But it was just our sin which messed up his perfectly loving plans for us.

If you just step out in a small amount of faith right now and give God a fair chance to reveal himself to you, he will show you there are many things in this life (like his love for you) that you can be certain of! Right now, God wants to give you yet another chance, simply because he loves you more than you know and wants you to be with him and share in his awesome eternal kingdom to come which, by the way, will blow the doors off anything this present world has to offer! But obviously, someday, all your opportunities to be right with God will run out. Someone once asked Jesus how many will be saved. And Jesus replied:

> **Make every effort to enter through the narrow door (and Jesus is that door—John 10:9), because many, I tell you, will try to enter and will not be able. (Luke 13:24)**

If you can see the obvious wisdom in receiving the eternal life insurance which Christ freely offers to all humanity right now while you still can and really want to experience his eternal love, I invite you to just take that first small step of faith by sincerely praying the prayer of salvation located at the end of this book. No matter what your past is like, God loves you and sincerely wants you to be a part of his awesome eternal kingdom!

> **Jesus said, "I am the resurrection and the life. He who believes in me, will live even though he dies; and whoever lives and believes in me will never die..." (John 11:25–26)**

OBJECTION 16

I Already Know the God of the Bible Is Real; I'm Just Ripping Mad at Him for All the Pain in My Life!

I think if we were all honest, we'd have to admit that we've all been mad at God at some time or another. In fact, much of the world may even be mad at God right now for some reason or another. After all, life is difficult for everyone, and it may only seem right that our very own creator who put us on this earth should catch the blame for all the suffering in the world. While all such notions may certainly *seem* right, what if we are actually believing some basic lies whenever we are mad at God for our sufferings? What if our personal sufferings (or even the sufferings of the whole world for that matter) are really not God's fault at all in any way? Since the above objection concerns *the God of the Bible*, would it not be only reasonable to see just what the Bible plainly teaches about God and his relationship to our sufferings before we should spend our whole lives mad at him?

Millions and millions of people have sincerely wanted to know how the God of the Bible could ever allow such suffering as our world has seen. But perhaps they assume some things which just aren't true, and the God they blame is not even actually the God of the Bible after all but rather just a distorted image of God which they've just assumed to be biblical!

Let's go right to the source and take a basic look at what the Bible has always taught about God and his exact relationship to human suffering in the world to see if we are even actually blaming the God of the Bible when we get mad at him for the suffering in the world or just some gross misrepresentation of him which we've just incorrectly assumed for years. After all, if the God we are blaming for all human suffering is not actually anything like the God of the Bible, why continue to blame the God of the Bible for all human suffering? It really doesn't make much sense now, does it?

> After all, if the God we are blaming for all human suffering is not actually anything like the God of the Bible, why continue to blame the God of the Bible for all human suffering?

Now let's consider the following basic teachings of the Bible as it concerns God and his relationship to all human suffering to even see if anger toward the God of the Bible for human suffering makes any sense at all:

1. God is Perfect—According to any Old or New Testament verses of the Bible, God himself is morally perfect in every way, and there is absolutely no evil in him whatsoever (Job 34:10; Psalm 19:9, 25:8, 92:15; Isaiah 53:9; Habakkuk 1:13; Matthew 19:17; Romans 9:14; 1 Corinthians 14:33; James 1:13, 1:17; 1 Peter 2:22; 1 John 1:5, 2:16, 3:3). And this, of course, would only make sense if God must also be an eternal being as the Bible has also plainly taught (see 1 Timothy 1:17, 6:16; Revelation 22:13). For even our conscience (and/or common sense) would tell us that no being could ever be "eternal" without also being morally "perfect," for nothing imperfect would ever last forever! Thus, if indeed God must be morally perfect, he could never be the author of anything evil, and that's exactly just what the Bible has always taught. Please consider the following verse:

    > **When tempted, no one should say, "God is tempting me." For God cannot be tempted by**

**evil, nor does he tempt anyone (with evil)...
(James 1:13)**

In addition to all the verses which plainly teach us that the God of the Bible is morally perfect in every way, one cannot find even one verse which teaches us otherwise! Therefore, if the God of the Bible is indeed morally perfect, he himself could never be the *cause* of any human suffering! It would be an absolute impossibility. And if he is not at all the cause of human suffering, of course, it makes no sense to blame him for it. If, in fact, God ever was the cause of any evil to even a slight degree, he would immediately cease to be an eternal being and could never even offer anyone eternal life. And that, my friend, is just the biblical truth.

2. Everything which God originally created was "*very good*," and it was only human sin which destroyed his perfect creation (Genesis 1:31, 3:16–19). By the end of the sixth day of creation, God had finished making everything which he had made during creation week and declared that it was *all* "*very good*." Six times during creation week, God had pronounced his work "*good*;" but at the end of creation week, he pronounced it all "*very good*." And the Hebrew word for "*very*" here really means "exceedingly," and the Hebrew word for "*good*" means "moral purity." Therefore, God pronounced all his creation work as being "*exceedingly morally pure*," which could also be understood as "*morally flawless*." This must include not only all living things on earth, but also the angels which were created before mankind.

3. All human suffering is only the result of human sin which all entered God's perfect creation *totally against God's will*. In Genesis, God makes it real clear that man's sin entered God's perfect creation totally against his will. In fact, God was "playing very fair" in that he clearly warned both Adam and Eve way ahead of time of the severe consequences should they disobey him and eat from the Tree of the Knowledge of Good and Evil (see Genesis 2:16–17). Adam and Eve could eat from any of the other trees in the garden, just not from that one single tree.

Why would God do something like that? We cover this subject more thoroughly in Objection 23, but the condensed answer is simple—it was absolutely necessary for God to ultimately test Adam and Eve's love for himself by placing that simple restriction on that one tree out of all others they could eat from. And because both Adam and Eve were disobedient (after plainly warned of the consequences), they both failed the test of heart and the curse of man's disobedience then entered and corrupted God's entire perfect creation.

But some might ask, "Why would God allow the corruption of his entire perfect creation just because Adam and Eve ate a piece of fruit from a tree?" Because Adam and Eve did fairly represent the entire human race which followed them, and their simple test of obedience was also a fair reflection of their love for God, which obviously was no small issue to God who is absolutely perfect in his love!

It is important to understand that the whole test was indeed a love issue to God, even though it was admittedly condensed down into a very simple test. And because God is defined by perfect love, it is this absolute moral perfection which many are ignorant of. Therefore, because all human suffering has *only* been the result of man's sin, which entered God's perfect creation totally against his will, how much sense does it make to blame God for *any* human suffering in the world, since that was never his loving will for us? Thus, it makes no sense whatsoever to blame God for even things like natural disasters, wars, sickness, accidents, etc., which are all just a result of man's sin corrupting God's perfect creation. Even the weeds in your garden are only the result of man's sin (Genesis 3:17–19)!

Conclusion

While man can choose to blame some twisted God of their own making for all the human suffering in the world, it is *honestly impossible* to actually blame the God of the Bible for the human suffering in the world if, in fact, the Bible clearly teaches us that all sin and suffering entered his perfect creation *totally against God's will*. However, because *some* may not want to take personal responsibility for even their own moral failure, they might just find it easier to blame the God of the Bible. But you certainly don't have to be that person. You do have a choice, and no one can take that power away from you! While "*ignorant* gross misrepresentation" is not probably a moral failure, we all know that "*deliberate* gross misrepresentation" is a moral failure. Many may not know just what the Bible has always taught about God and his relationship to human suffering, because they are ignorant.

But for man to continue to blame the God of the Bible for human suffering, when they know nothing in the Bible supports such blame, is to just prove that man's sin is the real cause behind all human suffering, because one has to *dishonestly* misrepresent the true God of the Bible in order to do so. *As* Jesus plainly taught in John 8:32, the truth of God will *always* "*set you free.*" If one is not "set free" and is ripping mad at God or is bogged down with other such spiritual problems, then it just means they do not yet know or believe the real truth of God and are believing lies about him (Please see Objections 18 and 23, which expound much further on God's relationship to human suffering).

Nobody likes pain in this life, but the good news is that all Bible-believing Christians have God's promise of a *pain-free* eternity! But unfortunately, those who continue to reject Christ don't even have that. As it concerns believers in Christ, Revelation 21:3–4 clearly teaches:

> **[B]ehold, the dwelling place of God is with men, and he will live with them, and they shall be his people, and God himself shall be with them, and be their God. And God shall wipe away all tears from their eyes; and there shall be no more death, neither sorrow, nor crying, neither shall there be any more pain: for the former things are passed away.**

The Bible teaches us that God is love, and everything he does has his perfect loving motive behind it (1 John 4:8). And if you don't yet know Christ personally, even now he offers you yet another opportunity to become part of his awesome eternal kingdom, which by his promise will be full of his love and goodness and absent of all pain. Perhaps you are beginning to realize all your anger toward God just stems from actual lies you've been believing about him. If you are one who is tired of running from God and you want to personally experience his awesome unconditional healing love for you, I invite you to just take that first small step of faith by sincerely praying the prayer of salvation located at the end of this book. None of us are any better than anyone else. And every one of us can escape the destruction of our own sin nature if we want to. No matter what your past is like, God loves you right now and sincerely wants you to be a part of his awesome eternal kingdom!

Jesus said, "I am the resurrection and the life. He who believes in me, will live even though he dies; and whoever lives and believes in me will never die..." (John 11:25–26)

OBJECTION 17

I Believe the Reason for the Moral Collapse of Mankind Is Because Many Won't Get More Involved in Politics

Even if the moral collapse of man is partly due to people neglecting their political responsibilities, one still must ask just what causes man to neglect his political responsibilities? And as good and responsible as it is for one to get involved and make a difference in the political arena, history has consistently shown that ultimately, the underlying reality is that the "morality mankind simply cannot be legislated!"

Why would this be? It is simply because any outside political or lawful attempt to change the heart (or spirit) of man goes against our "basic order of function." Just what do I mean by man's "basic order of function?" According to the Bible, science, and just plain general observation, man is made up of three basic entities—body, soul (mind, will, and emotions), and spirit (which includes the conscience). When we realize how these different entities basically operate in relationship to each other, then it becomes easier to understand why societies are *not necessarily* changed by passing better laws or political reform agendas. In fact, if you reasonably think about it, if it really worked that way, political reform would have created a permanent utopia a long time ago! But as it is, mankind is still just trying not to self-destruct after 6,000 years of recorded human history.

Man's Basic "Order of Function"

Scientists have easily confirmed that our body is controlled by our mind, and although we cannot see man's spirit (or spiritual heart), most would agree with the Bible that man's heart (or spirit) controls his mind. So to understand man's basic "order of function" correctly, the spiritual heart of man controls his mind, and his mind, in turn, controls his body—in that order. Therefore, in order for man to have a change of mind and bodily behavior, we must back all the way up in the "chain of command" of man's basic order of function and get permission from his spiritual heart first. In other words, before political societies can change, man must first have a "change of heart;" otherwise, any political attempts to change man's behavior from the outside in is like trying to stop an army without first negotiating with its commander!

Dictatorship governments would be an obvious example of man trying to change society from the outside in. Granted, most dictatorships are trying to lead men in the wrong direction, but even if they were to force men to do that, which is good (kind of like the Roman emperor Constantine tried to do), then that too fails, because dictatorships of any kind simply do not follow the "proper chain of command" in man's basic "order of function." Whenever the human mind and body is told what to do from a forceful outside influence without an appeal first to the spiritual heart of man, then rebellion is often the result, simply because the mind and body of a man only takes its direction from the inside influence of his own *spiritual heart*.

> Before political societies can change, man must first have a "change of heart;" otherwise, any political attempts to change man's behavior from the outside in is like trying to stop an army without first negotiating with its commander.

Therefore, to try to change society from the outside in is not only a lot more work, but also, it just doesn't work! It is really no different than trying to make a withering tree healthy by working on the trunk and branches. Most tree nurseries will undoubtedly tell you, you must focus on the roots of a tree first, simply because it is the roots which ultimately determine the whole health of a tree. Why? Simply because only the roots are connected to the tree's only source of life (from which it came)—the soil with its nutrients.

So to try to have a healthy tree by working on its trunk and branches is actually just delaying the only possible means for that tree to become healthy, because the roots (which are connected to its only source of life) are being neglected. In fact, if one persists in addressing the trunk and branches of a withering tree and refuses to properly address its roots, then that person is actually "a part of the problem" and not "a part of the solution." The very same could be said of those who insist on political involvement and reform to change society while they continue to reject Christ who is the only chance man has for a "change of heart."

The spiritual heart of man cannot be observed in a test tube, simply because it is spiritual and not physical. However, this in no way means it has no influence upon his mind or physical body. It is much like the wind, which we cannot see either, yet we know it has its real and powerful influence around the world! Just because a thing cannot be seen with our physical eyes does not make it fiction or a thing of no influence. The spiritual world is just as real as the wind; hence, all the churches in the world. In fact, that which is *most powerful* is unseen, just like the roots on a tree. In fact, it has been believed that one of the most powerful things in life is man's freewill heart choices, because no one (not even God) can interfere with them. And it is this elusive unseen spiritual entity of man which ultimately controls and determines the quality of his whole life from cradle to grave! So if man first has to have a real change of heart before his life and political society can change, just how does man obtain such change of heart anyway?

The very same way the roots of a tree become healthy—by being connected to our only source of life from which we came, namely our creator. To expect man to have a healthy change of heart (which in turn makes political society healthy) without being directly connected to his own creator and only source of life is like expecting an uprooted tree to live on and produce good fruit! It just ain't gonna happen!

Am I suggesting political involvement is wrong? Not at all. But if political reform (on any level) is pursued by a man while he continues to ignore the needed change of heart in others, which they can only obtain by being connected to their own creator, then the result is not only wrong (because man's only source of life is ignored) but always destructive to society. Why? Because any changes sought after (however "good" they would be) simply do not address the "root" or "heart" of man for a *permanent change* to his behaviors. It is like trying to save a sick, poisoned man with all manner of "good" medicines but never giving him the only real antidote to the poison!

> To expect man to have a healthy change of heart without being directly connected to his own creator and only source of life is like expecting an uprooted tree to live on and produce good fruit!

The Bible has always taught that the spiritual heart of man can only get its life and true health from a *"right relationship"* with his true creator (which just makes sense). And no clever substitute of man will work simply because God himself made us that way quite on purpose! Neither mere religion (just following religious rules apart from a right relationship with God) nor secular humanism (man's own humanistic efforts apart from a right relationship with God) will suffice. They can't suffice because with either of them, man is still disconnected from his only source of life; thus, a true and lasting change of heart cannot and will not occur.

For example, in mere religion, it is very possible for many who claim to have a right relationship with God to actually not have a right relationship with God. Not too long ago, it was reported in our nation that a supposed pastor was sleeping with the head deacon's wife. You see, just because someone goes to Bible seminary school (which itself is not even really biblical) and puts a "God stamp" on the outside of their life for all to see doesn't necessarily mean they've had the real change of heart that comes with a real and right relationship with God. In 2 Timothy 2:17–19, the Apostle Paul exposes a couple of "fake believers" in his own day and then ends by saying:

> **Nevertheless, God's solid foundation stands firm, sealed with this inscription: "The Lord knows those who are his," and, "Everyone that confesses the name of the Lord must turn away from wickedness."**

The bottom line is if we do not truly have a *"right relationship"* with our creator, we might as well be a vacuum cleaner which is unplugged and disconnected from its only source of power. How can you get your carpets cleaned that way? So either we are actually plugged in or we are not—it is that basic and that simple. So now, two basic questions remain:

1. If a healthy society truly hinges upon man having a "change of heart," and a man's healthy change of heart all hinges upon a "right relationship" with his one and only creator, then how indeed does a man obtain this "right relationship" with his creator?
2. And why would the Bible even teach that we need a "right relationship" with our creator? Why not just a relationship?

To start, let's answer this second question first:

Question # 2: Why would the Bible even teach that we need a "right relationship" with our creator? No man is going to see his need for a doctor if he doesn't first honestly see that he has a disease. Not only does the Bible plainly teach that all mankind has been plagued with the "disease" of sin ever since the first man Adam disobeyed God, but also the very bloody, painful, and destructive history of man should confirm to the honest soul that man has a basic problem which he simply cannot fix despite *all* his human efforts. And as each century has passed, sin itself seems to have only compounded and gotten worse. Today, with nuclear capabilities, many wonder if man will even be able to keep from complete self-extermination. Does this honestly sound like man is basically "good?" Or is it strong evidence of man's ongoing battle with sin?

On a more personal level, man has never been able to come close to living up to even his own God-given conscience. We all know it is wrong to *lie,* because it hurts to be lied to. Yet, everyone has lied, if we were *honest* with ourselves. We all know it is wrong to *steal,* because it hurts to get stolen from. Yet, everyone has stolen, if we were to be *honest* with ourselves. We all know it is wrong to *lust, gossip, dishonor parents, complain, be prideful,* have *unforgiveness,* etc., simply because all these things cause hurt to ourselves and others. Yet, we all have fallen into these things more times than we care to count, if we were to be *honest* with ourselves. The list, of course, goes on as we discuss more thoroughly in our Objection 19.

And the Bible teaches us that it is precisely these many sins which have "separated" us from our own creator who is absolutely perfect and eternal. The credible Apostle Peter as well as all the apostles who personally walked with Christ for three years said about him as a matter of fact in 1 Peter 2:22: "(Christ) *who did no sin, neither was guile found in his mouth....*" This word, *found,* must imply the obvious. They were all looking for sin in his life but could find none!

I think any of us would do the very same if for three years we were walking alongside of anyone claiming to be the Son of God. Especially the Jews would have done this with anyone claiming to be their Messiah. And when Jesus walked the earth, even his enemies could not find moral fault with him. Josh McDowell's book, *Evidence that Demands a Verdict,* is really a thorough convincing source on this whole subject.

According to the scriptures, the only reason Christ was crucified was simply because he claimed to be the Son of God, which certainly isn't a moral failure if it was true! But to the unbelieving Jews, this of course was "blasphemy," and to the unbelieving Romans, Christ was a political threat. Therefore, from their *unbelieving* perspective, Christ had to die, not because they found any moral fault in him, but simply because they refused to *believe* that he was actually just who he claimed to be—the Jewish Messiah and Son of the Living God.

Ironically, before Christ was crucified, the Jews looked for their perfect Messiah for over 1,000 years. Then when he finally did come, they nationally refused to believe it and crucified him. When the imperfect is confronted with the perfect, the imperfect is most often very threatened and reacts with fear.

I know it is difficult for any of us to comprehend God's absolute perfection, just because we are all forced to look through the dirty glasses of our own imperfect human nature. However, if God wasn't absolutely perfect, it just goes without saying that he surely could not then be an *eternal* being. But someone has been running this awesome universe for millenniums which must maintain just the right conditions to sustain delicate life on earth, and it sure isn't you and me!

And so in summary, because God is perfect, then his perfect justice must also be satisfied. And whenever we fail to keep his moral standards, all sin must be justly punished; otherwise, God would have to compromise his own character, which is impossible, because again, he is perfect and eternal.

If we would not respect a human civil court judge which lets the guilty go free, how much more so is our perfectly just creator unable to let sin go unpunished? Therefore, according to the Bible, God has determined that the just punishment for our many sins can be no less than eternal separation from himself. That's our problem. But hang on, because the Bible also gives us God's awesome solution to our problem! God (who is all knowing, which must be a part of his perfection) knew ahead of time that we would choose (he gave us a free will) not to live up to his perfect moral standards. So he decided to do something radical to save his much loved creation (you and me) from eternal destruction and restore our relationship with him. Very radically, he decided to take the just punishment for all our sins upon himself! Wow! When you think about it, that's a lot of love!

Question #1: How indeed does a man obtain that "right relationship" with his creator? The answer must, of course, be "his way and not our way!" Many try to obtain God's favor or eternal life their way. But God says to us through the prophet Isaiah:

For my thoughts are not your thoughts, neither are your ways my ways... For as the heavens are higher than the earth, so are my ways higher than your ways, and my thoughts than your thoughts. (Isaiah 55:8–9)

Proverbs 14:12 just adds to it by saying, "*There is a way that seems right unto a man, but in the end, it leads to death.*" If it is God's eternal life that he's willing to share with us, shouldn't a "right relationship" with him have to be done his way to obtain it? If God created everything, then does he not have the perfect right to tell us just how things have to be done within his own creation?

Again, the fact that there is only one way for man to be right with his own creator has nothing to do with God being on some power trip. Remember, he's not like us! He's perfect. And according to God (who "*cannot lie*"—Titus 1:2), there simply is no other possible way for man to be right with him other than the way he offered through his Son. And this reality may not even occur to many who persist in rejecting Christ.

In John 3:2, Nicodemus, a religious ruler of the Jews (who had a good reputation among his people) came to Jesus and said: "*Rabbi, we know that you are a teacher come from God: For no man can do these miracles that you do, except God be with him.*"

At this point, Nicodemus still believes Jesus is just a good moral "*teacher come from God*" and cannot yet see that Jesus is indeed just who he always claimed to be—the actual Son of God who came down to earth to redeem his own creation from sin. Because Nicodemus couldn't yet see this, he couldn't have a "right relationship" with God. Why? Simply because his sins still separated him from God if he didn't yet see that Christ was actually the Son of God who came to reconcile him with God.

> According to God, who cannot lie, there simply is no other possible way for man to be right with him other than the way he offered through his Son.

Simply put, the Bible describes Christ as the only "right relationship bridge" between God and man and that man must spiritually walk across the "bridge of Christ" if he is to be reconciled or "rightly rejoined" with his creator (1 Timothy 2:4–5). And if Nicodemus did not yet believe that Christ was the "bridge" between God and man, he certainly couldn't have walked across it yet!

This is why Jesus next replied to Nicodemus in verse 3: *"Truly truly, I say unto you, unless a man be "born again" he cannot see the kingdom of God* (by coming into "right relationship" with God)."

Not understanding that Jesus was speaking of a *spiritual birth* for a change of heart, Nicodemus, thinking of only the physical, then says, *"But how can a man be born when he is old? Can he enter a second time into his mother's womb, and be born?*

Then Jesus plainly says to him, *"[u]nless a man be born of the Spirit, he cannot enter the kingdom of God."*

So just like we need a physical birth to enter into this physical world, we also need a spiritual birth (being "born again") in order to be reconciled with God (because our sins have separated us from him) and enter his spiritual eternal kingdom. Both are necessary miracles which must come from God to give us his life—the only difference is one is physical and the other is spiritual.

So how does Christ say Nicodemus gets this "spiritual birth," which everything hinges upon? Here's the key that ends up changing the world. In verse 16 and 17, Jesus gives Nicodemus the answer by saying:

For God so loved the world that he gave his one and only Son (to die on the cross for our

sins and satisfy the justice of the Father), that whoever believes in him shall not perish but have eternal life. For God did not send his Son into the world to condemn the world, but to save the world through him.

The Bible plainly teaches us that when we simply believe that Jesus was indeed the Son of God and came to earth to take the just punishment for our sins upon himself (satisfying the perfect justice of God), we are then "born again" and made right with God, having that change of spiritual heart we can only get from a spiritual birth. And the moment we do sincerely believe who Jesus really was and why he had to come to earth and die on the cross, there's actually something incredible which the Bible also says happens inside our spiritual heart. The Holy Spirit actually comes to live inside our spirit (or spiritual heart; Romans 8:11)!

> Just like we need a physical birth to enter into this physical world, we also need a spiritual birth to enter God's spiritual kingdom and obtain his eternal life.

When this happens, our uprooted dying "tree roots" (or dying spirits) are finally reconnected to the nutrient soil (or our creator) from which we came, and we then cannot only have God's eternal life, but we are also internally governed by his Spirit living inside us for the rest of this life and eternally beyond. Wow! Pretty amazing, huh?

Since the Holy Spirit lives inside the spiritual heart of all believers in Christ, God's Spirit then connects with our spirit and gives us the change of heart we need to *live more like God himself.* Thus, the saying, "Either you are pregnant, or you are not." This and only this will give man his needed change of heart which will in turn reform political society *from the inside out.* And it just makes sense that God made it this way so we will always truly need him for a healthy life and society.

When the roots of society are healthy by people getting reconnected to their one and only creator, then the health of the political trunk and branches will automatically follow and show this! Some have thought that just because "all men are created in the image of God" that this makes men good enough for political reform. However, neither the Bible nor history itself bears witness to this simple notion. Why? Simply because the Bible teaches us plainly that "being created in the image of God" has been corrupted ever since the first man and woman fell into disobedience. And this is exactly why Christ told Nicodemus that he and all men must have the very necessary *second spiritual birth*. As Romans 5:12 states:

> **[s]in entered into the world through one man (Adam), and death (both physical and spiritual death) through sin, and in this way death came to all men, because all sinned...**

When someone is in the political arena who is really a believer in Christ and following him, they will not, of course, be perfect (because only God is, and Christians still have a sin nature to contend with). But nobody has to look after them and constantly spend all of their time and energy, making sure they are not having affairs or trying to pass immoral laws, etc.! Why? Because if they are truly walking with Christ, they will just *not want to* do anything which would grieve the Holy Spirit inside them, even though they are still "imperfect" human beings. One should be able to see that true Christians are following after Christ (even though imperfectly); but how can non-Christians follow after Christ if they don't believe in him and have his Spirit living inside them directing them to do so? And if non-Christians do not follow after Christ, they can only be left with "sin" and "self," which at times may appear to be good, but simply cannot lead man to real lasting life if God himself is the only source, and they are disconnected from that source. Thus, anything non-Christians would do to genuinely solve man's problems is an exercise in futility from the start, because they are disconnected from the only real solution.

Everyone Needs the Same "Oversight?"

It is true that because all men have a sin nature within them that all men need "oversight." That's why governments have been a necessary institution created by God (*Romans 13:1–5*). However, because Christ following Christians are actually connected to God in their spiritual heart and have a loving relationship with him, they actually want to do what is right through that change of heart, which only he can give them.

In this real sense, Christians (true Christians who are truly following Christ) simply do not need the great "oversight" which non-Christians constantly need. However, all throughout man's history after the first man, Adam, brought sin into the world, the political arena across the world has always been dominated by non-Christians as all the "world dominating empires" have been largely ruled by non-Christians. And this is because the Bible teaches us that we are living in the "*times of the Gentiles*" within God's overall prophetic plans for man (Luke 21:24).

When Christ said "*Gentiles*" here in Luke 21:24, he simply meant nations that do not know God. But why would God allow the whole world to be dominated by Godless nations for a certain time period within his overall plans for man? The answer is simple. So all mankind can see once and for all time that man apart from his creator simply does not have the answers for his own political/spiritual well-being! And as we can see plainly throughout history, the world has just gotten worse and worse as sin in the heart of man never stays the same but actually compounds with time. And this is exactly why all the "oversight" in the world will be to no avail in this age as we race toward Armageddon.

Why would God allow the whole world to be dominated by godless nations for a certain time period? So all mankind can finally see that man apart from his creator simply does not have the answers for his own political/spiritual well-being!

The problem with stepping up political "oversight" to solve our moral heart problems is that history has shown that even the "oversight," if it is not wanting to follow Christ through a right relationship with him, just creates more problems, simply because it has more power ungoverned by God, like dictatorships. But since God is the only pure authority worthy to govern his own creation correctly, true lasting political reform simply cannot happen until Christ returns to set up his eternal reign on earth, which all true Christians will be a part of (Daniel 2:44).

But right now, God is not only allowing godless men to dominate the world (by not interfering with their free wills), but also allowing Satan to be the ruler of this world, who appeals to the sin nature of godless men, helping them into positions of power. And ultimately, God has to allow all this before the return of Christ in order to test the hearts of men (Ephesians 2:2, 6:12; 1 John 5:19).

Will More "Oversight" Solve Our Political Problems?

It may very well be true that more oversight is necessary in some professions than others, just because of the nature of their vital impact upon the well-being of society. And the political profession may very well be one such profession which needs more oversight. However, remember, more imperfect human oversight has its real limitations as we just emphasized! It doesn't really matter how much oversight you give to the political arena. If that oversight is disconnected from the only solution which can bring a change of man's heart, then it will truly avail us nothing. In fact, as we can see with dictatorships (which is extreme oversight), it may just compound our problems. And for some to believe that everyone should be involved with politics to the point of babysitting all the politicians and making sure they all do what is right so evil will not get the upper hand is simply unrealistic.

When you stop and think about it, in normal society, no one really even has the time to "babysit" others and make sure they are doing their job, no matter which job that is. If I'm a carpenter, do all the politicians make sure I'm doing my job correctly by actually pounding nails with me? No. If someone is an electrician, do they have to constantly get involved with the hospital board of directors just to make sure the doctors and nurses are doing their job? No. Neither does anyone realistically have the time to *constantly and closely* babysit politicians, and that's exactly why not many people do or ever will. No one realistically has the time, money, or energy to do their own job correctly and constantly make sure the many politicians do theirs correctly as well.

Just what am I saying? If politicians (and the people they govern) are not reconnected to their true creator and only source of life, there is simply no hope for political reform! It's an inside job, not an outside job. And that's exactly why when the Son of God did have his short three-year ministry on earth (which had more impact upon cultures and societies of man than any other event in human history), he just preached the Gospel which reconnected men to their one and only creator and source of life, simply because he knew everything else would follow! There's not one single recorded statement of Christ (or his apostles) in the entire New Testament where they called *anyone* to even try to reform the political arena of their day through any type of involvement in politics—not one! And I might add that the political arena of their day was in extreme dire need with the cruel Roman dictatorship completely controlling their nation of Israel.

> If politicians (and the people they govern) are not reconnected to their true creator and only source of life, there is simply no hope for political reform!

So if everything else will follow man's change of heart through Christ, then why haven't societies been revolutionized for the better since Christ? Well, they have. In fact, if the *true* Christian Church hadn't been on earth since Christ, it is doubtful mankind would have fared half as well up to this point or even survived. For one example of many, without true Christians, would we really have won World War II? It is really rather doubtful considering all those in our military (and England's) who sincerely believed in Christ.

Look at all the food, shelter, and clothing needs of people met by the worldwide true Church over the centuries. Most all agencies supplying basic humanitarian needs to man throughout the church age were started by the Church. Even many hospitals were started by the Christ-believing Church; that's why they are often named after men or women in the Bible (for example, St. John's Hospital). Many natural disaster relief organizations among many other human need organizations were founded by Christ-believing organizations, and the list goes on and on—you get the point. The Church has truly been a light in this dark world and a restrainer of evil, just as the Bible plainly teaches us it will be (Matthew 5:14; 2 Thessalonians 2:6–8).

Is the Church perfect? No, far from it, I can assure you. But Christ never promised that his Church would be perfect (because only he is, and that's why Christians need him) or that the moral condition of the Christ-rejecting world would get better and better during the Church age. He just promised that the *"gates of hell"* would not prevail against his Church as long as it was on earth (Matthew 16:18). This just means his Church would *"restrain evil"* from overrunning the world as long as his Church was on the earth (2 Thessalonians 2:7). In fact, the Bible teaches us that because most will reject Christ (Matthew 7:13–14), who is their only hope for a change of heart, the "church age" itself (the age we are now living ever since Christ) will just keep getting worse and worse morally until Christ returns to set up his "theocracy" kingdom on earth (2 Timothy 3:13).

Because men have a God-given free will, we must realize that even many of those who push for political reform are not after the truth of God or a true change of heart for their fellow man, which can only come from being restored to their own creator. They just want the selfish things they want, which is usually money, power, and fame! Yes, our God given free will is among the most powerful things man possesses. Just why do some men want the lasting political transformations, which can only come through right relationship with their own creator, and others just settle for the mere appearance of political reform and outward good deeds while they really go after power, fame, and money? Who can say, other than God, who will judge the secrets of man's heart when we will all stand before him (*Romans 2:16*)?

Because most will reject Christ who is their only hope for a change of heart, the "church age" we're living in will just keep getting morally worse and worse until Christ returns to set up his "theocracy" kingdom.

Conclusion

The bottom line is that the job of achieving a healthy political society requires our spiritual transformation, which can only come from being reconnected in right relationship with our true creator. The spiritual must always come first, simply because the spiritual drives everything else. It always has and it always will, simply because that's how our creator made us.

Quite on purpose, he made us to need him! And there is simply no way around it. Thus, man's greatest need is for a change of heart first, which only our own creator can give us. As it has been said, "If our greatest need was money, God would have sent us a banker. If our greatest need was physical health, God would have sent us a doctor. If our greatest need was political reform, God would have sent us a politician. But our greatest need was a spiritual right relationship with our creator, so God very wisely sent us a savior—knowing everything else good would follow."

According to his own promise, Jesus is coming back soon and will establish his far better kingdom on earth, which will certainly not have the many political problems we see in society today. Why? Simply because all those in his government will not only have a right relationship with him, but according to scripture, it will literally be impossible for mankind to commit any moral wrong in his resurrected state, because he will no longer have a sin nature!

Are you spiritually ready for Christ's soon return and his awesome eternal kingdom through a heart belief in what Christ did for you on the cross? If not, but you would like to be, I invite you to just take that first small step of faith by sincerely praying the prayer of salvation located at the end of this book. No matter what your past is like, God loves you and sincerely wants you to be a part of his awesome eternal kingdom!

> **Jesus said, "I am the resurrection and the life. He who believes in me, will live even though he dies; and whoever lives and believes in me will never die..." (John 11:25–26)**

OBJECTION 18

If the God of the Bible Created Everything and Is Perfect and Loving, Then Where Did Evil Originally Come From?

While this age old question may seem quite reasonable, for many skeptics of the Bible, it may very well have a basic double false assumption built right into it. And that double false assumption is that evil itself is "something;" therefore it had to be something "created." Since this question concerns the "God of the Bible," it is only reasonable to answer it with the Bible, and for that, we must refer to the account of origins in Genesis chapters 1–3. Genesis chapters 1–2 discusses the origin of the physical universe, and Genesis chapter 3 discusses the origin of evil. Let us start with some obvious biblical facts.

> And that double false assumption is that evil itself is "something;" therefore, it had to be something "created."

The Bible is clear that God not only created everything that exists but that he himself existed before everything—*"that in all things, he might have preeminence"* (John 1:3; Colossians 1:15–18). Also in Genesis 1:31, it teaches us that by the end of the sixth day, God had finished making everything which he had made during creation week and that it was all *"very good."*

Six times during creation week, God had pronounced his work *"good,"* but at the end of creation week, he pronounced it all *"very good.*" And the Hebrew word for "*very*" here really means "exceedingly," and the Hebrew word for "*good*" means "moral purity." Therefore, God pronounced all his creation work as being "*exceedingly morally pure,*" which could also be understood as "*morally flawless.*" This must include not only all living things on earth, but also the angels which were created before mankind.

It is more than interesting that God actually attached morality to his physical creation of everything during creation week. Even though we might not necessarily associate morality with a physical creation, evidently, according to God, the two are indeed linked and inseparable.

In the Old English language, our term, *good,* is actually directly related to our English word, *God*—and that is why they are only one letter away. *Some* etymologists may try to insist that our words *God* and *good* have no relation to each other whatsoever, but not all etymologists agree on this notion. According to the Bible, all true "goodness" originally comes from God (James 1:17), and only God himself is the true source of all "goodness" (Matthew 19:17).

Thus, for these two words to be directly related to each other in our English language just makes sense, seeing the English-speaking world has a strong history of believing the Bible. The fact that King James created the King James version of the Bible in 1611 is just proof of that.

In addition, our English word for *evil* is only one letter away from our English word, *devil.* Just another coincidence? I don't think so, even though some etymologists will again try to convince you they too are *completely unrelated.*

Often, in our search for truth, if we start with the obvious facts, which we can be certain of, then whatever deductions we are forced to conclude in light of those facts must be the truth remaining. And since we know from all scripture that:

1. God himself is morally perfect;
2. God existed before everything;
3. And God created everything which exists;
4. And literally *everything* which God created during creation week was exceedingly morally flawless;

Then logically, evil itself:

1. Could not be a "created" thing;
2. Could not have come from God.

Often, in our search for truth, if we start with the obvious facts which we can be certain of, then whatever deductions we are forced to conclude in light of those facts must be the truth remaining.

So then, just what is evil and where did it come from? Now we are asking the right questions! To answer those questions, we must turn to Genesis chapter 3 where evil itself first manifested—*long after* God created everything perfectly good.

But first, let's firmly establish that according to all collective scripture pertaining to it, God himself is morally perfect in every way, and there is absolutely no evil in him whatsoever. This just makes sense if God is also eternal—past, present, and future as the Bible teaches—for nothing imperfect would ever last for eternity (see 1 Timothy 1:17, 6:16; Revelation 22:13). We've already cited both James 1:17 and Matthew 19:17, but the following scriptures also verify the absolute moral perfection of God (Job 34:10; Psalm 19:9, 25:8, 92:15; Isaiah 53:9; Habakkuk 1:13; Romans 9:14; 1 Corinthians 14:33; James 1:13; 1 Peter 2:22; 1 John 1:5, 2:16, 3:3). The entire word of God is not only clear on the fact that God is absolutely morally perfect but also that he never changes in his moral perfection (Hebrews 13:8; James 1:17). Also, another biblical reality which fully cooperates with the absolute perfection of God is that he is indeed *all-knowing*—past, present, and future (Romans 11:33–36; Col. 2:3).

In addition to all these verses and many more, which undeniably affirm God's absolute perfection, there is not one single verse in the entire Old or New Testament word of God which teaches us anything to the contrary! As we've already mentioned, if God were the source of evil, then he himself would have to be evil. And if he were evil even in the slightest degree, it would be impossible for him to be an eternal being. Additionally, if he were evil, then he himself could not conquer or triumph over death, which is just the result of evil. If God could not triumph over evil and death, he certainly could not save us from evil and promise the whole human race eternal life through his Son. Therefore, if there is absolutely no evil in God himself, the source of evil must logically be outside of God.

> The entire word of God is not only clear on the fact that God is absolutely morally perfect but also that he never changes in his moral perfection.

The Bible and Darwinian Evolution Don't Mix

Additionally, if God used any kind of Darwinian macro "evolution" to create during creation week, it would automatically necessitate evil, because the theory of Darwinian evolution requires death, suffering, and decay, which are only fruits of evil. If there was any evolutionary evil within the process, which God used to create during creation week, then God himself would have to be a source of that evil. And if God were even slightly evil, then he would not be eternal or able to conquer evil. Therefore, an eternal perfect God could never have used any kind of a Darwinian evolutionary process to create during creation week.

> If there is absolutely no evil in God himself, the source of evil must logically be outside of God.

This also is a major blow to the idea that the perfect God of the Bible used Darwinian evolution to create as the "Day-Age" and

"Gap" theories ignorantly suggest. In this real sense, when the problem of evil in the Darwinian evolutionary process is considered, the Bible and Darwinian evolution simply cannot mix at all!

Now that we've established that there is absolutely no evil in God and that he could not have used death and decay to bring all things into being, let's take a look at the first appearing of evil in Genesis, the third chapter, in order to determine just what it is and where it came from. In Genesis 3:1–19, we see the fall of mankind into sin. However, the first source of evil mentioned is the *"serpent"* who *"beguiled"* Eve into disobedience. The Bible teaches us that the *"serpent"* was just one of many other *"very good"* creatures in the garden which God had originally made (Genesis 1:31, 3:1). So if everything God had made was *"very good,"* how could this particular *"serpent"* animal in the garden be evil?

If there was any evolutionary evil within the process which God used to create during creation week, then God himself would be a source of evil.

The animal wasn't, since "morality" in general is not assigned to any animal within God's word. Obviously, according to Genesis's account, with this particular serpent animal who beguiled Eve, we are not just dealing with a mere animal who would certainly have no real ability to talk to and tempt any man with premeditated lies and deception.

According to the rest of scripture, it was Satan who just possessed the *"serpent"* animal's body to tempt and deceive Eve (see 2 Corinthians 11:3; 1 Thessalonians 3:5; 1 Corinthians 7:5). The scriptures teach us that long before he tempted Eve, Satan himself is the very first source of evil which manifested in God's creation. In fact, Satan (or the devil) used to be Lucifer, one of God's highest-ranking angels who was perfectly created by God in every way to worship him (Ezekiel 28:12–19). He was actually the one of the most beautiful angels as he was literally covered with precious stones and even had musical instruments built right into his body! According to scripture, he was "*full of wisdom and perfect in beauty*" (Ezekiel 28:12) and was, in fact, "*perfect in his ways from the day that he was created, until sin was found in him*" (Ezekiel 28:15). And what was his sin? The answer is basically his "pride" of wanting to take the place of God and is explained in Isaiah 14:12–17. But unfortunately for him, the job was just not available!

> So technically, Satan himself is the very first source of evil which manifested in God's creation.

So then the question remains, if God created Lucifer to be "*perfect in his ways*," just how could evil have been "*found in him?*" Well, to answer that, we must first acknowledge another biblical fact, which has real relevance to both the fall of Lucifer and the fall of man into disobedience. And that is that when God perfectly created both angels and men, he had to give them the "free will" which his true love absolutely required. There are literally hundreds of scriptures throughout God's Word which directly teach that all mankind (as well as the angels) have a built in God-given freewill choice, whether or not to love God and have a right relationship with him (Galatians 6:7–8; Revelation 22:17).

You see, love is only meaningful and true when there remains a choice not to love. God could have forced his creation to love him and obey him, but then it would not have been "true love" any more than it would be true love for a bride to love her groom at gunpoint. The truth is, any forced love is not really love at all! And God who is absolutely perfect, of course, knew all this and simply could not force his creation to love him and remain loving himself. He had to give both man and angels a perfect free will to choose love over hate, good over evil, and truth over deception.

> Love is only meaningful and true when there remains a choice not to love.

The Biblical Differences Between Angels and Mankind

According to collective scripture on the subject, there are some basic differences between angels and men. For example:

1. Angels were not born into sin, because they cannot physically reproduce, whereas sin genetically spread from Adam and Eve to all mankind through procreation.
2. Angel's just had a one-time testing, whereas mankind is typically tested many times throughout his natural life.
3. Once angel's fell into their sin, they could not repent (turn from their moral wrongs) and become right with God again, because evidently, they seared what conscience they had. However, mankind sins many times before, and after he becomes right with God and can repent of his sins (if he does not persist in his rebellion to the point of "searing his conscience"). Because angels had a one-time testing, and those angels who failed their test seared their conscience and could not repent, Christ did not die for the sins of angels, but he did die for the sins of men because we can repent.

However, the fact remains that both angels and men have a God-given free will and conscience; therefore, both could be right with God if they chose to. We may certainly never be able to fully understand our God-given free will, why some men ultimately choose good over evil and others choose evil over good. However, according to scripture, our choice between good and evil is a very *necessary test* of our love for God himself (*James 1:12*). But just because we will never fully understand free will or the heart choices of men, this does not mean we should just throw away those things we cannot fully understand in this life. Just because biblical Christianity may certainly go way beyond our reasoning in many respects, we must understand that does not mean it ever goes against it!

Where the Bible goes beyond our human reasoning is exactly where "faith has its place." But if everything we do know about God through his word to us does not go against our reason, then our faith is not at all "blind faith" but rather only a "reasonable faith."

Evil Defined

So just because we may not yet understand just why some men choose evil over good within their God-given free will, does that mean the fault must lie with the free will which God gave man? No, certainly not, because remember, everything which God created (including our free will) was *very good*" (Gen. 1:31). Adam and Eve's free wills were uncorrupted by sin before the first sin, and yet they sinned anyway. And even though our free will (after the fall of man into sin) was undoubtedly affected by sin to some degree, we all still have the basic power of choice which cannot be interfered with. Like our conscience, the free will of man is still basically operational after sin invaded God's perfect creation. Thus, man is still responsible for his bad moral choices! Therefore, the best way to think of "evil" is not that it is "something" created but rather just the lack of something "good."

> If everything we do know about God through his word to us does not go against our reason then, then our faith is not at all "blind faith" but rather only a "reasonable faith."

Just put it this way in your mind: Evil itself is not a plus; it's a minus. Evil can't be created, because evil itself doesn't exist as something created. Evil is not a substance, entity, force, or a being or even anything spiritual. Evil is not the presence of something. According to the Bible, it is defined as the absence or lack of something good. Evil is just the lack of a spiritual good. Similarly, darkness is just the absence of light.

In other words, for man (or angels) to disobey God or rebel against him is for man (or angels) to initiate evil. Even though evil is not a created reality by God, it can have a real manifestation in God's creation but only when God's creatures go against their conscience and choose with their free will to disobey or do something less than moral perfection. According to the Bible then, evil *first* came into existence or manifested in God's perfect creation when Lucifer chose to disobey God with his perfectly good created free will. Then later, Adam and Eve did the same. Therefore, evil itself could simply be defined as "the lack of spiritual good within the free will heart choices of God's creatures when they go against their God given conscience."

> Evil itself could simply be defined as "the lack of spiritual good within the free will heart choices of God's creatures when they go against their God given conscience."

So again, where did evil come from? It simply came from "the lack of spiritual good within the freewill heart choices of God's creation when they go against their God given conscience." But once and for all, we must settle it in our hearts and minds that evil itself did not and could not have come from God who must be absolutely morally perfect in order to be an eternal being. Just as Isaiah 55:8–9 says, God himself is morally "transcendent" from his creation:

> **"For my thoughts are not your thoughts, neither are your ways my ways," saith the Lord. "For as the heavens are higher than the earth, so are my ways higher than your ways, and my thoughts than your thoughts."**

What About Those Verses Which Appear to Teach that God Created Evil?

In verses like Isaiah 45:7 and Amos 3:6, because of a poor translation, it may *appear* that the Bible teaches that *moral evil* is created by or comes from God. However, the original Hebrew words within these verses, if translated correctly, more accurately teach that in his sovereignty (his absolute control of everything), God does *allow Satan to bring evils* upon men to justly test their heart's love for him as it also clearly teaches in Job chapters 1–2 (see also 1 Peter 1:7–8). This is very different than God creating evil or being the source of evil as we will continue to discuss in the following objections. Just because God allows all men to be justly tested with the evil of the demonic realm to a controlled degree because it is actually necessary, this does not make God evil.

For example, in the book of Job, it wasn't God who actually brought the evil upon Job; it was Satan. God just allowed it for a season for the testing of Job's heart. And notice the whole time Job was being tested, God believed Job would pass the tests of his heart's love for God while Satan believed Job would not pass the tests. All throughout scripture, God hopes all men will pass their very necessary heart tests so they will be able to spend eternity with him.

Meanwhile, Satan hopes we will not pass our tests as he is just trying to hurt God and his creation in any evil way he can. There is a huge difference between those two motives. One is loving, and the other is not. Again, just because out of necessity, God allows all men to be justly tested with the evil of the demonic realm to a controlled degree, this does not make God evil.

What About the "Tree of the Knowledge of Good and Evil?"

Some may think that because God created "*the Tree of the Knowledge of Good and Evil*" before Adam and Eve even fell into sin that he must have created evil before Adam and Eve committed evil. However, once again, we must understand that the "*Tree of the Knowledge of Good and Evil*" itself could not have been evil, even though it had the word "*evil*" in its title given by God.

Just because out of necessity, God *allows* all men to be justly tested with

> the evil of the demonic realm to a controlled degree, this does not make God evil.

According to the Bible, not only have we already established that God himself is absolutely morally perfect but that *everything* which God created during creation week was "*very good*" according to Genesis 1:31. According to Genesis 2:9, both the "*Tree of Life*" and the "*Tree of the Knowledge of Good and Evil*" were "*pleasant to the sight and good for food.*" Therefore, there could not have been anything in the actual physical tree of the knowledge of good and evil which would harm man in any way as it was "*good for food.*" And as we've already established, evil itself is just anything that comes from "the lack of spiritual good within the freewill choices of God's creatures when they go against their God-given conscience," and is not anything created by God.

> There could not have been anything in the actual physical Tree of the Knowledge of Good and Evil which would harm man in any way as it was "good for food."

Therefore, the evil which entered God's perfect creation during the fall of man did not come from the "*Tree of the Knowledge of Good and Evil*; it was only something which simply came from "the lack of spiritual good within the freewill choices of Adam and Eve when they went against their God-given conscience." In fact, according to their descriptions, both the "*Tree of Life*" and the "*Tree of the Knowledge of Good and Evil*" were probably even better than all the other trees within the garden of Eden, because they were set apart from all other trees in the garden and planted in the very middle of the garden with their special purposes (Gen. 2:9). Therefore, the only thing which could have made the "*Tree of the Knowledge of Good and Evil*" as such was the fact that it was the only tree in the entire garden upon which God had placed a restriction. God "*commanded*" Adam and Eve *not to touch it or eat from it* (Gen. 2:16–17). This and only this is what made the "*Tree of the Knowledge of Good and Evil*" as such.

For true loving relationship with God, Adam and Eve must be free to reject their relationship with God, just as it is still true for all mankind today. And the minor restriction imposed upon Adam and Eve with the "*Tree of the Knowledge of Good and Evil*" was a very fair, simple, and straightforward test of their love for God. It was the only tree within the entire garden they could not touch or eat from among the many other beautiful and delicious fruit-bearing trees.

Just because of God's restriction, it was the only tree which had the potential to reveal "the lack of spiritual good within the freewill choices of Adam and Eve." Only when Adam and Eve first disobeyed God did they even know what evil was, and this was the only tree which could bring about that knowledge, because *it was the only tree which had the potential for disobedience through the breaking of God's restriction or law.* Once man disobeyed God, he had then essentially learned how to disobey God in virtually everything that was morally good. And, of course, history has shown that to be true, and that is why the "*Tree of the Knowledge of Good and Evil*" had the potential to reveal *all manner of evil* to man. However, there was nothing evil about the tree itself, and God probably could have used any given tree in the garden and called it the "*Tree of the Knowledge of Good and Evil*" as long as he placed that same simple restriction on it.

But Did the Fact that God Had "Evil" in the Title of "Tree of the Knowledge of Good and Evil" Actually Help Adam and Eve to Fall into Evil?

As we have already referred to God's perfect foreknowledge of all man's freewill choices, perhaps the word *evil* in the title of the "*Tree of the Knowledge of Good and Evil*" was a general title which encompassed God's foreknowledge of Adam and Eve's fall into sin before they actually committed evil by disobeying him. Because, let's face it, it was no surprise to God when Adam and Eve fell into sin as he had to have known it would happen in his perfect foreknowledge of the future.

Obviously Adam and Eve did know all about "*good*" before they ate from the "*Tree of the Knowledge of Good and Evil*," because everything which God had created was "*very good*" (Gen. 1:31). But we must remember that neither Adam nor Eve really knew what evil or sin even was before the very first time they disobeyed God.

However, according to Genesis 2:16–17, they did know that the word *evil* within the title of the "*Tree of the Knowledge of Good and Evil*" was connected to the "*death*" God warned them of in the case of their disobedience, and that it was not a good thing, just because God *pre-warned* them of it. Since God had never warned them before, it is only reasonable to assume that this new word, *evil*, which they knew nothing about was part of the test of their free will. And to be even curious about something which God commanded against was to go against the conscience which God had also given them. Therefore, as long as they loved their creator and did not go against the conscience he had given them, then they would not even be curious about the new word, *evil*, within the title of the "*Tree of the Knowledge of Good and Evil*," which God had warned them not to touch or eat from.

But How Could God Be Absolutely Morally Perfect and yet Have the Foreknowledge of All of Man's Evil Choices?

As we've already discussed, part of God being absolutely morally perfect is the fact that he is also "all-knowing" or "omniscient," which must include his perfect foreknowledge of the freewill choices of men. And obviously, God had the perfect foreknowledge that Adam and Eve would fall into "*evil*" disobedience when he tested their love for him. The fact that God had given the "*Tree of the Knowledge of Good and Evil*" a title with the word *evil* in it, even before Adam and Eve actually committed any evil simply revealed God's foreknowledge of evil, which he knew would enter his perfect creation through Adam and Eve's disobedience.

But does God's foreknowledge of man's evil choices make God himself evil? No, not at all. In Psalm 5:4, it teaches us that "*evil shall not dwell with God.*" But obviously, God can know all about evil

274

before and after man chooses it (because he is all-knowing) and not be evil himself as the evil did not originate from him but the freewill choices of his creation when they go directly against the conscience he had given them.

If God Tells Man Ahead of Time that He Will Sin, Does that Actually Help Cause that Man to Sin?

While this is an interesting question, the technical answer must again be no, if man has a God-given free will and conscience which really cannot be controlled by an outside influence. In the Gospels, we read of Jesus telling his disciple Peter that he will deny him three times, just before a rooster crowed twice (Mark 14:30). So the question is, when Jesus told Peter ahead of time that he would deny him, did Jesus then actually help Peter to deny him just because he told Peter he would? Not at all, simply because no one can make a man do anything against his free will and conscience—not even God.

That's the whole point of our God-created free will! Also, how could a perfect God possibly judge man for sinning if he influenced him in any way to do it? It just doesn't make any biblical sense whatsoever. However, the fact that no one can make a man do anything against his own will (not even the Devil) is probably more proven than anything in human history. And if we are talking "influence," if anything, Christ's prediction that Peter would deny him would have set Peter on his guard and influenced Peter to confess that he knew Christ, especially since Jesus foretold that Peter would deny him right in front of the other disciples. And this is evident from Peter's response to Christ as Peter immediately insisted that he would never deny him or be offended of him (Mark 26:33,35).

> If anything, Christ's prediction that Peter would deny him would have set Peter on his guard and influenced Peter to confess that he knew Christ...

Man Is Responsible for His Own
Consistent Moral Choices, Not God

All throughout scripture, the Bible teaches that man is responsible, because he has freewill choices to make and will be judged some day for those choices. We must understand that if God himself ultimately interfered with our moral freewill choices, it would make absolutely no sense for him to judge us; not to mention, he'd compromise his own perfect loving character in the process. We must once and for all understand that man is responsible for his *own* choices, not God. For example, in Joshua 24:15, Joshua says to the nation of Israel, "*Choose this day whom you will serve.*" In Genesis 4:7, God says to Cain who murdered his brother Abel:

If you do well, will you not be accepted? And if
you do not do well, sin is crouching at the door;
its desire is for you, but you must master it.

Other examples within Scripture indicate that God will give men what they are continually bent on choosing, be it bad or good. Psalm 37:4 teaches us that if we "*delight ourselves in the Lord, he will give us the desires of our heart.*" However, passages like 2 Thessalonians 2:10–12, Proverbs 17:11, and 1 Kings 22:1–28 teach us that if one continually rejects the truth of God, then God will actually send them the strong deception they really want by way of deceiving demonic spirits.

In other words, if we continually rebel against the truth of God, whatever our hearts choose and really want, God will eventually give it to us as again, he really cannot ultimately interfere with our consistent freewill choices and remain loving himself. And the list goes on of similar verses which clearly teach we are responsible for our moral freewill choices, such as Romans 8:13–14, Galatians 6:7–8, etc. So from all collective scripture, we know that it is simply impossible for God, who is perfect, to interfere with the moral freewill choices of man and actually cause us to sin against him or not sin against him in any way. As James 1:13–14 clearly teaches:

> **Let no man say when he is tempted, "I am tempted by God:" for God cannot be tempted with evil, neither tempteth he any man. But every man is tempted, when he is drawn away of his own lust, and enticed.**

However, while God may not interfere in the overall consistent freewill moral choices of men, in his love, he does intervene in the overall affairs of men just to preserve and love his own creation.

So even though God does not interfere in the moral freewill choices of man, does that mean God does not have any influence in the affairs of men at all? Obviously not. First of all, you were born without a choice and put on an awesome planet called earth. Actually, there are many such things which man does not have a choice in. We have to breathe air. Human males and females must reproduce to preserve the human race. The list goes on—you get the idea.

Yes, according to scripture, even though God cannot and will not actually cause men to make good or bad moral choices, he still has his just and loving influence in the lives of men for the loving preservation of the human race. Just for some examples, if God did not have any influence at all in the human race, which overrides the freewill choices of men, he would:

1. Not indwell all believers in Christ with his Spirit to help them live good and godly lives (Romans 8:1–11).
2. Not stop evil men influenced by the demonic realm from taking over the world and destroying mankind (Job Chapters 1 and 2; 1 Corinthians 10:13).
3. Not stop the demonic realm from killing off mankind in an instant.
4. Not keep all the planets in their basic alignment so as to preserve all life on earth.

However, please notice that all of these major influences do have an obvious motive of love on the part of God. And there are even some scriptures which indicate that God actually has influence in the very heart of man as well for his same loving purposes of preserving the human race.

For example, Proverbs 21:1 talks about God's influence in the hearts of national rulers which says, "The king's heart is in the hand of the Lord, as the rivers of water, he turns it wherever he wills" (see also Ezra 6:22). But again, based on collective scripture which touches upon this subject, the evidence shows that ultimately, God gives mankind just what his heart is consistently bent on—be it good or bad.

Another example is how God worked in the heart of the Pharaoh of Egypt during the time Moses delivered his people from him. More than one place in the book of Exodus, it does say "*the Lord hardened Pharaoh's heart*" (Exodus 7:3 and Exodus 10:1).

> Based on the collective scripture of God's word which touches upon this subject, the evidence shows that ultimately, God gives mankind just what his heart is consistently bent on—be it good or bad.

But scripture also says in several places that Pharaoh hardened his own heart against God as well (Exodus 7:23, 8:15,19,32). So when we consider all scripture on this matter, God just gave Pharaoh what he knew his heart continually wanted, and when Pharaoh's heart was hardened, it was all because Pharaoh "*sinned*" by rejecting the truth of God first (see Exodus 9:34).

Let's face it; long before Moses set the Israelites free, the Pharaoh of Egypt did not at all believe in the Hebrew God of the Bible; he believed in the idols of Egypt! And because he rejected the truth of God *first*, then God gave him over to strong deception, just like it teaches in 2 Thessalonians 2:1–12. Thus, there is absolutely no compromise of God's perfect character involved. It's not like God just said for no reason—"I think I'll just harden the Pharaoh's heart!" Nor does God role dice in heaven to decide his dealings with men. We must understand once and for all that God ultimately goes by our continual heart choices to determine his own influence with men, and he also has his needed influence in the hearts of men with a pure loving motive.

Fulfilled Bible Prophecy Had to Involve God's Perfect Foreknowledge of the Freewill Choices of Many Men

As we've already mentioned in the introduction of this book, there are about 2,500 predictions of the future which God made throughout his word, which in most cases involve the freewill choices of many men. And all but 20 percent of them have come to pass, just as God foretold in his Word to us.

For example, God foretold through the prophet Daniel the last three world-dominating empires, which came into power (the Medo-Persian empire, the Greek empire, and the Roman empire) in their exact sequence hundreds of years in advance. Even though those prophecies involved millions of moral freewill human choices, scripture indicates that they were also brought about by God as he does shape even basic history to his will by working in the hearts of men.

In Daniel 2:21, it says that God *"removes kings and sets up kings."* And in Psalm 75:7, it teaches us that God essentially promotes or demotes all men, whether they be kings or not! But again, according to collective scripture, God's motive is always love, and his loving mercy sometimes is to *not* give us what we want, just like a parent with their children.

However, ultimately, even in all his loving influence to retard evil, he basically does not interfere in the overall moral freewill choices of mankind at the same time. Again, this is because mankind during his natural state is in a needed time of testing. When it comes to God's dealings with men, God has largely chosen to ultimately make his influence with men based upon man's consistent freewill choices. And when he does so, we must once and for all understand that he always does it in such a way which never compromises any aspect of his perfect loving character in the process.

The additional following scriptures also reveal that many times, God in his mercy does actively bring about his own plans when the plans of man are not conducive to his life and love. Yes, God does not always let man have what he wants. If he always did, perhaps we would have destroyed ourselves long ago. For example, in Proverbs 19:21, it says:

> **Many are the plans in the mind of man, but it is the purpose of the Lord which shall be established.**

In John 3:27, it says:

> **A man can receive nothing, except it be given him from heaven.**

However, if our choices as believers in Christ are conducive to the life and love of God, then scripture indicates that God will give us what we ask of him. Proverbs 16:1–3 says:

> **The plans of the mind belong to man, but the answer of the tongue is from the Lord. All the ways of a man are pure in his own eyes, but the Lord weighs the spirit. Commit your work to the Lord, and your plans will be established.**

1 John 5:14 says:

> **And this is the confidence that we have in him, that, if we ask anything according to his will, he hears us. And if we know that he hears us, whatsoever we ask, we know that we have the petitions that we desired of him.**

But If God's Influence and Dealings with Men Ultimately Revolve Around the Moral Freewill Choices of Men, Doesn't that Make Man in Control and Compromise the Total Sovereignty of God?

The answer is "certainly not," any more than it would compromise a parent's complete authority over their children, just because they are allowing their children to make their own decisions to some degree and learn from their mistakes! Similarly, just because God has allowed man to have moral freewill choices, it certainly does not nullify his complete sovereignty. Let's face it; just because we have free will, there is certainly a God-given limit to our God given free will as well. For example, we could not become God, even if we chose to. Nor could most of us be the US president, even if we chose to. In fact, the higher up in authority you go, the less power men have to bring about their own desires.

In other words, God's sovereignty is not at all threatened by the very limited freewill choices he gave us. Trust me, God is still completely in control of every single molecule of his own creation (see Colossians 1:17). And just like he gave the oceans a limit to their power when they fall upon the beach, God also gave mankind a reasonable limit to the power he has exercising his free will.

We must understand that right now, in this stage of God's prophetic program for man, God's dealings with us do mainly revolve around our choices and not his, simply because we are the only ones who need to be tested and have something to learn! God already knows he loves us, because he's perfect. But right now, it is our love for him which he is testing, simply *because it is absolutely necessary*. In his awesome love, God has decided to focus on mankind, his recent creation. And this is just as reasonable as a married couple focusing on the needs of their children as they bring them up in the world.

But just why an absolutely perfect God would even want anything to do with us, much less offer us his awesome eternal life when we often hurt him and break his moral standards is, of course, beyond our comprehension. But we sure can be glad he does! However, just because God has been focused on the needs of his own creation and, in his love, granted us limited power of freewill choice, it certainly does not at all mean that he's compromised his total sovereignty in doing so.

> God already knows he loves us, because he's perfect. But right now, it is our love for God which is being tested, because it is absolutely necessary.

If a Group of Men Believe Strong Enough that Another Group of Men Will Do or Not Do Something, Do They Actually Cause It to Happen?

Even those who don't yet believe in Christ can see that within the world today, the stage is being largely set for the book of Revelation to unfold. For example, since everything is going "global" with the aid of computer technologies, they can easily see that a one-world government controlled by an Antichrist is becoming more realistic with each passing day. In fact, many people become Bible-believing Christians, simply because they can plainly see the accurate foreknowledge of God coming to pass within Bible prophecy, even 2,000 years after the book of Revelation was written! However, though it seems rather absurd, some non-Christians will actually accuse Bible-believing Christians of somehow causing the book of Revelation to unfold, just because they really "believe" it will take place. But, obviously, this unrealistic notion is rather ridiculous.

Most Bible prophecies involve the freewill choices of many other men and in many cases the freewill choices of those who do not even believe in God or the Bible. But obviously, no man can control the freewill choices of other men and make Bible prophecy come true, just because they strongly "believe" it will come true. God himself only knows what will happen, simply because he has perfect foreknowledge of what all men will choose to do or not do. Not to mention, he has his needed influence, which again is based upon what men will choose. Besides, if Bible-believing Christians are actually causing the book of Revelation to unfold in the world just by strongly believing it will happen, then how do you explain the lack of opposite influence from the many more non-Christians who strongly do not "believe" that the book of Revelation will take place?

If Bible-believing Christians are actually causing the book of Revelation to unfold just by strongly believing it will happen, then how do you explain the lack of opposite influence from the many more non-Christians who strongly do not "believe" that the book of Revelation will take place?

Conclusion

Because "evil" itself is best defined as "the lack of spiritual good within the freewill choices of God's creatures, when they go against their God-given conscience," it is not even a "created" thing. Nor could it be a thing created by God, for he himself is both perfect and eternal and perfectly created all things. Therefore, as we have already mentioned, the simple truth is that God tempts no man and that "*every man is tempted when he is drawn away of his own lust, and enticed*" (James 1:13–14).

While some men wait for our perfect creator to take responsibility for all the sin and evil in the world, he continues to wait for each one of us to be honest enough with ourselves to admit that it was sinful man who destroyed his perfect creation with evil. And ironically, when we blame our perfect creator for the world's evil, which only mankind himself is responsible for, it is just more of that same sin and rebellion against him!

If you don't yet know Christ as your personal Lord and Savior, a new life and far better future is just waiting for you to *choose* it. If you'd like to finally be part of the solution to all the evil in the world and do not wish any longer to be a part of the *basic* problem, then I invite you to just take that first small step of faith by sincerely praying the prayer of salvation located at the end of this book. No matter what your past is like, God who is only the source of all that is good, loves you and sincerely wants you to be a part of His awesome eternal kingdom where there will literally be no more evil, pain, nor human suffering for all eternity (Revelation 21:4).

> **Jesus said, "I am the resurrection and the life. He who believes in me, will live even though he dies; and whoever lives and believes in me will never die..." (John 11:25–26)**

OBJECTION 19

I'm a Good Person, and I've Done the Best I Can

If you were to walk down the street and just ask people if they believed they were basically "good," most people would probably say "yes." And those that would say "yes" would probably also say that the whole human race (minus the "Hitlers," of course) is also basically "good" as well. Of course, all of us are capable of "doing some good things," but is that really the same thing as "being basically good?" And really, anyone can say or even "believe" they are basically "good," but does that just automatically make it true? It may even make us feel good about our lives just to believe we are "a good person." But are the feelings of man always in line with reality? And whose standards would we use to measure "goodness" or "evil" for that matter anyway?

Well, it has been said that if you let the students grade their own papers, they will get "good" grades every time! But the simple truth is only the teacher is qualified to grade the students. Similarly, if we are our only judge, then we too will just compare ourselves with the murderers, thieves, and gutter drunks and believe afterward that we are basically "good."

But really, isn't "being good" a little more involved than just not being as bad as the murderers, thieves, and gutter drunks of society? How then do we determine just how "good" a person has to be in order to satisfy the true definition of "goodness?" What does the word *goodness* really mean anyway? Well, as we have already pointed out, many times man's definition of "goodness" can be quite far from moral perfection.

But to get to the real definition, let's start with the actual word itself. Where did our modern English word *good* even come from? Some etymologists may try to assert that our English word *God* and our English word *goodness* are totally unrelated and have nothing at all to do with each other. However, within Klein's *A Comprehensive Etymological Dictionary of the English Language*, it can be found that *goodness* used in the sense of "kind" or "benevolent" during the mid-fourteenth century was, in fact, a reference to either persons or God.[36] Like many of our other English words, their spellings aren't nearly the same because of mere coincidence. And that's why when you look up the word *goodness* in some of our modern dictionaries, it will define it by saying something like "moral excellence," or even a "substitution for God" himself!

When someone says with surprise, "Oh my goodness!" it is essentially the very same as saying "Oh my God!" simply because in the biblical understanding, God himself is morally perfect and the only source of all true goodness. So when talking about "goodness," if we are talking about the "goodness" of God, and not man's compromised definition of goodness, this does indeed connect it to "moral excellence" or "moral perfection."

> When you look up the word *goodness* in our modern dictionary, it will define it by saying something like "moral excellence" or even a "substitution for God" himself!

Yes, many may truly believe they are a "good person," because they don't rob banks or murder people; however, it is for this very reason that many may not even see their need for Christ, their very own creator and savior. After all, if they are basically "good," what do they need to be "saved" from? And if one doesn't see that he has a terminal sickness, why would he even see his need for a doctor? And

---

[36] Klein, Dr. Ernest. *Klein's A Comprehensive Etymological Dictionary of the English Language.* Amsterdam, London, New York: Elsevier Publishing Company. 1966

this is exactly why it is quite critical indeed to understand what true "goodness" even is.

Is Any Man Really Good?

Yes, we can use our own compromised definition of "goodness" to judge ourselves if we want to, but unless we can stand in the mirror and honestly say we created ourselves, it may be as meaningless as the student grading his own paper by his own compromised standards. If one doesn't use the actual "morally perfect" definition for "goodness," which came from the word *God*, then we are simply left with a whole barrage of man's opinions which will vary greatly from one another in their degrees of moral perfection. And who's to say which "less than perfect" definition for the word *goodness* is the right one?

Once the "compromised definition" door is opened for this word, *goodness*, there is really no way to arrive at the truth of what our word *goodness* really means. In fact, one compromised opinion of what "goodness" means is just as meaningless as any another! However, when we understand where our word *good* actually came from, and that it is tied directly into the very character of God himself who is morally perfect, then this gives us the true moral standards to measure our life by in order to determine just how "good" we truly are.

The Outer Life of Man

Mere outward "Religion" or "Humanism" may say you are good if:

- You don't steal;
- You help people;
- You don't swear or cuss;
- You're a faithful church member;
- You don't smoke, chew snuff, drink, or do drugs;
- You read the Bible;
- You don't physically hurt people;
- You pray (or meditate);
- You don't commit adultery or fornication;

- You are responsible with money;
- You don't gamble;
- You keep a good job;
- You don't watch bad movies;
- You give money to church or other charities;
- You don't set fires to people's property;
- You sing in your church choir;
- You don't cheat on your taxes;
- You pray for others;
- You don't speed;
- You are a hard worker;
- You don't argue with your spouse;
- You *try* to get along with everyone;
- You don't agree with abortion;
- You like yourself;
- You do the best you can.

The Heart of Man

However, while God's standards in the Bible for being "good" may definitely include many of the standards of mere outward "religion" or "humanism," they clearly go far beyond them into the heart of man, teaching us that God ultimately looks at the heart, not just the outward appearance of a man's life (1 Samuel 16:7). And this is exactly why the Bible has always taught that only God himself is truly "good" (Matthew 19:17).

Yes, man may be capable of doing good things outwardly, but that is quite different than being pure of heart like God with good motives all the time. As history has proven over and over again, mankind (unlike God) is also capable of much evil as well. And if so, just where does his evil come from?

Well, we just answered that in our last Objection 18. Technically, even Satan can do outwardly good things and actually does with the evil motive to deceive men away from God. But of course, he is not good in his heart, because his motives are always evil. My point is that mankind definitely has an inborn sin nature that is against the very goodness of God, and his motives are also most often selfish, even when doing good things outwardly.

> While God's standards for being "good" may definitely include those of mere outward "religion" or "humanism"... God ultimately looks at the heart, not just the outward appearance of a man's life.

The "heart of the issue" is that you and I are "good" only if we:

- Never love some people more than others (James 2:9);
- Always love your enemies (Matthew 5:44);
- Never boast (1 Corinthians 13:4);
- Always love others as our self (Matthew 7:12);
- Never lie to others or our self (Revelation 21:8);
- Are always gentle and kind to others (Galatians 5:22–23);
- Never lust (Matthew 5:28);
- Are always completely humble (1 Peter 5:6);
- Never steal (includes over extending break time at work; Exodus 20:15);
- Always have complete self-control from all temptation (2 Peter 1:6);
- Never speak anything evil (Ephesians 4:31);
- Always help others when you have the opportunity and means (Galatians 6:10);
- Never gossip or speak evil of others (James 4:11);
- Always forgive those who hurt you immediately (Matthew 6:14);
- Are never rude or irritable in any situation (1 Corinthians 13:5);
- Always show perfect honor to your parents (Exodus 20:12);
- Never look down on (or judge) others (Matthew 7:1);
- Always thank God in all circumstances (1 Thessalonians 5:18);

- Never complain to God or others about anything (Jude vs. 16);
- Always do everything, having faith in God (Romans 14:23);
- Never doubt God or his promises (Luke 12:29);
- Always trust God perfectly in your sufferings (1 Peter 4:19);
- Never get angry without a true cause (Matthew 5:22);
- Always love God with all your heart, mind, body, and soul (Matthew 22:37).

Yes, indeed, according to this list, which of course is only a partial list, we can all easily see that only God himself is able to keep all his own perfect standards, just as the Bible has always taught us (Luke 18:19; 2 Corinthians 5:21; 1 Peter 2:22)! You see, only when we start to compare ourselves with God and not just murders do we begin to see our true sinful condition. As Romans 3:23 states:

> **For all have sinned, and come short of the glory of God.**

Many other scriptures of God's word also just confirm this basic truth:

> **Who can say, I have made my heart clean? I am pure from my sin? (Proverbs 20:9)**

> **The heart is deceitful above all things, and desperately wicked... (Jeremiah 17:9)**

In fact, the collective scriptures of God's word teach us that all men are actually born with a sin nature which was inherited from Adam:

> **[m]an is born into trouble as the sparks fly upward. (Job 5:7)**

> **Wherefore, as by one man sin entered into the world, and death by sin; and so death**

passed upon all men, for all have sinned. (Romans 5:12)

And so not only can no man come close to keeping the perfect moral standards of God, but whenever man even tries to earn a right standing with God by *trying* to keep his moral standards, he just shows God more of his sin, because he cannot even come close to doing it, just as Romans 3:20 states:

Therefore by the deeds of the law (our efforts to live God's perfect standards) there shall be no flesh justified (made right with God): for by the law (of God's standards) comes the knowledge of sin.

Since I've Done the Best I Could in My Life, Why Would a Loving God Reject that and Deny Me His Salvation?

It is certainly commendable that you are trying very hard to do what is right in your life. So many people have stopped doing their best and have, for the most part, settled for being far less than they could be. However, many who may attempt to obtain the eternal salvation of God through their own efforts (either religiously or through plain humanism) simply fail to understand *the absolute perfection of God and his perfect moral standards* described throughout his word. And even at the end of their whole life of trying to please God by being the very "best person" they could be, they still *cannot be sure* of their eternal destiny, simply because deep down, they know how short they really do fall from all God's perfect moral standards.

If you really want to be a "good person," you must first be *honest* with the fact that you are *not good* and only God alone is (Matthew 19:17)! Then at least God's goodness can be *given* to you through Christ, and you will have the truth, even though you may not be able to live it perfectly. But those who don't even know Christ and still insist that they are good do not even have the truth which they live so imperfectly.

> If you really want to be a "good person," you must first be *honest* with the fact that you are not good and only God alone is. Then at least God's goodness can be *given* to you through Christ and you will have the truth even though you may not be able to live it perfectly.

You see, even if you were a very good swimmer, you still could not swim across the Pacific Ocean by yourself, unaided! You might make it further than many because you are a good swimmer, but let's be *honest*, your "best" would simply not be even close to good enough. Similarly, this is just the way it is when we try to earn the eternal salvation of God Almighty through our own very imperfect merits. However, the moral gap between us and our perfect creator is even much wider than any earthly ocean!

The above list of perfect moral standards could be looked at as the great spiritual ocean some are attempting to swim across. And this is exactly why the Bible teaches that we all need salvation through Jesus, and there is absolutely no hope of eternal life without him! When Christ was asked by his disciples in Luke 13:24 just how many would make it into his eternal kingdom, he responded by saying:

> **Strive to enter in at the strait gate: for many, I say unto you, will seek to enter in (through their own means) and shall not be able.**

We must understand that God is perfect love, and if he's offered us no other way to get into his eternal kingdom other than through his Son, then there simply is no other way possible. He loves you very much, enough to tell you the truth of your true spiritual condition way ahead of time so you are not deceived and can be with him for all eternity. Like many other things in life, unless we are in perfect alignment with the correct solution to a problem, we can try as many other things as we want, but we will never get the victory we need.

When you are attempting to open your house door with a key when it is twenty below zero outside, within the whole surface area of the outside of your house, there is only one small hole which will allow you safe passage to the inside of your nice warm home. If you compare that one small key hole with all the other outside surface area of your whole house, you can surely conclude that life-giving "truth" by definition is most of the time *very narrow,* whether we like that reality or not! And because he loves us, with no games, our loving creator has told us plainly that Jesus himself is, in fact, the only narrow door to the eternal life of almighty God (John 10:9).

> Many who may attempt to obtain the eternal salvation of God through their own efforts simply fail to understand the absolute perfection of God and his perfect moral standards described throughout his Word.

Other Obvious Examples of Man's True Moral Condition

1. The selfish inborn nature of children—For a simpler example of all mankind being born into moral failure and not basic "goodness," let's look at children who have not yet even had the opportunity to be corrupted by the world's evil. When observing all children growing up from six months on, it is a constant battle for parents to teach their children just how to "be good." But what parent has ever had to teach their children how to misbehave or be selfish? No parent, because everyone knows that bad or selfish behavior just comes inherently natural for all kids! Younger children must always be taught to share their toys but never need to be taught how to be selfish! If man was "basically

good" as some false religions or belief systems assert, this my friend, would certainly not be the case.

2. The basic need for human government—Another major obvious indication that man is not "basically good" is the fact that "governments" have always been a necessity as far back as recorded history of larger populations takes us. Granted, some smaller "tribes" of people haven't had big political governments, but nevertheless, they've had their own smaller form of government, even if it consisted of one "chief" to maintain order in their tribe.

James Madison, the fourth President of the United States said that if men were "angels" (referring to good angels), governments would not be necessary. Other obvious indications that man struggles constantly with a basic destructive sin nature is the fact that prisons today are just as full as they have ever been. No modern government that I'm aware of has suddenly announced that the need for their prisons is becoming obsolete because their society "is morally *improving,* just because men are learning from their mistakes and evolving into a better race."

If men were angels, governments would not be necessary.

3. The "rotten fruit" of war—The many wars of history are just one more obvious example of man's immorality which we could cite, verifying that man has a serious *sin* problem. Why some religions or "humanistic belief systems" would even attempt to maintain that mankind is basically good when it is all we can do to not blow the whole world up with nuclear missiles is really beyond comprehension when you just think about it for a moment!

Again, basic honesty is the sacred key to arriving at the truth. Some may have prematurely thought that just because no nation has pushed any nuclear war head buttons yet that this somehow must indicate that man is "morally improving." However, since it has only been just decades since the last world

war which wiped out close to 100 million people, such a conclusion may be a bit premature indeed. Since all governments
know the awful repercussions of nuclear war, our refraining
from it may not so much be "moral maturity" as it is just pure
selfish survival so far!

Now, if all mankind started to actually disarm and get rid of
all our nuclear warhead missiles, then we might possibly believe
man was having a real change of heart and "morally improving."
However, the real honest truth is not only that just more nations
are being "armed to the teeth" with nuclear warheads every year,
but that just about every weapon which man has devised for war
in history, he has thoroughly used! So to believe we will also end
up using our nuclear warheads is not at all unreasonable, going
by our honest track record.

4. Abortion also strongly indicates man is not basically good.
    Abortion itself is also the taking of human life. According to the
    "California Prolife Council," from 1973 to 1997, approximately
    35 million human lives have been taken through abortion, and
    more human lives are taken through abortion every year (1.5
    million) than through all the major American fought wars com-
    bined (total American war deaths being 1,043,569)!

    Ever since the US Government made abortions legal, many
    have debated whether or not abortion was, in fact, "murder." But
    if, in fact, the brain waves of a human fetus can be measured or
    their hearts are, in fact, beating (as is the case with most aborted
    babies), then honestly, why isn't it considered the "taking of a
    human life?" Especially when that aborted baby would have in
    almost all cases been normally born into the world and become
    a person just like you and me had they not been aborted! As the
    saying goes, "Those who are for abortion would not even be
    here if their mothers believed as they do. Shouldn't a family be
    more united than that?"

5. All the obvious false "belief systems" and "religions" in the world
    most certainly confirm that mankind is plagued with moral
    failure. As we discuss more thoroughly in Objection 41, after
    comparing all the obvious *conflicting* doctrines of all the basic

different religions in the world, simple logic would dictate that only *one of them* can reasonably be the truth. But is it that narrow truth which is so shocking? Or is it all the lies and deception of all the false religions which are so shocking? We all know in our conscience that ultimately, the truth will always "give mankind life" and not harm; simply because when we are told the truth, it always helps us in some way in the big picture of things. But when we are deceived or lied to, it always leaves a wake of destruction, pain, or harm and does not give us the life we need.

Many will repeat the old saying that only "the truth hurts." But is it really the truth itself which hurts us or only the lies and deception which the truth just exposes? For example, when someone finds out the truth of their spouse cheating on them, was it really that "truth" which hurt them? Or was it really the lies and deception of their spouse? Some may have "run from the truth" their whole life, simply because they've heard that "the truth hurts." But really, it's only lies and deception they should be afraid of, because really, it is only lies and deception which hurt us. However, the truth never does hurt us as it just sheds light on the lies and deception.

> Many will repeat the old saying that "the truth hurts." But is it really the truth itself which hurts us or only the lies and deception which the truth just exposes?

And going by the fact that all the different religions in the world but one must be wrong according to simple reasoning because all their basic doctrines conflict with each other, what does that in itself *honestly* say about the true moral condition of all men adhering to all the false religions in the world? If all religions out there but one cannot be truly representative of reality as all of their adherents dogmatically claim, then there is certainly more going on than mankind just being "imperfect." At some point, we must realize that mankind as a whole must have a major problem with moral failure within all the false religions of the world, not just "mere imperfection." In fact, there are only so many realistic possibilities for those who just continue to dogmatically adhere to their false belief systems. Please consider the following:

1. They may be genuinely ignorant—Yes, admittedly, there is a real place to be "ignorant" in this life. But usually, this ignorant stage of life is more prominent between ages one and twelve for most people who do not have a mental handicap of some kind. Why? Simply because the root word of *ignorance* is *ignore* and as one gets older, it is virtually impossible not to collect more information about what is supportive of reality and what is not. And reasonably, the more information supportive of reality we obtain, then the more accountable we become to believe the truth; at least, that is what any good judge in a court hearing would rule.

    You see, even if we choose to just "ignore" the truth we encounter and "believe in nothing," that in itself is a moral failure. It may be a moral failure of "omission" (not doing something one should do) rather than "commission" (doing something which one should not do); but nevertheless, it is a moral failure. For example, if you were drowning, and someone walking by just "ignored" a life preserver which they could easily throw out to you, would you not think it morally wrong, even though that person was not at all to blame for you drowning and has their own life to live? Similarly, as it concerns adults of society, is it not just as morally wrong when they constantly ignore the spiritual truth which could help themselves and others who are drowning in spiritual deception and getting hurt by it?

    For example, if a parent constantly ignored the spiritual truth they encountered just because "it is their life," to say it would not affect their children in a loveless way would be rather skewed and unrealistic. No parent, when you think about it, is "privileged" enough to just believe anything they want to spiritually, just because "it is their life." The truth is, they are morally responsible to believe in the spiritual truth if, in fact, their spiritual beliefs have a basic impact on the spiritual well-being of their children (not to mention their eternal destiny!). However, if you think about it, if a parent is always being dishonest with themselves about the spiritual truth they encounter, then they would also be quite capable of being dishonest about the fact that their lack of spiritual convictions have a harmful effect on their family members as well.

The point is that even mere "ignorance" in the many cases when adults choose to just keep "ignoring" the spiritual truth they encounter is also a serious moral failure which really does negatively affect them and everyone in their lives. Modern dictionary definitions for the word *ignorant* typically do not attach any moral failure to the word. However, they strangely treat its root word, *ignore*, a bit different. They define ignorance by saying it's just "lacking knowledge or experience" while they define *ignore* by saying its "intentionally disregarding" something.

While it is technically possible to "intentionally disregard" something and have no moral failure doing it, one must admit that when it comes to purposely ignoring the truth, which helps one's self and others, it must involve moral failure. And this is exactly why the Bible itself has actually attached moral failure to spiritual "ignorance," especially when one has actually encountered the spiritual truth many times and just keeps on ignoring it (Romans 10:3). The Bible refers to this kind of immoral "ignorance" as "willful ignorance" (2 Peter 3:5).

Even though it is "your life," and technically you are not committing any moral failures of "commission" when you just ignore a drowning person, because you are choosing to not do anything "right" in the situation and help that person in need (a moral failure of "omission") when you could, this would be a moral failure for any honest individual.

In the very same way, it becomes a moral failure not to believe in the spiritual truth as well when we encounter it. Just because it may be "your life" and "you can believe what you want," to say your "unwillingness" to believe in the spiritual truth will not affect those you love or even strangers, for that matter, is simply not realistic any more than it is honest. Therefore, we must sensibly conclude that the many millions of adults worldwide who dogmatically adhere to their false belief systems and or religions year after year and continually reject that which they know in their hearts to be the truth are themselves a strong example of the moral failure of mankind.

> Just because it may be "your life" and "you can believe what you want"…to say your "unwillingness" to believe in the spiritual truth will not affect those you love, or even strangers for that matter, is simply not realistic.

2.   Genuine Deception—Yes, like ignorance, there is a real place for "genuine deception." But also like ignorance, the place for it is rather small. All of us can be "tricked for a time" due to the lack of experience, evidence, or information. But even if some, who may be in a false religion, are "genuinely deceived" for a time due to the lack of experience, evidence, or information, they really can't be for very long, if they really want the truth! But when you look at it, most people adhering to false religions generally do so for longer periods of time, which is not exactly a moral "feather in their cap," because it indicates that the lack of experience, evidence, or information is really not their problem. Reasonably then, just what is their problem? Please consider the following real possibilities:

    A.   They are not sincerely searching for the truth. Many in false religions (or humanistic belief systems) may not really be sincerely searching for the truth, simply because they like their life the way it is. However, if you look at such reasons, we must conclude that they are basically "selfish" in nature, because they are not concerned with the "truth" or "what is right," which again can only give man the real life and healing he needs. For example, anyone can just lazily say that Jesus Christ was just some "phony" (and continue to reject biblical Christianity) without giving any substantial honest evidence to back up their claims. But isn't that just like believing bad things about others based on mere hearsay without bothering to get all the honest evidence, especially their side of the story? Therefore, even "not sincerely searching for the truth" while in a false belief system or religion is a moral failure.

B.   They are purposely and consciously running from or pushing away the spiritual truth when they encounter it. In this case, why don't false religion adherents push away the deceptive false doctrines of the belief system they are tangled in if they have the strength to constantly push away the truth? This too is an obvious moral failure. In many cases, the reason some may stay in their deception is simply because there is "something in it for them." For example, parents may want to stay in a false religion, just because of the help and support they might receive from the leadership of that religion. Or children raised in false religions may just want to please their parents because of all the help in life they know they will get from them (financial help, emotional support, etc.).

One has to ask why false religion adherents don't push away the deceptive false doctrines of the belief system they are tangled in if they have the strength to constantly push away the truth?

And aside from pleasing family members for selfish motives, most false religions also have things built into them which naturally appeal to the selfish sin nature in man as well. For example, some attracted to false religions may be just seeking "power" or "importance." Every person is important, and we all need a little bit of power in this life, but obviously, there is a healthy way to get importance and power in this life and an unhealthy way to get it. We all learned this in grade school. Many people will compromise their conscience in what is right just to be "important" or fulfill their inborn need (which we all seem to have) "to belong" to a group. However, this too is moral failure to desperately seek self-importance with the sacrifice of truth.

Money, drugs, sex, and or materialism are also main attractions in many false religions as well. Obviously, it is not wrong to have some money or material things, but when these things become an underlying motive to belong to a false religion, which has clearly compromised the truth, then this too is an obvious moral failure.

For some examples, Islamic suicide bombers are promised seventy virgins awaiting them in heaven if they carry out their destructive task. Mormon beliefs allowed polygamy for many years. Many modern TV preachers have promised money and materialism, just so they can get more money and materialism for themselves. Sadly, they even use Christ or the Bible in their spiritually sick tactics, but if one even bothers to crack the Bible for themselves, they can *easily see* that Christ and his apostles did not teach or live that way! Thus, such people are not at all a reflection of Christ, just themselves.

Aside from these obvious things, even the false doctrines of false religions appeal to many. How could a false doctrine possibly appeal to anyone? Well, the answer can be rather simple. When we carefully consider that man is an "emotional being," who may very well have hidden fears, we then can begin to understand just why anyone could fall for a doctrine which is obviously false if, in fact, they thought it "eased their fears" in some way. And unfortunately, many people make many decisions in life, not because "it is the truth" or "the right thing to do," but just because they may think it "protects their fears," which again is a moral failure.

Upon simple examination, one will find that the *many false doctrines* of many false religions attempt to "protect the fears of man" in some way. However, to compromise the truth just in order to protect one's fears is also an obvious moral failure. The bottom line is that all these shallow reasons for staying in a false religion would also be a moral failure, because if they really loved God and cared about their family, they'd want the truth above all else, simply because that would be the best for their family as well, especially if the eternal salvation of their family members is on the line!

3. Genuine Dishonesty—It is also obvious within the false religions of the world that many of their false religious leaders are knowingly dishonest as well. Money, fame, sex, and materialism have all proven to be the unhealthy motives for the dishonesty of false religious leaders in the past. They claim to love God, but they obviously love those "things" and "power" much more. While such false religious leaders may "play God for a fool," he is not at all "fooled by their play;" and trust me, their "day of reckoning" will come soon enough!

The Inevitable Conclusion of Man's True Moral Condition in Light of All the World's Conflicting Religions

Therefore, any which way one would look at it, when considering all the obvious false belief systems and or religions in the world, our world is a "moral mess;" seeing those adults adhering to them must be a decent chunk of the world's population! To make our basic point of man's immorality even more obvious in light of all the conflicting religions of the world, let's use a quick simple analogy.

If twelve different people who did not even know each other all went to the same play and came back, telling you completely different conflicting stories of what the basic plot of the play was, what could you safely conclude (providing none of them slept through it)? Not only that one or none were correct, but that at least eleven of those twelve people were either:

1. So disinterested in the play that they didn't keep track of its basic plot, even though they were firsthand, completely competent eyewitnesses of the play (which is very hard to believe);

2. Or *purposely dishonest for some selfish motive* (protecting personal fears, wanting money, power, etc.).

In this real sense, just because of the widespread moral failure which must be attached to the adult adherents of all the conflicting false religions of the world, we are once again forced to conclude that the moral condition of man as a whole is not good but sinful, just as the Bible has always taught. However, as we've already discussed, all the different conflicting religions of the world are just one of many indicators that man has a constant "moral failure" problem and is not just "merely imperfect" or just "spiritually evolving" by learning from his mistakes. The basic point here is to permanently establish that in light of the obvious evidence, which we've cited in this objection, man cannot possibly be "basically morally good" to the honest soul.

> Just because of the moral failure which must be attached to the adherents of all the conflicting false religions of the world, we are rather forced to conclude that the moral condition of man is not good.

Why All Sin Must Be Punished

What most people may also fail to realize is that because God himself is *absolutely morally perfect*, all sin (or the compromise of his perfect moral standards) must be justly punished. God himself really does not have a choice in the matter, simply because he cannot go against his own perfect character and must be perfectly just when it comes to our breaking of his many moral standards. You see, sin not only hurts man but actually hurts God as well, and all sin goes directly against God's love. And for this reason, God himself could not and would not tolerate sin in his presence for even one moment where he resides in heaven (see Psalm 5:4; 1 John 1:5; 1 Timothy 6:16).

Added to this reality, the Bible actually teaches us that if we only broke one of God's commands, it would be essentially the very same as breaking them all (James 2:10–11). How can this be?

Simply because all of God's commands, which we break every day, actually represent the pure heart and mind of God who is a person, not merely just some list of do's and don'ts. Therefore, when we break only one of God's commands, it is like someone coming up to you and breaking only one of your fingers! Even though only one of your fingers are broken, it has deeply offended your whole person, simply because your single finger is quite connected to your whole person!

> God himself is so perfect that he cannot live in the presence of any sin for even a moment.

Likewise, if someone came up to you and broke only one of your fingers, would not your relationship with that person be broken right along with your finger? Well, that's the very same way it is with our relationship with God. Even if we were to only break one of his perfect standards during our entire life, our relationship with him would still be broken for all eternity until our relationship with him is restored his way.

So really, according to James 2:10–11, then we all actually break all of God's commands every day! And considering we all actually break many of God's perfect moral standards every day, our relationship with God is irreparably broken many times over every day. And unfortunately, this is exactly why the Bible says that God (who we must remember is absolutely perfect) had to determine that the just punishment for our many sins must be eternal separation from him, in the lake of fire, being punished for our sins day and night forever (Rev. 20:10–14).

Wow. This not only shows us how far we all fall short of God's standards (because we are not even close to his perfect standards), but also just how serious sin is to God. And both of these critical realities are something that many who may try to earn their eternal salvation through their own efforts simply fail to understand.

> When we break only one of God's commands, it is like someone coming up to you and breaking only one of your fingers!

But isn't God merciful? Why can't he just overlook all our sins and forgive us? He can through what his Son did for us on the cross, but we must be forgiven his way and not ours if his perfect justice is to be satisfied. Because he is absolutely perfect, he simply cannot forgive us with the compromise of his own perfect character. And according to his perfectly "just" character, of course, all sin must be justly punished! If, in fact, God just excused all of our many sins against him without his Son taking the just punishment for them, he would actually have to compromise his own perfect character millions of times over and over again to do it.

Would we even respect a human judge in our civil courts who constantly let the guilty go free? Not at all, because more people would just get hurt, and because it goes against love of our fellow man, society would not allow that. And all the more, God who is perfect love simply cannot allow that either. If your family member was murdered, and the judge just let the murderer go free, would you not be enraged? Even if someone stole your car and the judge just let them go free, wouldn't you demand justice? Even if a stranger came up to you and broke only one of your fingers, you would likely want civil justice, would you not? And if we, who are very imperfect, insist on perfect justice when wronged, how much more would God, who is perfect, insist on perfect justice when He is wronged? So the just punishment for our many sins has already been sentenced. However, hang on, because here's the good news…

The Only Exception

Because God is love (1 John 4:8), and his great mercy triumphs over his judgment (James 2:13), God, in His love for us, devised the only plan of salvation possible (without the compromise of his own character) through his Son, Jesus Christ. It miraculously gives everyone an opportunity to be right with him and obtain his eternal salvation, even though we have all fallen so far short of his moral standards (Romans 3:23). Determined to save his much-loved creation (you and me) from eternal destruction, God did something radical. Knowing that all sin had to be justly punished according to his perfect character, God himself decided to actually take the just punishment for all our sins himself!

If we, who are very imperfect, insist on perfect justice when wronged, how much more would God, who is perfect, insist on perfect justice when He is wronged?

Wow. This just shows us how much God must really love us (1 John 3:16)! You see, God loves us because of who he is, even in our sinful state. And this is exactly why God decided to send his Son, Jesus Christ, to earth to die for all our sins on the cross, even though we all hurt him deeply through our sins. Since Christ himself is perfect (1 Peter 2:22) and didn't at all deserve the just punishment of his own fallen creation, *only he alone was qualified* and able to take the punishment for our sins and satisfy the perfect justice of the Father. And all God wants from us now (in order to be right with him) is to just believe in what Jesus did for us on the cross! As John 3:16 says:

For God so loved the world that He gave his one and only Son, that *whoever believes in him* shall not perish, but have eternal life.

> Knowing that all sin had to be justly punished, God himself decided to do something radical and take the just punishment for all our sins upon himself! Wow. This just shows us how much God must really love us!

God himself is, in fact, the only one who can save us from our sins, simply because he is the only one who can keep all his own perfect moral standards. And now that God's own Son has lovingly and humbly taken our just eternal punishment upon himself when he died on the cross, it is easy to see why it is an *absolute insult* in the eyes of God for any man to continue to try to obtain his eternal life through their own efforts apart from believing in what his perfect Son did for them on the cross.

It is like if your neighbor's son died and you went over and just gave them a dollar for the life of their son! What an insult to your neighbor, right? This is why according to the Bible, only those who believe in what Christ did for them on the cross are reconciled with God and have his eternal life. Ephesians 2:8–9 states:

> **For by grace are you saved through faith; and not of yourselves. It is the gift of God, not of works, lest any man should boast.**

Salvation through believing in Christ (what he did for us on the cross which we could not do for ourselves) is so simple that many "hard cases" of humanity completely miss it and continue to try to earn heaven through their own methods and merits, not at all realizing that their own miserable efforts are at best an insult to our perfect creator *(Luke 18:10)*. My friend, it doesn't matter if you've been a faithful church member for fifty years; that cannot begin to save you!

As Jesus said to Nicodemus, an "outwardly good" religious ruler of his day:

[I] tell you the truth, no one can see the kingdom of God unless he is born again. (John 3:3)

We were all, of course, born physically in order to enter a physical world, but what Jesus was saying to Nicodemus is that we must all have a "spiritual birth" as well (being "born again") by simply believing in what Christ did for us on the cross if we are to be right with God and enter his spiritual eternal kingdom. Yes, God is very merciful and does not want to be separated from any of us for all eternity. That's why he offers all men his eternal life as a *free gift* (which cannot be earned in any way) if they just believe in what Christ did for them on the cross. And that's exactly why Psalm 103:10 says:

He does not treat us as our sins deserve or repay us according to our iniquities.

Conclusion

Many in the world today will continue to believe and teach that mankind is basically good and does not even have a "sin nature." However, it is actually impossible to deceive others without first deceiving yourself. The Bible clearly teaches us that our sin nature in and of itself is deceitful and wicked, more than any other thing (Jeremiah 17:9). In fact, one of the very first things it will try to convince you of is that you don't have a sin nature despite all the honest evidence we've just discussed!

Those refusing to admit that they have a sin nature are kind of like someone with the circular problem of not being able to find their glasses because they just can't see well enough. And that's exactly why we all need our perfect creator to give us the basic spiritual vision we need to see his love and truth.

After thirty-five years of being a Christian, I can personally testify that it was God's love which ultimately changed my life for the better. But if I had never given Christ a chance to even reveal himself to me after I was shown his love, then I know I would have never gotten the healing I needed. If you are one who is tired of running from God and you want to personally experience his awesome unconditional healing love for you, I invite you to just take that first small step of faith by sincerely praying the prayer of salvation located at the end of this book. No matter what your past is like, God loves you and sincerely wants you to be a part of his awesome eternal kingdom!

> **Jesus said, "I am the resurrection and the life.
> He who believes in me, will live even though
> he dies; and whoever lives and believes in me
> will never die..." (John 11:25–26)**

OBJECTION 20

Aren't We All Children of God?

Often in the world, especially in cases of prejudice, it is quickly echoed that all men are "children of God." For example, when someone is being practically "partial" toward another due to their race, color, or religion, such discrimination is often met with the defending statement that "we are all children of God." And in a "created" sense, we are indeed all "children of God" in the respect that we are all created equally in the image of God just as the Bible plainly teaches us (Gen. 1:27).

In other words, just because all men are created in God's image, all men should be treated without prejudice or discrimination, and all men should be given the basic respect they are entitled to just because they too are a valuable human being created by God himself. However, this title, "children of God," in a "created" sense should not be confused with the title "children of God" in the "spiritual" sense. For while we are all certainly "created in the image of God" with a conscience and a moral compass that sets us apart from the animal kingdom, the Bible also makes it clear that all men are born into sin as well, which has separated us from our creator (Job 5:7; Isaiah 59:2). As Isaiah 64:6 states:

> **We are all infected and impure with sin. When we display our righteous deeds, they are nothing but filthy rags. Like autumn leaves, we wither and fall, and our sins sweep us away like the wind.**

The title, "children of God" in a "created" sense should not be confused with the title "children of God" in the "spiritual" sense.

And because our sin actually separates us from God, we must be in agreement with God about that sin and what Christ did for us on the cross in order for our spiritual relationship with God to be restored. As God says to us in Isaiah 1:18:

> **Come now, and let us reason together...though your sins be as scarlet, they shall be as white as snow; though they be like crimson, they shall be as wool.**

And other verses such as the following, specifically tell us just how our relationship with God is restored through faith in Christ:

> **For God so loved the world, that he gave his one and only Son (to die on the cross), that whoever believes in him (and what he as God, did for us on the cross) shall not perish, but have eternal life. (John 3:16)**

> **[I]f you confess with your mouth, "Jesus is Lord" (that he is God), and believe in your heart that God raised him from the dead (as God), you will be saved. For it is with your heart that you believe and are justified (made right with God just as if you had never sinned), and it is with your mouth that you confess and are saved. (Romans 10:9–10)**

Conclusion

So until we choose to be reconciled with our creator in this respect *on his terms* by truly believing in what Christ did for us on the cross, we simply cannot claim that we are "children of God," spiritually and "heaven bound," even though we are, of course, still created in his image and "children of God" in the created sense. In fact, before we are born spiritually, by believing in Christ and what he did for us on the cross, God actually refers to us as *"children of wrath,"* simply because until we believe Christ took the punishment for our sins, we are all scheduled to undergo the eternal punishment (or wrath) of God for those sins (John 3:36; Ephesians 2:3).

Additionally, Jesus told the religious Pharisees that were looking to murder him that they were actually children of the devil, simply because they were really serving the devil and not God (John 8:44). And so it is with all men who are not yet right with God through Christ, simply because we cannot actually serve God and live for him until we are first "right with him" on his terms. And if we are *not right with God* and serving him, then we are just serving ourselves and the cause of the devil and his demonic host, whether we realize that fact or not.

And that is exactly why Jesus also told even Nicodemus (whose religious life certainly looked good on the outside) that unless he was born spiritually, he could not see the kingdom of God either (John 3:3). Thus, only when we are born spiritually can we call God our "Father" in the spiritual sense and know we are "his children," obtaining his eternal life (Romans 8:15). Someone once asked Jesus how many will be saved. And Jesus replied:

> **Make every effort to enter through the narrow door (namely Jesus—John 10:9), because many, I tell you, will try to enter (through their own methods) and will not be able. (Luke 13:24)**

And the moment we choose to be right with God on his terms by believing in what Jesus did for us on the cross (that we could not have done for ourselves), the Holy Spirit will come and live inside us and bear witness in our hearts that we are truly *"children of God"* (Romans 8:16). Wouldn't you like to accept God's wonderful invitation of salvation through his Son and know for sure that you too have his complete forgiveness and eternal life? If so, I invite you to just take that first small step of faith by sincerely praying the prayer of salvation located at the end of this book. No matter what your past is like, God loves you and sincerely wants you to be a part of his awesome eternal kingdom!

> **Jesus said, "I am the resurrection and the life. He who believes in me, will live even though he dies; and whoever lives and believes in me will never die..." (John 11:25–26)**

OBJECTION 21

I Don't Believe in Sin

As we already discussed quite thoroughly in Objection 18, sin, evil, and suffering only came into the world through man's sin of disobedience. And according to the Bible, sin is simply defined as the breaking of God's laws or moral standards (Romans 3:20). And as we already discussed quite thoroughly in our previous Objection 19, all of us probably break God's perfect moral standards many times a given day.

While the Bible specifically refers to "*sin*" itself roughly 450 times, it refers to the very concept of sin many more times than that, using different words for it, etc. But what if you still just don't believe in "sin?" Well, I guess we are all privileged enough to choose our own spiritual beliefs, but this doesn't mean they are necessarily connected to reality or that we will avoid the sure consequences for those beliefs should they be false.

For a simple example, there was a time when many sincerely believed the world was flat. But reality itself proved them wrong in time. However, just giving credit where it is due, the Bible has always taught that the world is spherical (see Isaiah 40:22). And ironically, even though the many influential men of the time who sincerely believed the world was flat had full access to the scriptures of God's Holy Word, they still insisted that the world must be flat.

Once I met a street person with long hair and beer breath who was sleeping on my front porch bench. And when I woke him up, he sincerely tried to convince me he was Jesus Christ. Another time, I met a fellow restaurant worker who sincerely tried to convince me that he was actually an angel; he just hadn't gotten his wings yet! But I knew he was no angel and probably just got done watching the Jimmy Stewart movie, *It's a Wonderful Life*.

> We are all privileged enough to choose our own spiritual beliefs...but this doesn't mean they are necessarily connected to reality or that we will avoid the sure consequences for those beliefs should they be false.

Yes, we can all choose to believe anything we wish, but that doesn't necessarily mean our beliefs are connected to reality. And if they are not connected to reality, really, what good are they when we run into reality and we just get hurt?

Similarly, some today actually do not believe that the WWII Holocaust ever really happened and that it was just some big made-up hoax. But try telling that to the relatives of those who really went through it! Talk about man's incredible ability to deny reality! However, for those *honest*, there is plenty of overwhelming honest evidence that the Holocaust really did happen. Millions of eyewitnesses and family members personally testify that it was indeed a very real experience for their close relatives.

Others continue to deny the historical fact that we even landed on the moon, even though many credible people who were a part of us landing Neil Armstrong on the moon are still alive today to testify of its real occurrence. Millions of alcoholics commonly "live in denial" of their drinking problem, and indeed, the list of people flatly denying reality could go on and on for some time...but you probably get the idea.

Mankind in general has always had a decent ability to dishonestly deny reality, even though there's plenty of overwhelming honest evidence to the contrary. But the problem is that when we do, we just continue to hurt ourselves and others, because only by embracing reality can we avoid the pain we often encounter when we deny it.

All the Different Religions in the World Also Show Us Man's Great Ability to Deny Reality

We already know that all the different religions in the world cannot all be right, because they all conflict with each other in their basic beliefs of who God is, who man is, heaven, hell, and how salvation is obtained, etc. In fact, of all the religions in the world, logically, we are rather forced to conclude that only one of them is correct or none of them are correct if they all disagree with each other in their basic beliefs.

For example, just take Darwinian evolution, agnosticism, Hinduism, Islam, New Age movement, and biblical Christianity. Logically, *only one or none* of them could be correct. And this being the case with all the different religions in the world, we can also be sure then that at least all but one is false and not even connected to reality! My point once again is that man is very capable of denying obvious reality, even though there is plenty of honest evidence for it! You mean to say that some people may just dishonestly choose not to believe in certain aspects of reality because that's part of their own sin nature to do so? Yes, all down through recorded history, human nature has often "denied reality" when confronted with it. Therefore, when man, who has a sin nature, does not believe in sin, he is a lot like someone who cannot find their eyeglasses, simply because they can't see well-enough to find them! So what am I saying? I'm saying it is quite possible for some people to actually deny the reality of man's sin, simply because it is part of their own sin nature to do so!

However, the truth is that if you ask most of the human race, they would *easily admit* that there are *all kinds of honest evidence* (which we just discussed in Objection 19) that man has this basic moral problem, which the Bible calls "sin" and that they themselves are very far from the perfect moral standards of God. As we have already mentioned in Objection 19, it is quite easy to see that all babies are born with a sin nature, just as the Bible has always taught (Job 5:7). Some may refuse to call it "sin" and may prefer to call it "moral imperfection." But really, what's the difference?

The Bible also refers to sin as "evil," "transgression," "lawlessness," or "iniquity." But whatever name you give it, the very concept of it is still the same, and all mankind is still born with the basic problem of moral failure and selfishness to the hurt of his fellow man and God.

> It is quite possible for some people to actually deny the reality of man's sin simply because it is part of their own sin nature to do so!

So why get hung-up on terms when the basic concept of what the Bible calls sin has always been undeniably prevalent in the world all throughout recorded human history? And since man's sinful condition on a world scale has just compounded and gotten worse with time, it is pretty tough for honest men to ignore its reality. Especially when there's around thirty to forty wars going on in the world at any given time, and mankind in general has historically always been his own worst enemy! Personally, I have also found that those who flatly deny the reality of "man's sin" often have just been *decently sheltered* from some of sin's harsher consequences. However, it becomes harder and harder to discount the reality of "man's sin" the more one personally experiences its harsh consequences.

For example, those who have gone through wars or tortures (like the Jews during the holocaust), they have a pretty good understanding of "man's sin." They are full believers! All throughout history, we find man capable of denying reality, but that doesn't mean we can just make negative realities disappear simply because we deny their existence. In fact, it is to your full advantage to believe in reality, just as it truly is as quickly as you can, so you can avoid those harsher consequences of just denying it! Those better connected with reality in man's history have always had the advantage of survival, whether it be physical or spiritual. In fact, history has always proven it to be quite dangerous most of the time man denies reality. And the more important the aspect of reality which is denied, the harsher the consequences.

So it is quite to our own advantage to make sure we are connected to reality in our spiritual beliefs and not just denying an unpleasant aspect of it *for purely emotional reasons.* Typically, belief systems such as Darwinian evolution, agnosticism, Hinduism, Buddhism, the New Age movement, and probably more tend to deny the reality of man's sin. But the Bible teaches us that without the acknowledgment of sin, one simply cannot be right with God and have His eternal life! This makes our belief in sin rather critical to say the least!

However, it becomes harder and harder to discount the reality of "man's sin" the more one personally experiences its harsh consequences.

The Strong Evidence for the Effects of Sin in the World Is Abundant

As we've already mentioned, technically, sin is defined as the breaking of God's moral law (Romans 3:20). However, the root of all sin is first doubting God's word to us, and that's why we end up breaking God's laws. This truth is easily seen in the original fall of man when Adam and Eve first doubted God's Word to them before they actually disobeyed God (Genesis 3:1–6). Therefore, evidence for sin in the heart of man is actually as abundant as man's doubt of God's word! And the effects of man's sin after Adam and Eve's disobedience actually manifested in the form of a physical curse upon God's perfect creation. The corruption of that which was perfect can be seen literally everywhere in God's creation all the way on down into the subatomic world. There's what we call the normal, but then there's always the mutation or corruption of the normal called "abnormal."

For some obvious examples, cancer cells are, of course, a corruption of the normal cell. When a person is born with deformities, this too is all part of the effects of man's sin. When a tornado rips through the countryside and leaves a wake of destruction behind it, this too is all because of the effects of man's sin upon God's originally perfect creation. Even the very elements were corrupted by man's sin. Rot, rust, and decay would not exist if it were not for man's sin which entered God's perfect creation. Additionally, there would be no aging of the human body without sin corrupting it. The scientific evidence for the effects of sin within nature is simply overwhelming as it is one of the most well-proven laws in science called the Second Law of Thermodynamics or the Law of Entropy. This scientific law simply states that "everything left to itself tends to ruin and disorder," which ironically is the very opposite of what would make Darwinian evolution even possible.

Conclusion

Therefore, since:

1.   The united conscience of mankind down through recorded human history has always acknowledged that man has a problem with moral failure;
2.   And God's word has always plainly taught us about its reality and consequences;
3.   And the well-proven scientific law of "entropy" testifies to the effects of sin upon God's perfect creation;

Then it is only reasonable to believe those flatly denying the existence of sin in the heart of man are only dishonestly denying that aspect of reality, because it is just part of their sin nature to do so! According to the Bible, a basic part of "repentance" is man agreeing with God about the reality of sin and that God can completely cleanse us of it if we just believe that Christ took our full punishment for it on the cross (Isaiah 1:18, 53:5; 1 John 1:9).

The good news is that because God has told us ahead of time throughout his word about the reality of sin with its eternal consequences and that Christ himself is our only savior from it…*all men* can choose to be honest with themselves and God about their own true moral condition and obtain his awesome eternal life as a result!

Truly, no one on the planet can be connected to reality *without basic honesty.*

If you are one who knows in your heart that you too fall short of God's perfect moral standards and you want to personally experience his awesome unconditional healing love and forgiveness for you, I invite you to just take that first small step of faith by sincerely praying the prayer of salvation located at the end of this book. No matter what your past is like, God loves you and sincerely wants you to be a part of his awesome eternal kingdom!

Jesus said, "I am the resurrection and the life. He who believes in me, will live even though he dies; and whoever lives and believes in me will never die…" (John 11:25–26)

OBJECTION 22

All Spiritual Truth Is Just Relative to One's Own Perspective

We've all heard people parrot the saying, "All truth (which includes spiritual or moral truth) is just relative to one's own perspective." Even our public school systems have taught children that they need to discover and establish their own moral values in classes like "values clarification." In such classes, students have essentially been taught that values do not come from without, like from parents, God, or the Bible; but rather, they really come from within, meaning whatever you yourself think best at the time. In other words, if it's true for you at the moment, then it's true, period.

However, as appealing a relative spiritual truth and morality is for some, there is some real unsolvable problems with such a notion which plagues even those who fiercely promote it. For if all truth is just relative to one's own perspective, then one person's truth is just as representative of reality as another person's truth is. However, obviously, the "truth" of reality by definition cannot contradict itself, because the moment it does, it no longer qualifies as the reliable truth and falls into the realm of "falsehood," or worse yet, deception. If you had two "final authority" bosses at work, which told you to do two opposite things, confusion and the loss of your job would be the result if that pattern continued! Very similarly, world peace is absolutely impossible for those who believe in "relative morality."

And very reasonably, only those who believe in absolute universal truth even have a chance to obtain the real moral truth to discern rightly with, because they are the only ones who even have a chance of not contradicting themselves with the conflicting opinions of men. Since all those who believe in absolute universal truth must have a singular unifying agent (such as God and his word, the Bible), we also know that it is truly impossible for them to even have any basic contradictions among themselves, if they truly believe in their unifying agent.

Since we know that the universal "Golden Rule" truth which applies to all (which is the only truth we should use to discern right from wrong with in the lives of others) really cannot and should not ever contradict itself, then we also know those who believe in "relative morality" (which must contradict itself) really cannot have the universal truth they need in order to discern rightly.

> Obviously, the "truth" of reality by definition cannot contradict itself, because the moment it does, it no longer qualifies as the reliable truth and falls into the realm of "falsehood," or worse yet, deception.

Just what are we saying? Ultimately, one must certainly have a "power source" much greater than just their *mere opinion* if they are going to convince anyone of any truth. There are many contradicting religions in the world, which all claim to have the truth, but only one of them has even openly demonstrated the necessary power which convinces us it could not have come from imperfect man. Since the world is full of contradicting opinions, why should anyone just take the word of someone who believes in contradicting relative morality? Anyone can give an opinion which has no real power to back it. Obviously, there is more than one kind of truth, so let's just list several of those different kinds common to man's experience:

1. Rational truth—that truth which can be conceived by the human mind.

2. Empirical truth—that truth which is perceived through our five senses.
3. Utilitarian truth—the practical truth; if it works, it's true.
4. Scientific truth—observable truth which can be made to re-happen.
5. Legal/historical truth—court of law evidence confirmed by oral and written testimonies and physical exhibits.
6. Spiritual truth—revealed truth which is not only experienced but confirmed through man's conscience and all the other kinds of truth listed above.

However, no matter what kind of "truth" we wish to contemplate, it simply cannot contradict itself; otherwise, it is not the truth! For example, *rational* truth cannot contradict itself. Mathematics is a good example of rational truth which cannot contradict itself. If we all know that 2 + 2 = 4, someone cannot just come along and insist it actually equals 5, just because they believe it does. They could certainly do that, but everyone *honest* would know they didn't have the truth.

Empirical truth cannot contradict itself. If everyone knows it's a cloudy rainy day and many people see the same clouds and feel the same rain, someone else cannot come along and just claim it's a bright sunny hot day, just because they personally wish it to be so! They could certainly do that, but again, everyone *honest* would know they didn't have the truth.

Utilitarian truth cannot contradict itself. If everyone knows that one cannot just jump on a trampoline and bounce to the moon, someone cannot claim that they could do so just because they believe it strong enough. Again, they could certainly do that, but everyone *honest* would know they didn't have the truth.

Scientific truth cannot contradict itself. If the scientific community has already established the first and Second Laws of Thermodynamics, which are consistently repeatable truths under observation with the five senses, then someone cannot just come along and claim those scientific laws are obsolete without any honest evidence to back them up. They could certainly do that, but again, everyone *honest* would know they didn't have the truth.

And last, but not least, *spiritual* truth cannot contradict itself. If one person believes in "monotheism" (the belief in a singular supreme personal God), and another person believes in "Pantheism" (the belief that everything is God), and another person believes in "Polytheism" (the belief in many different gods), and another person believes in "Atheism" (the belief in no God or gods), we can know for certain that no two of these positions can even be correct. It is simply an impossibility!

Logically, we know that either one of them is correct or none of them are correct. And if one of them is true, then all others are necessarily *false*. Philosophers call this the law of "noncontradiction." Try as you may, you just cannot (sanely or honestly) get around it.

Yet Another Test of Truth

We all know intuitively in our conscience that those who claim to have the truth will also have genuine love as well. And similarly, we all know that those who claim to love will also have the truth, which does not contradict itself. Hence, the simple but profound true saying:

"Truth without love cannot be the whole truth, and love with contradicting truth cannot be true love."

Interestingly enough, the Bible has also always taught that truth and love are married together as one as 1 Corinthians 13:6 plainly states: "*Love…rejoices in the truth….*" Is it just a mere coincidence that the Bible teaches us the very same as our collective consciences bear witness? If the very same God who gave us our conscience also wrote the Bible, then I guess it just makes sense, does it not? And if the very same God is, in fact, the only source of all real love and truth, then man's collective conscience sensibly expecting both love and truth to be "married" together only makes good sense as well.

The Philosophy that "All Spiritual or Moral Truth Is Just Relative to One's Own Perspective" Simply Does Not Work in Real Life

It is more than interesting to note that those who would insist that "all spiritual or moral truth is just relative to one's own perspective" do not even begin to hold to their own philosophy in real life. For example, they certainly expect their interactions with other people to be characterized by absolute truth, which would apply to all men and have no relativism or self-contradictions. If they are sick, they expect the doctor's advice to not be just relative to his own perspective. They expect it to be the medical truth backed by honest evidence, which any certified doctor would consistently relate to any patient without self-contradictions.

They certainly expect their banker to be honest with all their money transactions and not handle their money just as they see fit. If they are flying in an airplane, they certainly expect their pilot to land on the narrow runway and not just anywhere using any method they want at the time.

If they are married, they certainly expect their spouse to be honest, loving, and faithful to them and not just live out any morality that would suit them at the time. They also expect their president (and or other politicians) to be truthful, have good character, and not just live anyway they want. They expect their news station to report the actual truth of events without any deceptions which would alter the truth.

The list, of course, could continue, but you get the idea! Those who supposedly believe in "relative truth" certainly expect absolute truth without any personal relativism when it comes to every other kind of truth, which would affect them directly. However, when it comes to spiritual truth, all of a sudden, they very *inconsistently* insist that "it is just relative to one's own perspective!" Hmm...certainly "something is rotten in Denmark" with all that hypocrisy. Can you see it too?

Those who supposedly believe in "relative spiritual truth" *inconsistently* expect "absolute" truth without any personal relativism when it comes to every other kind of truth which would directly affect their well-being.

We've already plainly shown that *no kind of truth* can contradict itself and remain the truth, so how does it make any sense at all for them to make an exception for spiritual truth and insist that only it is relative to one's own perspective? The truth is, it doesn't, not only because it is morally inconsistent (or hypocritical), but also because their "relative morality" doesn't even begin to work in the rest of life! On the other hand, Bible-believing Christians, of course, believe in absolute spiritual and moral truth in every area of life across the board, which is the same for every soul on earth. This is simply because they believe that the singular source of all perfect truth (which does not contradict itself) is essentially Christ their creator, the very person of God himself who never changes (John 14:6; Colossians 2:3; James 1:17; Hebrews 13:8). And of course, this whole belief about absolute spiritual truth also fits wonderfully with the fact that all mankind literally needs absolute truth (which does not contradict itself) in all other facets of life to even *survive* every day!

In other words, Bible-believing Christians reasonably treat all the different kinds of truth the very same, expecting them all to be absolute (without inconsistent relativism), knowing that it is literally a matter of life and death to not have contradicting truth. However, as we've already shown, those who insist that just spiritual truth is relative to one's own perspective are rather *forced* to be very inconsistent.

Ironically enough, those believing in moral and spiritual relativism often also claim to be "tolerant" of all spiritual beliefs, which obviously contradict each other. However, at the same time, they are often even inconsistent with that claim as well because of their obvious intolerance toward those Bible-believing Christians who very reasonably are consistent and expect all truth (even spiritual and moral truth) to be absolute without self-contradicting relativism.

As we already mentioned, if any statement of truth does not have some basis of fact or honest evidence which supports it, then it falls in the realm of either falsehood or even deception. And the truth is that historically, neither falsehood or deception can be relied upon to give man life and not harm. Yes, the unique power of the absolute truth (which does not contradict itself) is its ability to consistently give man life and wellness. But quite to the contrary, the deception of contradicting falsehood has always had the consistent reputation to do mankind harm and ultimately give him death. Thus, the battle for truth is literally a matter of life and death for all men—*whether they realize it or not*. The life and death experienced by man in his battle for truth can be both physical and spiritual.

And that's exactly why it is important for all men to take the personal responsibility required to find the singular truth on a given important subject, which does not, in fact, contradict itself through relativism. Let's again be honest—no one can do that for you or me. We must sort out the spiritual truth for ourselves using the mind, five senses, and conscience which God gave each of us for that very purpose! And if you are reading this book right now, then you are hopefully doing just that. It is difficult enough to discover the truth when one really wants to know just what the truth really is. But if you really *do not want to know* what the life-saving truth actually is, then your ability to find it is greatly decreased! No man can change the life-giving truth of reality. We can only trust in it and gain life from it, or we can ignore it to our own hurt or twist it to our own destruction.

In every search for truth known to man, no matter what the issue, there have always been a lot of people convinced on all sides of it. Man as a whole has always been self-contradicting within his own society. This is one of the greater proofs that even though man can indeed discover the truth, truth itself could not have originated with man. The many voices of society echoing opposing viewpoints may make the search for truth much more challenging. However, if one with patience and sincerity continues to add up the honest evidence, the truth is really not anymore unknowable than life is meaningless.

Obviously, if we believe the truth comes from within mankind, then it will *always* contradict itself, simply because all men will always have differing opinions. This is one main reason we can be absolutely *sure* that the truth (no matter which kind it is) must come from outside of mankind and not from within! So if one really wants to find the real spiritual truth, surrendering to the fact that it must come from a perfect source outside themselves (and the rest of mankind) *is the very first step.*

Anyone can say they've discovered truth, and many do. But how do the fruits of their discoveries fair? The truth will always ultimately bring life, not harm. If one has discovered the truth of good health and nutrition, would it not give them long life and manifest in their body for others to see? If one has discovered truth of whom to wed, would not their marriage ultimately bring to them deep blessing and unity in love for others to witness? If one has discovered truth of occupation for themselves, would they not use the gifts given them in a trade that brings purpose and fulfillment which others can see? If one has discovered spiritual truth, would not they experience God and his love in a way others can see?

> If one really wants to find the real spiritual truth, surrendering to the fact that it must come from a perfect source outside themselves *(and the rest of mankind) is the very first step.*

He who speaks the truth provides honest evidence (Proverbs 12:17). The search for truth is messy for most all but leads to life and awesome blessing for the serious searcher. Honest evidence has never guaranteed man's belief in the truth if his heart *does not sincerely want the truth.* But for those sincere and honest, the weight of honest evidence has always had plenty of convincing power. Reasonably, it only makes sense that only the source of all truth can aid our discovery of the truth. And as millions have discovered, the source of all truth is not some eternal list of just facts, but rather the very person of the living God himself who is more than willing to help you find the truth, if you ask him (John 14:6; Matthew 7:7–11).

Honest evidence has never guaranteed man's belief in the truth if his heart does not sincerely want the truth. But for those sincere and honest, the weight of honest evidence has always had plenty of convincing power.

Conclusion

As we've already mentioned, because truth of any kind (even spiritual or moral truth) simply cannot contradict itself, we can reasonably know for certain that it cannot come from within mankind who will always have opposing opinions. Thus, the statement "All truth is just relative to one's own perspective" must certainly be false. And because we can know for certain that all perfect moral truth (which does not contradict itself) must come from outside of mankind, we can also reasonably conclude that the source of all truth is a singular source, which is perfect and simply cannot contradict itself in any way.

And all this being the case, a single supreme monotheistic God (who is perfect and not self-contradicting) who is the very source of all truth is really the only reasonable option left open to us if we are once again honest with those facts. And obviously, such a reasonable conclusion also lines right up with the monotheistic God of the Holy Bible who has plainly revealed himself to us through his creation (Romans 1:20) the many fulfilled prophecies of his word (Isaiah 46:9–10) and the divine Christ when he walked the earth (1 John 1:1–3). Therefore, it is not only reasonable to believe that our monotheistic creator is real but that he also desires to have a right and loving relationship with each and every person whom he's created just as the Bible teaches us.

The Prayer of Salvation

Because the Bible also teaches us that it is sin which separates us all from God (Isaiah 59:2), our sins must first be dealt with before our relationship with him can be restored. And the Bible teaches us plainly that *only through Christ* can our relationship with God be restored so he can grant us his eternal life.

> **Jesus said, "I am the way and the truth and the life. No one comes to the Father except through me." (John 14:6)**

Someone once asked Jesus how many will be saved. And Jesus replied:

> **Make every effort to enter through the narrow door, because many, I tell you, will try to enter and will not be able. (Luke 13:24)**
>
> **Jesus said, "I am the door: by me if any man enter in, he shall be saved..." (John 10:9)**
>
> **For God so loved the world, that he gave his one and only Son, that whoever believes in him shall not perish, but have eternal life. (John 3:16)**

If you'd like to know for certain that you too are right with God and have his eternal life, I invite you to take that first small step of faith by sincerely praying the following prayer of salvation sincerely from your heart. No matter what your past is like, God loves you and sincerely wants you to be a part of his awesome eternal kingdom!

Dear Lord Jesus, I easily admit that I cannot come close to keeping all the perfect moral standards of your word through my own efforts and this is what your word, the Bible, calls "sin." And because my sin is what separates me from you, I believe that in your great love for me, you humbly came to earth and died a brutal death on the cross, taking my punishment for me, even though you yourself are perfect and didn't even deserve it. Just because I believe in what you did for me on the cross that I could not do for myself, I believe according to your own word that the justice of the Father is now satisfied and my relationship with you is now restored. I ask your forgiveness for all my sins, and I humbly give you the rest of my life from here on, no longer living for myself, but only for you to the best of my ability. Thank you for what you did for me on the cross and for your free gift of eternal life! Amen.

> **Jesus said, "I am the resurrection and the life. He who believes in me, will live even though he dies; and whoever lives and believes in me will never die..." (John 11:25–26)**

1 John 1:9 says:

> **If we confess our sins, he is faithful and just to forgive our sins, and cleanse us from *all unrighteousness*.**

And now that you have come into a right relationship with God through Christ, for your personal spiritual growth, it is important to:

1. Talk to God (pray) as much as you can every day with thanksgiving and praise (Romans 12:12; Philippians 4:4–7; Psalm 145:3).
2. Read God's Word (the Bible) as much as you can every day to get to know the Lord better. Ask the Holy Spirit to help you understand, and don't be discouraged if there are some things you don't understand for a while. The book of John and the other Gospels are good books to start with (John 8:31–32, 15:7; 2 Peter 3:14–18; 2 Timothy 3:14–17).
3. Attend a Bible-believing church and stay in fellowship with them and other Christians as much as you can. If the church

you attend has small groups or home groups, this will greatly aid your spiritual growth as well (Hebrews 10:25; Acts 2:42; Ephesians 2:19). If you are one who'd prefer not attending a traditional church in some church building, a "home church" with just friends is a very good option, which many do not even know about. In fact, such a church model is just as biblical as the first Christians also met in homes (Matthew 8:14–17; Acts 28:30–31).

Jesus plainly stated that when two or more are gathered in his name, there he is in the midst of them (Matthew 18:19–20). Let's face it; the entire worldwide Church will not fit into one building! When it comes to a quality church experience, bigger is not necessarily better. The main thing is that there is at least one elder who's teaching the Bible accurately with the literal method of interpretation, and Christ is worshiped in Spirit and in truth. There's absolutely nothing in God's Word which insists that teachers or even pastors for that matter must graduate from some Bible seminary school in order to be qualified to teach in church. In fact, many Bible seminary schools today are even teaching false doctrines, because they've drifted from the truth of God's Word through the allegorical method of interpretation. We must remember, it's all a heart issue with God, not an issue of "high education."

4. If one truly believes in what Christ did for them on the cross in their heart, they will actually show it by following after Christ and not sin. This, of course, does not mean as a Christian, you will be perfect (if you were, you would not need Christ), but the "rudder on your ship" should be basically pointed in the direction of Christ and not sin (2 Corinthians 5:15; 1 John 2:6). If you just remember that God always loves you and that nothing can separate you from his love (Romans 8:35–39), then you will just be inspired from the inside to live for him with all your heart.

5. Share your faith with others so they too can know Christ and have his eternal life. The Christian faith was never something which God intended the Christian to keep to himself. If we

truly love God, we'll love others. And if we love others, we'll want them to have God's eternal life too! Truly there is a grand variety of ways we can share our faith in order to help others into God's kingdom. Just choose the one which uses the gifts which God gave you, and have a good time doing it!

May God truly bless you in your new relationship with him, and always remember your future with Christ is far greater than any of your problems and far better than anything this world can offer! As Revelation 21:3–4 clearly teaches:

> [B]ehold, the dwelling place of God is with men, and he will live with them, and they shall be his people, and God himself shall be with them, and be their God. And God shall wipe away all tears from their eyes; and there shall be no more death, neither sorrow, nor crying, neither shall there be any more pain: for the former things are passed away.
>
> No eye has seen, no ear has heard, and no mind has imagined what God has prepared for those who love him. (1 Corinthians 2:9)

ABOUT THE AUTHOR

Not having been raised with any particular religion at all, it wasn't long before author Ted Even did discover real hope when, at age 18, he decided to give Christ a chance and become a Bible-believing Christian. If the Christian faith did not really make good sense, Ted Even is probably one of the first to say that he most certainly would have abandoned his faith long ago.

But while he diligently studied the Holy Bible (as well as other sources) during the last thirty-six years, which followed his conversion, he only found that God's Word gave reasonable solid answers to even the harder questions which many skeptics have probably wrestled with ever since Christ. In his *Answers for the Honest Skeptic* four-part series, Ted Even reveals just what he has discovered as he responds to eighty-five different objections which skeptics often have had to biblical Christianity.

CPSIA information can be obtained
at www.ICGtesting.com
Printed in the USA
FSHW011244210920
73907FS

9 781098 037338